| DATE | | | |
|---|---|---|---|
| FEB 17 1997 | | | |
| | | | |
| | | | |
| | | | |
| | | | |
| | | | |
| | | | |
| | | | |
| | | | |
| | | | |
| | | | |

The Reaffirmation of Republicanism

ʃᴥ *Twentieth-Century America Series*

# The
# Reaffirmation

EISENHOWER AN[

# of Republicanism

## THE EIGHTY-THIRD CONGRESS

### *by Gary W. Reichard*

THE UNIVERSITY OF TENNESSEE PRESS

*Ɉ۰ Twentieth-Century America Series*

DEWEY W. GRANTHAM, GENERAL EDITOR

Copyright © 1975 by The University of Tennessee Press / Knoxville.

*Library of Congress Cataloging in Publication Data*

Reichard, Gary W    1943–
   The reaffirmation of Republicanism.
   Bibliography: p.
   Includes index.
      1. Republican Party. 2. Eisenhower, Dwight David,
Pres. U. S., 1890–1969. 3. United States. 83d
Cong., 1953–1954. 4. United States—Politics and
government—1953–1961. I. Title.
JK2357 1953.R43      329.6      75–1017
ISBN 0–87049–167–9

Historians have shown a surprising lack of interest in Dwight David Eisenhower's place in recent American political history. Neither the belated succession to the White House of his chosen heir nor the recent Republican electoral revival seems to have produced any marked interest in Eisenhower or his influence on the party. Indeed, historians have been largely content to accept and perpetuate existing stereotypes without subjecting them to the test of critical analysis.

Almost from the time of Eisenhower's election to the Presidency in 1952, verbal pictures of him have been drawn in broad, rough strokes without much attention to detail. The descriptions which have been offered, moreover, have not been based on any sort of systematic or rigorous analysis. Not surprisingly, a number of simplified stereotypes of Eisenhower have therefore emerged. Some of these are mutually contradictory; none is really accurate. Some observers, for example, have emphasized Eisenhower's "nonpolitical" nature. Since he was elected on the basis of his own popularity and proved unable to transfer that popularity to other Republican candidates, it is argued, he was a man above—or at least apart from—the mainstream of two-party politics. Furthermore, this argument continues, he was a political innocent who, as President, possessed neither the political understanding nor the ambition necessary to make a lasting impact on his party—or even on his country. On the other hand, many of Eisenhower's admirers have glorified him as a virtual savior of the Republican party: one who, after winning the 1952 nomination over the objections of the party's Old Guard, brought about the emergence of a "New Republicanism." In this view, Eisenhower's election ensured that the party would adapt itself at last to the political realities of a nation which had experienced successive wrenching dislocations from the Great Depression, the New Deal, and World War II.

This study aims to define more systematically Eisenhower's political views, expertise, and overall impact. Along the way, several questions present themselves. Was Eisenhower a strong or weak leader in the White House? Did he want to produce change in his party? How well did Republicans in Congress work with the President, and to what extent did their cooperation or obstruction reflect the quality of White House leadership? The answers to such questions, of course, reveal as much about the modern Republican party and the American system of government as about Eisenhower and his leadership.

In 1953–1954, Dwight Eisenhower was new to the White House, possessing the vast power and prestige of a newly elected, highly popular President who was eligible to run again. Those first years also saw, in the Eighty-third Congress, the only Republican congressional majorities which he was ever to enjoy. After twenty years of Democratic rule, moreover, the time was ripe in 1953 for the revived Republican party to assert itself and place its own ideological brand on public policy. The combination of the President's personal power, the majority status of his party in Congress, and the opportunity for charting a new course unhampered by the commitments of recent Republican administrations makes the period 1953–1954 an appropriate time in which to analyze Eisenhower's political impact.

In this study "Eisenhower Republicanism" is analyzed in two ways. In addition to describing the specific programs Eisenhower presented and supported in 1953 and 1954, I have also examined the nature of the Republican support and opposition these various programs received. Very often, the political meaning of a program is clearly revealed by the kinds of friends and foes it has. Therefore, in each of the following chapters dealing with particular legislation, as well as in the conclusion, I have employed quantitative techniques to measure the response of congressional Republicans to the Eisenhower program.

The policy views and inclinations of the Republican representatives and senators themselves were of course crucially important to the future of the President's program in the Eighty-third Congress. In order to define those views, I examined the 1952 campaigns of incoming Republican freshmen in both houses and developed ideological classifications (through use of the scalogram technique devised by Louis Guttman in the early 1940s) for GOP incumbents returning from the previous Congress. This background information on congressional Republicanism, together with a brief study of Eisenhower's 1952 presidential campaign, provides a useful context for understanding the policies and legislation emanating from the Eighty-third Congress.

Legislative history can be overwhelming if its focus is not limited. To keep this study manageable, I chose four major topical areas which together differentiated shades of Republican ideology in the 1950s: foreign policy, fiscal and economic policy, welfare policy, and policy related to power and resource development. Limiting the study to these four areas obviously leaves out a number of considerations of great importance in the Eighty-third Congress, including defense reorganization and appropriations, internal security legislation, and "McCarthyism." These subjects, while intrinsically interesting and significant, did not serve really to differentiate political ideologies within the Republican party in the early 1950s. On national defense questions, party members were virtually united in their support for the "New Look" (reduction in ground strength and increased air power), even though many Democrats criticized it sharply. Nor did Republican legislators differ much in their attitudes toward Communist subversion. Although Senator Joseph R. McCarthy's conduct and ultimate censure in late 1954 did finally divide the party, Republicans—like Democrats—continued to adhere to a zealously anti-Communist line. In the face of party unanimity behind the internal security legislation of 1954, important intraparty ideological differences over the "communism" issue do not seem to be indicated by a split Republican vote on the McCarthy censure of late 1954.[1]

In order to keep the number of specific issues considered to a sensible minimum, I chose to examine congressional action only on matters which interested President Eisenhower directly. Finding these issues was relatively simple. After selecting the four policy areas, I consulted the *Congressional Quarterly Almanac* for the "Eisenhower issues" before Congress in 1953–1954 which fit them. I then used roll-call votes on these "Eisenhower issues" as the basis for my quantitative determination of "Eisenhower support" by Republicans, individually and collectively, in the Eighty-third Congress.[2]

The study points to certain judgments of the Eisenhower Presidency. Many critics have underestimated the depth of Eisenhower's political beliefs. On the other hand, some of his admirers have incorrectly implied that he held and promulgated a set of beliefs more progressive than those characterizing the rest of the party. Very conservative in fiscal affairs and devoted to the principle of local responsibility in power and resource development, President Eisenhower acquiesced in certain New Deal programs but did nothing to expand on them, and he remained philosophically opposed to much of the spirit of both the New and Fair Deals. His acquiescence in programs like social security and limited public housing reflected political inevitability by the 1950s, not the triumph of a "moderate" or "liberal" wing within the Republican party. The generally strong support for Eisen-

[1] See Robert Griffith, *The Politics of Fear: Joseph R. McCarthy and the Senate* (Lexington: Univ. Press of Kentucky, 1970), 223, 283–84, 292–94, 316.

[2] See *Congressional Quarterly Almanac*, Vols. ix (1953), 83, and x (1954), 54–57. *CQ* lists 198 "Eisenhower issue" votes in 1953–54 (126 in the Senate and 72 in the House). Of these, 131 fit into the four policy areas. In addition, I have included four Senate roll calls on questions relating to control over foreign policy, as distinct from the substance of that policy. The study thus deals with 135 roll-call votes: 86 in the Senate and 49 in the House.

hower programs among traditional (or conservative) Republicans in the Eighty-third Congress tends to support this interpretation. Only in foreign affairs did Eisenhower effect any real conversion of his party colleagues in Congress. Yet here, too, one might argue that basic acceptance of the nation's world responsibilities had become a necessity for any party in power during the 1950s.

Most observers have also sold short Eisenhower's qualities of leadership and political understanding. The activities of recent Presidents are obscured to history by both the existence of the telephone and the caution of public officials in committing themselves to paper, and the Eisenhower Presidency is no exception. Yet there are indications of President Eisenhower's astuteness and firm hand in the political clinches during 1953–1954. Incontrovertible evidence of the President's personal activities on behalf of a given bill is, unfortunately, frequently missing. Yet many surviving pieces of evidence—reports of his command over legislative leadership conferences, his own written and spoken words, and the rare glimpses of genuine presidential activism— suggest that Eisenhower did exercise leadership, and that he had a keen sense of his role as party leader.

As President, Dwight Eisenhower turned out to be what one might have expected: a competent leader and a fairly orthodox Republican. The story of Eisenhower and the Republican Eighty-third Congress, then, demonstrates the reaffirmation— rather than the renovation—of Republicanism.

ACKNOWLEDGMENTS

This book began as a doctoral dissertation at Cornell University, where I had the good fortune to receive help and guidance from Professors Richard Polenberg, Walter LaFeber, and Joel Silbey. Professor Polenberg, especially, gave unhesitatingly of his time and energies in criticizing every portion of the initial drafts. I am indebted to him for the insightful and demanding criticisms he provided as a teacher and scholar, but equally for the support he provided as a friend.

I wish to thank also Professor James R. Bartholomew of Ohio State University and David D. Lee, a graduate student at the same institution, both of whom read the entire manuscript with great care and keen critical faculties. Professor James T. Patterson of Brown University generously shared with me his knowledge of the Taft-Eisenhower relationship and of the politics of the period in general. Professor Donald R. McCoy of the University of Kansas provided me with a number of invaluable suggestions for improving the manuscript. The editor of this series, Professor Dewey W. Grantham of Vanderbilt University, not only gave me the benefit of his criticisms on this work but has been an inspiration to me in academic and professional life since my first days as a graduate student. To him I am profoundly grateful.

The staffs of various libraries I visited in the course of my research have been of inestimable assistance. I wish to thank those many persons who helped me at the George Arents Research Library, Syracuse University; Baker Library, Dartmouth College; the Collection of Regional History and University Archives, Cornell University; the Dwight D. Eisenhower Library, Abilene, Kansas; the Manuscripts Division of the Library of Congress; Lilly Library, Indiana University; the Ohio Historical Society; Princeton University Library; and the Wisconsin State Historical Society. I am grateful also to the Honorable John W. Bricker, who consented to an interview during my early research and who has been helpful to me on a number of subsequent occasions. Mrs. I. Jack Martin of Kensington, Maryland, granted me access to certain of her late husband's papers and showed me the gracious hospitality of her home while I worked there.

The later research for this study was supported, in part, by the Ohio State University Development Fund through its Faculty Summer Fellowship Program. I am grateful also to the Department of History at Ohio State, which made available the clerical assistance necessary for the production of the manuscript, and especially to Nancy L. Hines, who cheerfully and efficiently typed the finished product.

To the members of my family, who suffered various deprivations while I worked on this project, I can only say thank you and promise that this book, at least, should cause them no further anguish.

# CONTENTS

*To Marcia*

# CHAPTER ONE

# The New Republicans

Political events of 1952 left the future direction of the Republican party uncertain. Dwight D. Eisenhower's nomination, following a hard-fought contest with Senator Robert A. Taft of Ohio, signified to many observers that the party would finally break away from its conservative traditions.[1] Indeed, fewer than half of those who voted for Eisenhower in November even regarded him as a "real" Republican.[2] Yet in retrospect such a view seems to have been largely the product of the wishful thinking of liberals and the paranoia of conservatives.

The list of General Eisenhower's early political champions did make him seem the candidate of party liberals. Of the twenty Republican congressmen who wrote to him in Europe during February of 1952 urging him to run for President, nearly half were identified with the party's liberal wing.[3] But while the

[1] See Samuel Lubell, *The Future of American Politics*, 3rd ed., rev. (New York: Harper, Colophon Books, 1965), 220–21; Conrad Joyner, *The Republican Dilemma: Conservatism or Progressivism* (Tucson: Univ. of Arizona Press, 1963), vi; Paul T. David, Malcolm Moos, and Ralph M. Goldman, eds., *Presidential Nominating Politics in 1952*, 5 vols. (Baltimore: Johns Hopkins Univ. Press, 1954), I, 67–68; and Joseph Harsch, "Which Road? The Chicago Choice," *The Reporter* 7, No. 2 (July 22, 1952), 5.

[2] Angus Campbell, Gerald Gurin, and Warren E. Miller, *The Voter Decides* (Evanston, Ill.: Row, Peterson [1954]), 64, Table 4.18.

[3] The 20 co-signers included 14 Republican House members who would return to the 83rd Congress: James Auchincloss, Clifford Case, and Robert Kean (N.J.); Sterling Cole, Jacob Javits, and Walter Riehlman (N.Y.); Norris Cotton (N.H.);

"Eastern establishment"—men like Senators Henry Cabot Lodge and Leverett Saltonstall of Massachusetts and Governor Thomas E. Dewey of New York—was much in evidence among the early Eisenhower-boosters, so too were prominent Midwesterners such as Senator Frank Carlson and ex-Senator Harry Darby of Kansas and Roy Roberts of the Kansas City *Star*. Actually the General's early advisers were in far from perfect accord, either ideologically or in the tactics they urged on their candidate. Probably the strongest single bond uniting them was a pragmatic desire to win the November election.[4]

The "modern" wing of the party claimed victory after the convention, but the platform indicated a mixed outcome. The document was fairly moderate on foreign policy: while denouncing in strong terms the policies of Truman and Acheson, it declared in favor of continued aid to Europe and, significantly, did not condemn either the NATO pact or Truman's commitment of troops to Korea in 1950. The chief architect of the foreign policy plank, John Foster Dulles, had been acceptable to the Taft forces, but he was himself an Eisenhower supporter and an internationalist of long standing.[5] In the platform's domestic sections, traditional Republican conservatism was much in evidence. The 1952 party program differed sharply from the Democratic in favoring revision (rather than repeal) of the Taft-Hartley Act, vaguely de-

---

Gerald Ford (Mich.); John Heselton (Mass.); Clifford Hope (Kans.); Walter Judd (Minn.); Winston Prouty (Vt.); Hugh Scott (Pa.); and Thor Tollefson (Wash.). The others were Claude Bakewell (Mo.), Albert M. Cole (Kans.), Harmar Denny, Jr. (Pa.), Christian Herter (Mass.), Thruston Morton (Ky.), and Edward Sittler, Jr. (Pa.). Other GOP leaders, including Sens. Carlson, Lodge, and James Duff (Pa.), and Governors Sherman Adams, Dan Thornton, Arthur Langlie, and Dewey, had already been urging such a course on General Eisenhower, but the events of February and March seem to have been decisive.

4 Harsch, *The Reporter* 7, No. 2, 7; David F. Schoenbrun, "The Ordeal of General Ike," *Harper's Magazine* 205, No. 1229 (Oct. 1952), 29–30; and John H. Kessel, *The Goldwater Coalition: Republican Strategies in 1964* (Indianapolis: Bobbs-Merrill, 1968), 35.

5 David et al., *Presidential Nominating Politics*, I, 90. On Dulles's role, see Dwight D. Eisenhower, *The White House Years: Mandate for Change, 1953–1956* (Garden City, N.Y.: Doubleday, 1963), 41; and Barton J. Bernstein, "Election of 1952," in Arthur M. Schlesinger, Jr., and Fred L. Israel, eds., *History of American Presidential Elections*, 4 vols. (New York: Chelsea House, 1971), IV, 3233.

4

termined flexible (rather than rigid) farm price supports, and state and local autonomy (as opposed to federal aid) in education. Other areas were noncontroversial, undisputed, or otherwise obscure. Content analysis of the platform reveals that, overall, Republicans paid greater than usual attention in 1952 to foreign affairs, defense, and "governmental" concerns (criticisms of the in-party as well as statements on purely institutional and bureaucratic matters).[6]

Eisenhower's own preconvention comments were no more suggestive of liberalism than either the collective profile of his early supporters within the GOP or the party's platform. His first major address as a candidate for nomination, delivered at a "homecoming" celebration in Abilene, Kansas, in early June 1952, contained little but clichés and vague platitudes, and he did not become much more specific at any time before his nomination. Consequently, as the campaign began, there was little hard evidence on which to judge the temper of Republicanism in 1952. The party's campaigners—presidential and congressional —were to play important roles in defining that temper and foreshadowing the direction of the GOP beyond the November election.

### Eisenhower and the "Mandate for Change"

Electoral mandates are difficult to measure in American politics. In 1952, the immense personal popularity of Dwight D. Eisenhower made the problem of measurement more complex than usual. Those who interpret the election as a purely personal triumph for Eisenhower implicitly suggest that the Republican party received no mandate at all,[7] but this is far too simplistic. Survey researchers later established that a Republican majority

6 Gerald Pomper, " 'If Elected, I Promise': American Party Platforms," *Midwest Journal of Political Science*, 11, No. 3 (Aug. 1967), 331.

7 See, e.g., Emmet Hughes, *The Ordeal of Power: A Political Memoir of the Eisenhower Years* (New York: Atheneum, 1963), 47; Richard H. Rovere, *Affairs of State: The Eisenhower Years* (New York: Farrar, 1956), 50; and Milton Viorst, *Fall From Grace: The Republican Party and the Puritan Ethic* (New York: New American Library, 1968), 182.

existed in 1952 before the party conventions and merely increased in size after the nominees were known.[8] When the votes were counted in November, moreover, President-elect Eisenhower's margin of victory was not overwhelmingly greater than his party's; excluding the South (where in several districts the party failed to field a candidate), Republicans running for the House of Representatives polled a combined 54.8 percent, compared to Eisenhower's 56.4 percent.[9] Despite the preponderance of registered Democrats, in November 1952 the American public expressed a clear desire to put the Republican party in power.[10]

If there was a mandate for Republicans, however, it was largely negative. The voters knew what they did not want. There is broad agreement that the victory was produced by three issues: Korea, Communism, and Corruption. All three evils were popularly associated with the Truman administration. Of the three, the Korean War, in which the United States had been embroiled for more than two years, dominated the field.[11] Aside from Eisen-

[8] Campbell et al., *The Voter Decides,* 14–15.

[9] Louis Harris, *Is There a Republican Majority? Political Trends, 1952–1956* (New York: Harper, 1954), 203.

[10] Elmo Roper estimated in June 1952 that 50 percent of all registered voters were Democrats. and only 34 percent were Republicans. Roper, *You and Your Leaders: Their Actions and Your Reactions, 1936–1956* (New York: Morrow, 1957), 247.

[11] See, e.g., Bernstein, *History of Presidential Elections,* IV, 3250; Eric F. Goldman, *The Crucial Decade—And After: America, 1945–1960* (New York: Vintage Books, 1960), 224; Harris, *Is There a Republican Majority?,* 23, 25; Ronald J. Caridi, *The Korean War and American Politics: The Republican Party as a Case Study* (Philadelphia: Univ. of Pennsylvania Press, 1968), 209; Malcolm E. Jewell, *Senatorial Politics and Foreign Policy* (Lexington: Univ. of Kentucky Press, 1962), 39, 187; Joyner, *The Republican Dilemma,* 79; V. O. Key, Jr., with the assistance of Milton C. Cummings, Jr., *The Responsible Electorate: Rationality in Presidential Voting, 1936–1960* (Cambridge, Mass.: Harvard Univ., Belknap Press, 1966), 75; and Roper, *You and Your Leaders,* 249.

Conversely, some observers have suggested that the impact of both communism and corruption has been overestimated. On the communism issue, see Campbell et al., *The Voter Decides,* 52; Harris, *Is There a Republican Majority?,* 32; Morris Janowitz and Dwaine Marvick, *Competitive Pressure and Democratic Consent: An Interpretation of the 1952 Presidential Election,* No. 32 in Michigan Governmental Studies (Ann Arbor: Univ. of Michigan Institute of Public Administration, 1956), 43–44; Roper. *You and Your Leaders,* 250–51; and Michael P. Rogin, *The Intellectuals and McCarthy: The Radical Specter* (Cambridge, Mass.: M.I.T. Press, 1967), esp. 224–25.

On the corruption issue, see Samuel Lubell's conclusion early in the campaign

hower's widely heralded promise to "go to Korea," first uttered at Detroit on October 24, 1952, none of these issues involved a specific mandate for the GOP if it should win.

Public unrest over the Korean War, however, produced important "trailer issues" involving both economic and foreign policy. In his treatment of these off-shoot issues, General Eisenhower provided some insight into the construction he would place on the "mandate" of national victory.

Eisenhower spoke with some ambiguity about foreign policy. Steering clear of the Old Guard's scathing denunciations of American involvement in the Korean War, he accepted the original necessity for participation in the conflict and contented himself with indicting the Democrats for their general pre-1950 foreign policy and making vague promises of peace. "I believe that the decision to fight to hold Korea . . . was inescapable," Eisenhower proclaimed in mid-campaign, but "I deplore . . . the incompetence of political leaders which made military action necessary." In his noted Detroit speech a month later, however, the candidate altered this argument, stating that the war "was never inevitable, . . . never inescapable." [12] Criticism that his statements on Korea were ambiguous and contradictory did not shake Eisenhower. At one point he neatly turned the tables on his detractors, charging in self-righteous indignation that "any [Truman] Administration apologist should make up his mind whether he wants to charge me with embracing, in 'me too' fashion, his party's foreign policy too warmly, or with criticizing it too harshly." [13] But it mattered not who won the debate on points. The public cast its votes for Eisenhower.

---

that it ranked "well down the list of issues splitting off one-time Democratic voters" (New York *World-Telegram and Sun,* Sept. 24, 1952); and the assessment of *U.S. News & World Report* that corruption was "an issue in third or fourth place, not first" (Oct. 10, 1952, p. 12).

12 Sept. 22 speech at Cincinnati, *New York Times,* Sept. 23, 1952. See also Eisenhower's statement of Aug. 21 at Kansas City and the Detroit speech (*ibid.,* Aug. 22, Oct. 25).

13 For a critique of Republican arguments about Korea, see Henry Steele Commager, "The Republican Dilemma," *The Reporter* 7, No. 8 (Oct. 14, 1952), 7. Eisenhower's statement from Oct. 5 press release, *New York Times,* Oct. 5, 1952.

On broader questions of foreign policy, too, the Republican candidate's public position was somewhat blurred. Having begun his campaign with an ill-starred announcement of a "liberation" policy for dealing with worldwide communism, Eisenhower backed down in subsequent speeches until, within a few weeks of his first such utterance, the *New York Times* could assure the public with accuracy that there was a "considerable rapprochement of views" between the two parties "regarding both the goals of our policy and the means of attaining them." The pro-Eisenhower Washington *Post* simply dismissed the announced "liberation" policy as an "unfortunate" verbal slip and proceeded to treat it as a non-event.[14]

General Eisenhower's foreign policy statements during the campaign—including the "liberation" pronouncement—were consistently internationalist in tone. "The vast majority of Americans of both parties," he declared at Detroit, "know they bear a majestic responsibility for freedom throughout the world." To resolve any further doubt, he stated a week later: "I have long insisted—and do now insist—that isolationism in America is dead as a political issue." Repeatedly during the campaign Eisenhower stressed the importance of a system of collective security in general, and of the United Nations in particular.[15] He also spoke up in support of continuing both the reciprocal trade and foreign aid programs, though he occasionally hedged his support for the latter with comments about the impossibility of "buying" allies.[16] As final confirmation of his internationalist sympathies, the General even spoke of the need for making the nation's immigration

[14] For the initial "liberation" declaration, see Eisenhower's speech before the American Legion National Convention on Aug. 25 (*New York Times*, Aug. 26, 1952). For contrasting later statements, see speeches at Philadelphia (Sept. 4), Los Angeles (Oct. 9), and Worcester (Oct. 20), *ibid.*, Sept. 5, Oct. 10, Oct. 21. The editorials are from *ibid.*, Sept. 13, and Washington *Post*, Sept. 5.

[15] Speeches of Oct. 24 (Detroit) and 31 (Chicago), *New York Times*, Oct. 25, Nov. 1, 1952. On collective security, see speeches of Oct. 1 (Flint), 14 (San Antonio), 27 (Pittsburgh), and 30 (New York), *ibid.*, Oct. 2, Oct. 15, Oct. 28, Oct. 31.

[16] For the latter allusion, see San Antonio speech of Oct. 14. Statements of support for "trade and aid" appear, e.g., in his speeches of Sept. 4 (Philadelphia), Sept. 9 (Indianapolis), and Oct. 21 (New York), *ibid.*, Oct. 15, Sept. 5, Sept. 10, Oct. 22.

8

laws more liberal.[17] Eisenhower's 1952 campaign represented a sharp break with the nationalist-isolationist wing of his own party, even though those who voted for him were not necessarily making such a break.[18]

Eisenhower held more true to Republican tradition in his handling of the other main "trailer issue" to the war, the resulting economic dislocation. When, late in the campaign, the candidate proposed to bring about "prosperity based on peace," he was summarizing the essence of his party's economic appeal in the election.[19] On this issue, the Democratic party was highly vulnerable. Prosperity was not lacking in 1952, but—as Eisenhower's phraseology suggested—since it was accompanied by war, the in-party was unable to cite national economic well-being in defense of its policies. Furthermore, the prosperity which existed was badly undermined by both inflation and ever-increasing taxes which seemed to be producing no tangible benefits for the public.[20] Explicit in the GOP appeal, as expressed both by General Eisenhower and by Republican candidates for other offices, was a promise to do away with inflation and reduce taxes, not only by ending the war but also by controlling the excesses of Democratic "big government." In thus assailing the scope of federal activity, the Republican party was repeating an attack it had been mounting with quadrennial regularity since the 1930s.

Eisenhower's traditional Republican leanings were especially apparent in his statements regarding economic issues. In a speech advocating economic policies "designed to give this country and its people prosperity and economic growth under the opportunities of peace," he observed that government policies, instead of

17 See speeches of Oct. 17 (Newark), 20 (Bridgeport), and 29 (New York), *ibid.*, Oct. 18, Oct. 21, Oct. 30.

18 On the divergence of Eisenhower and Stevenson voters on foreign policy issues, see Janowitz and Marvick, *Competitive Pressure and Democratic Consent*, 46.

19 Speech at Chicago, Oct. 31, *New York Times*, Nov. 1, 1952.

20 Lubell, *Future of American Politics*, 3. Actually, the sharp inflation which had set in during 1950 had begun to level off by late summer of 1952, but, as Louis Harris says, "public opinion has always shown a notorious lag in catching up with what the BLS Price Index shows" (*Is There a Republican Majority?*, 35–36). See also Harold G. Vatter, *The U.S. Economy in the 1950's: An Economic History* (New York: Norton, 1963), 79.

espousing "high-handed interference and regulation . . . must give free play to the individual." At other points in the campaign, General Eisenhower blamed Democratic practices for producing inflation and delivered scathing denunciations of the "whole-hog theory" of government and "the alien philosophy that our national destiny lies in the supremacy of government over all."[21] He emphasized that if the economies and reductions of governmental activities which he proposed were put into effect, lower taxes would inevitably follow. Although he eschewed promising immediate tax cuts, always carefully tying them to prior reductions in federal spending and a balanced budget,[22] the frequency of Eisenhower's references to tax reduction reflected a continuation of traditional Republican economic policy.

It was not clear from the candidate's more specific comments, however, where the promised savings would come from. On domestic issues, Eisenhower played his own version of the artful dodger throughout the campaign. Even while lashing out against the evils of "big government," the General repeatedly assured the voters that he accepted the social gains of the previous twenty years as a "solid floor" of protection for the welfare of individual citizens.[23] In an important policy speech at Los Angeles, Eisenhower promised Republican support for extension of social security benefits, unemployment insurance, and public housing, describing such programs as "a sound investment in a sounder America."[24] Significantly, however, he never clarified the relative value he attached to these social welfare schemes compared with the goal of economy in government.

The Republican candidate plainly revealed an aversion to "big

[21] Speeches of Oct. 2 (Peoria), Oct. 6 (Seattle), and Sept. 9 (Indianapolis), *New York Times*, Oct. 3, Oct. 7, Sept. 10, 1952.

[22] See, e.g., speeches of Oct. 2 (Peoria) and 20 (Worcester), *ibid.*, Oct. 3, Oct. 21. See also Hughes, *Ordeal of Power*, 27.

[23] Speeches of Aug. 20 (Boise), Sept. 17 (AFL Convention in New York), and Oct. 20 (Worcester), *New York Times*, Aug. 21, Sept. 18, Oct. 21, 1952.

[24] Los Angeles speech of Oct. 9; see also speeches of Oct. 13 (New Orleans), 17 (Newark), 27 (Pittsburgh), and Nov. 3 (Boston), *ibid.*, Oct. 10, Oct. 14, Oct. 18, Oct. 28, Nov. 4.

government" in his pronouncements regarding power and resource development. Outlining his "partnership concept" even
before the campaign had officially begun, Eisenhower reiterated
often—especially in the West—his view that "local agencies and
officials" should have a strong voice in the use of any federal funds
provided for water storage, power production, and reclamation
activities. While confessing that he had "no pat and detailed
plan" for implementing the partnership concept, Eisenhower did
suggest "a new interstate body" to oversee "the planning, management, and coordination" of all such activities in the Northwest.
And though he promised in Memphis not to "impair the effective
working out of TVA," he stated definitely that Republicans would
not "look upon the TVA as a rigid pattern for . . . other regions."
Eisenhower also promised to end the long-standing controversy
over legal title to national resources in offshore waters within the
three-mile limit (erroneously known as the "tidelands") in favor
of the states. All of these stands demonstrated the Republican
candidate's rejection of the proposition that the states should,
or could, depend on the federal government to meet their power
needs or to oversee the conservation and development of their
resources.[25]

Eisenhower did find it expedient to stress, especially late in the
campaign and in the Northeast, that Republicans would not
allow the machinery of government to lie idle if depression threatened. "Whenever there are the slightest signs of any boom-and-
bust cycle in our economy," he told an audience at Utica, New
York, "the full power of the Federal Government . . . will be

---

25 See Eisenhower's speeches of Aug. 20 (Boise) and Oct. 6 (Seattle), 7 (Portland),
and 15 (Memphis), and the "partnership plank" of his ten-point pledge issued on
Nov. 1, *ibid.*, Aug. 21, Oct. 7, Oct. 8, Oct. 16, Nov. 2, 1952. Also, Aaron Wildavsky,
*Dixon-Yates: A Study in Power Politics* (New Haven: Yale Univ. Press, 1962), 17.
Eisenhower also applied his "partnership concept" to soil conservation, as in his
speeches to farm audiences at Kasson, Minn., and Des Moines on Sept. 6 and 18,
respectively (*New York Times*, Sept. 7, Sept. 19). For the "tidelands" pledge, see
speeches of Oct. 13 (New Orleans), 14 (Houston), and 15 (Fort Worth), *ibid.*, Oct.
14, Oct. 15, Oct. 16.

mobilized to make certain that there are no breadlines."[26] But this probably represented no more than contingency planning in response to political necessity; in mid-October, the candidate was advised by his private polling expert that he might stop the apparent erosion of independent voter support by taking a more liberal line, especially in the populous Northeast. In the light of Eisenhower's other statements during the campaign, it is inaccurate to read this particular pledge as evidence that he viewed himself as a "New Deal Republican" in 1952.

Political realities worked to reinforce Eisenhower's own orthodox Republican tendencies. After the General's nomination, Senator Taft, who enjoyed the loyalty of great numbers of rank-and-file party workers, came around only slowly. "We may get a Republican New Deal Administration," he wrote to a colleague in August, "which will be a good deal harder to fight than the Democrats."[27] Despite overtures from Eisenhower campaign headquarters, the Ohio senator did not meet with the candidate until September, at the now famous Morningside Heights conference. His reason for delaying the political summit is clear. "It may be," he explained to an adviser, "that by . . . September they will be well scared and anxious to come around and really seek some advice. Up to date, my feeling is that they only want to give the impression that the Taft people are co-operating without giving them any real voice in the running of the campaign itself."[28]

Working through Senator Everett Dirksen of Illinois, Taft insisted as a precondition of his going to meet with Eisenhower on a number of "assurances (some of which might be made public and others not)," including the candidate's agreement to support

[26] Speech of Oct. 23, *New York Times*, Oct. 24, 1952; see also speeches of Oct. 20 (Worcester), 21 (Lynn), 25, 29, and 30 (all New York), *ibid.*, Oct. 21, Oct. 22, Oct. 26, Oct. 30, Oct. 31.

[27] Robert Taft to Herman Welker, Aug. 18, 1952, Robert A. Taft Papers, Manuscripts Division, Library of Congress.

[28] Taft to Paul W. Walter, Aug. 2, 1952; to Cole J. Younger, Aug. 7, 1952; telegram from Eisenhower inviting Taft to confer, dated July 17, 1952, all in Taft Papers.

specific reductions in federal spending, the basic principles of the Taft-Hartley Act, and the concept of flexible price supports for farmers, as well as to appoint Taft supporters to Cabinet-level posts "on approximately equal terms" with Eisenhower followers.[29] As a result of these prior negotiations, the Taft-Eisenhower conference on September 12 went well. When the Senator emerged from the meeting, he asserted that Eisenhower, like himself, viewed the Republican party's mission as the defense of "liberty against socialism" and the "liberty of the people against Federal regulation." Despite remarks in the press to the effect that the General had "surrendered" to the party's conservative wing, no less an authority than Eisenhower's closest adviser later confirmed that Taft's statement accurately reflected the candidate's own position.[30]

During the 1952 campaign, as afterward, Eisenhower characterized his political beliefs as a "middle way" between Old Guard conservatism and the "big government" philosophy of the New and Fair Deals.[31] Yet traditional Republican hostility to federal intervention in the economy was implicit in much of what the candidate promised in 1952—reductions in spending, eventual tax cuts, and the encouragement of private initiative. This bias also surfaced more directly on occasion. In a moment of candor during the campaign Eisenhower asserted that he was "never going to accept . . . Left-Wingish, pinkish influence in our life. . . . I am going to try to make them ["leftists" in Washington] see, either through argument or fight or persuasion that they have got to get away from that . . . kind of thing and get back to Ameri-

29 Taft to Everett Dirksen, Aug. 6, 1952; to Thomas Coleman, Aug. 14, 1952, Taft Papers. Also James T. Patterson, *Mr. Republican: A Biography of Robert A. Taft* (New York: Houghton, 1972), 574–76.

30 *New York Times*, Sept. 13, 1952; see also Walter Lippmann's comment in Washington *Post*, Sept. 16. The judgment is that of Sherman Adams, in his *Firsthand Report: The Story of the Eisenhower Administration* (New York: Harper, 1961), 23. Eisenhower, in *Mandate for Change*, failed to indicate any disagreement with the Taft statement after the meeting (64). Bernstein (*History of Presidential Elections*, IV, 3242) and Patterson (*Mr. Republican*, 578) basically agree.

31 See speeches of Aug. 20 (Boise) and Oct. 10 (Salt Lake City), *New York Times*, Aug. 21, Oct. 11, 1952.

canism."[32] Thus spoke the voice of modern Republicanism, swept into office in November 1952 by a huge popular majority.

## The Congressional Class of '52

Besides making Dwight Eisenhower President of the United States, the 1952 election also produced nine new GOP senators and fifty new Republican members of the House of Representatives.[33] Since the party held only slim majorities in both houses of the Eighty-third Congress,[34] these newcomers formed a significant bloc within the congressional GOP. An examination of their ideological leanings and public commitments in the 1952 campaign, therefore, helps to clarify the political outlook after the Republican electoral victory.

These campaigns are also worth studying because, in a sense, congressional contests can reveal more than national elections. Although local constituencies (and individual states) possess particular political idiosyncrasies, they are also subject to "national influences." Because the candidate running for election in a single district, or even in a particular state, is less restricted than

[32] *Ibid.*, Sept. 9, 1952.

[33] Actually, two new House "freshmen," William C. Cole (Mo.) and William Dawson (Utah), had served single terms earlier. In addition, two new GOP senators, Charles Potter (Mich.) and J. Glenn Beall (Md.), had served in the House, and one other—John Sherman Cooper (Ky.)—had sat in the Senate from 1946 to 1948. Because none of the five was running as an incumbent for the office he sought in Nov. 1952, I have included all of them as "freshmen."

My usual sources for campaign statements by these congressional candidates were leading local newspapers (see Tables 1 and 2). In the interest of economy, I have included in the footnotes only the sources for quotations or allusions within the text. Where newspapers were unavailable or insufficiently informative, I tried to get campaign literature or reminiscences from the candidates themselves, but with limited success. In all, I was able to secure adequate information on all nine senatorial campaigns and on 42 of the House campaigns.

[34] After the election, Republicans controlled the House, 221–214, and the Senate, 49–47. The margin of control changed slightly during the course of 1953–54, due to deaths and replacements, but the party retained its narrow majority at the close of the second session. In this study Wayne Morse (Ore.) is numbered among Senate Republicans even though he broke with the GOP during the 1952 campaign and styled himself an "Independent" in the 83rd Congress. Morse voted with the Republicans on organization in Jan. 1953, and he announced after Sen. Taft's death that he would do so again in the event the Democrats challenged Republican control of the upper house (see *New York Times*, Aug. 3, 1953).

a presidential candidate, who must reduce his campaign to a least common denominator to please a broad, diversified electorate, the "narrower" congressional campaigns sometimes provide a clearer indication of the nature of a party victory.[35]

## THE HOUSE

Not surprisingly, the freshman House winners in 1952 concentrated their campaigns more on domestic policy than on foreign affairs (see Table 1 for the data on which this section is based). The most prevalent issues in their campaigns were the cry of "Trumanism," implying government corruption, and an emphasis on inflation and its roots in excessive federal spending and waste. Thirty-four of the forty-two congressmen whose 1952 campaigns were examined stressed "Trumanism," and, even more significantly, thirteen centered their appeal on it. Those running against Democratic incumbents (Bonin, Bosch, Cretella, Dawson, Hillelson, Jonas, Mailliard, Merrill, Neal, Poff, Rhodes, Young) could make the connection between their opponents and the Truman "mess" easily enough. There were frequent references in their campaigns to incumbent Democratic opponents as men who had forsaken the wishes of their constituencies to become "vest-pocket" votes and "blind rubber stamp" legislators backing "Fair Deal bunk."[36]

Other GOP candidates, though deprived of incumbent opponents to tie to the Truman maladministration, were nonetheless equally vehement. They alluded disparagingly to the "Mink Dynasty" and "grafters" in Washington whose behavior, as one

[35] James M. Burns, "Congressional Contests and the Presidential Election," *Annals of the Amer. Acad. of Political and Social Science* 283 (Sept. 1952), 116; Malcolm Moos, *Politics, Presidents and Coattails* (Baltimore: Johns Hopkins Univ. Press, 1952), 116, 155.

[36] Mailliard in San Francisco *Chronicle*, Oct. 13; Neal in Huntington *Herald-Dispatch*, Oct. 15; Young in Reno *Evening Gazette*, Oct. 14; Rhodes in Phoenix *Gazette*, Oct. 21.

Table 1   Issues in 1952 Campaigns of Republican House Freshmen in Eighty-Third Congress[a]

| Name and District[b] | "Trumanism" | Inflation and Waste | Tax Levels | "Creeping Socialism" | Communism-in-Government | Korean War | Post-1945 Foreign Policy | Information Source[c] |
|---|---|---|---|---|---|---|---|---|
| Bentley, Alvin (Mich.-8) | * | * | | | ** | | * | Saginaw News |
| Bolton, Oliver (Ohio-11) | ** | * | * | | * | | | Warren Tribune-Chronicle |
| Bonin, Edward (Pa.-11) | ** | * | * | | * | ** | * | Hazleton Standard-Sentinel |
| Bosch, Albert (N.Y.-5) | ** | ** | * | * | * | * | * | (See note c) |
| Broyhill, Joel (Va.-10) | * | ** | * | | * | | | Washington Post |
| Cederberg, Elford (Mich.-10) | * | * | | * | ** | | | Bay City Times |
| Clardy, Kit (Mich.-6) | * | ** | | * | ** | * | * | The State Journal (Lansing) |
| Cole, William (Mo.-6) | * | ** | ** | | * | | * | St. Joseph News-Press |
| Coon, Sam (Ore.-2) | * | * | | | | | ** | East Oregonian (Pendleton) |
| Cretella, Albert (Conn.-3) | | ** | | | | ** | | Meriden Record |
| Curtis, Laurence (Mass.-10) | * | * | * | | * | | * | Boston Daily Globe |
| Dawson, William (Utah-2) | * | ** | * | ** | | | * | Salt Lake Tribune |
| Frelinghuysen, Peter (N.J.-5) | * | ** | * | ** | | | | (See note c) |
| Gubser, Charles (Calif.-10) | ** | * | * | | * | | * | San Jose Mercury |
| Hillelson, Jeffrey (Mo.-4) | ** | | | | * | | | Kansas City Star |
| Holt, Joseph (Calif.-22) | * | * | * | | ** | ** | * | Los Angeles Times |
| Hosmer, Craig (Calif.-18) | | * | | ** | ** | ** | * | Los Angeles Times |
| Hruska, Roman (Neb.-2) | * | ** | * | ** | | | * | Omaha Morning World-Herald |
| Hyde, DeWitt (Md.-6) | * | ** | * | | * | | * | Washington Post |
| Jonas, Charles (N.C.-10) | ** | ** | * | * | | | * | Charlotte Observer |
| Knox, Victor (Mich.-11) | * | * | | | * | ** | * | Sault Ste. Marie Evening News |
| Krueger, Otto (N.D.-A.L.) | ** | ** | * | | * | * | * | Fargo Forum |
| Laird, Melvin (Wis.-7) | ** | ** | * | * | * | * | ** | Wausau Daily Record-Herald |
| Mailliard, William (Calif.-4) | ** | ** | * | | | * | * | San Francisco Chronicle |
| Merrill, Bailey (Ind.-8) | ** | * | * | | * | * | * | Evansville Courier |
| Neal, Will (W.Va.-4) | ** | * | | | ** | * | ** | Huntington Herald-Dispatch |
| Oakman, Charles (Mich.-17) | * | * | * | | ** | * | * | Detroit Free Press |

| Candidate[b] | C1 | C2 | C3 | C4 | C5 | C6 | C7 | Newspaper |
|---|---|---|---|---|---|---|---|---|
| Pelly, Thomas (Wash.-1) | * | | | | ** | * | * | Seattle Daily Times |
| Pillion, John (N.Y.-42) | ** | ** | * | | ** | * | * | (See note c) |
| Poff, Richard (Va.-6) | ** | ** | * | | | | | Roanoke Times |
| Rhodes, John (Ariz.-1) | ** | * | * | | * | ** | * | Phoenix Gazette |
| Robsion, John (Ky.-3) | ** | * | * | | | ** | * | Louisville Courier-Journal |
| Scherer, Gordon (Ohio-1) | * | * | | ** | * | ** | * | Cincinnati Enquirer |
| Small, Frank (Md.-5) | * | * | ** | * | ** | | | Washington Post |
| Stringfellow, Douglas (Utah-1) | ** | * | ** | * | | * | | Ogden Standard-Examiner |
| Utt, James (Calif.-28) | * | * | * | | | | | Santa Ana Register |
| Wampler, William (Va.-9) | | | | | ** | ** | * | Bristol Herald-Courier |
| Warburton, Herbert (Del.-A.L.) | * | * | * | | *** | * | * | Wilmington Journal-Every-Eve. |
| Westland, Jack (Wash.-2) | ** | | | * | * | * | * | Seattle Daily Times |
| Wilson, Robert (Calif.-30) | | ** | | * | | * | * | San Diego Union |
| Young, Clifton (Nev.-A.L.) | ** | * | | | * | ** | * | Reno Evening Gazette |
| Younger, Arthur (Calif.-9) | * | * | * | | | | * | San Mateo Times |
| | | | | | | | | |
| Total References[d] | 34 | 39 | 23 | 15 | 21 | 26 | 27 | |
| Percent | 81 | 93 | 55 | 36 | 50 | 62 | 64 | |
| Total Times Main Issue | 14 | 10 | 2 | 4 | 4 | 8 | 0 | |
| Percent | 33 | 24 | 5 | 10 | 10 | 19 | 0 | |

[a] A single asterisk indicates that the candidate made use of the issue in his campaign; a double asterisk indicates that it seemed, on the basis of the source used, to serve as his main issue.

[b] Republican House freshmen not included in Table 1 are Frank Becker (N.Y.-3), Steven Derounian (N.Y.-2), Francis Dorn (N.Y.-12), Paul Fino (N.Y.-25), Edgar Hiestand (Calif.-21), John Ray (N.Y.-15), Walter Stauffer (Pa.-19), and Stuyvesant Wainwright (N.Y.-1).

[c] I was unable to secure a newspaper from the district of only one House candidate (Frelinghuysen). For the New York City and Long Island congressmen, I examined the New York Times, Herald Tribune, Journal American, and World Telegram, and the Brooklyn Eagle, which among them summarized adequately only the campaign of Bosch. In the cases of Hiestand, Pillion, and Stauffer, the newspapers I was able to obtain (Los Angeles Times, Buffalo Courier-Express, and Gettysburg Times, respectively) failed to give adequate coverage of their campaigns. In response to my letter asking for samples of 1952 campaign literature, Frelinghuysen and Pillion sent sufficient information for me to analyze their campaigns.

[d] "Total References" refers to the number of campaigns in the sample in which each issue explicitly appeared; the "percent" is that number as a percentage of 42 (the total sample). "Total times main issue" refers to the number of campaigns in which the issue appeared, to serve as the candidate's most prominent theme; the "percent" is that number as a percentage of 42.

candidate warned, might "numb" the American public to "rottenness in high places." In Hillelson's Kansas City district, where the charge had special local significance, Republicans gleefully linked "Pendergastism and Trumanism." Jack Westland of Washington's Second District headlined his election eve advertisement, "I WANT OUR KIDS TO GROW UP CLEAN," explaining ingenuously that he was "a newcomer to politics" but he did "know right from wrong." Perhaps the most colorful metaphor came from Maryland auto dealer Frank Small, running in that state's Fifth District. Electing the Democratic slate in 1952, Small claimed, "would be like putting a new pin in a soiled diaper."[37]

It is hard to separate attacks on "Trumanism" from Republican assaults specifically against Fair Deal "big government" and the inflation which allegedly resulted from such a wasteful monolith. Nevertheless, these lines of attack, usually taken in combination, were present in the campaigns of nearly all (93 percent) of the GOP House campaigns examined and were central to ten of them. Briefly, the Republican argument was that "Federal deficit financing is a chief source of our inflation." Accordingly the Democrats were accused of "fiscal hi-jinks" and labeled "spendocrats" who engaged in "installment buying" at the federal level, thereby bringing the nation to "the brink of financial disintegration." Delaware Republican Herbert Warburton, warming to the subject on one occasion, described Democratic wasteful "big government" as a "giant octopus with . . . thousands of feelers encroaching on all phases of individual activity." In Oregon's Second District, Republican hopeful Sam Coon repeatedly stressed his opposition to an overextended federal government, observing laconically that "big government makes little people."[38]

---

[37] Warburton in Wilmington *Journal-Every Evening*, Sept. 24; Merrill in Evansville *Courier*, Sept. 19; statement on behalf of Hillelson in Kansas City *Star*, Nov. 3; Westland advertisement in Seattle *Daily Times*, Nov. 3; Small in Washington *Post*, Sept. 18.

[38] Gubser in San José *Mercury*, Oct. 29; Cretella in Waterbury *American*, Sept. 25; Poff in Roanoke *Times*, Oct. 8; Frelinghuysen, undated and untitled clipping

Republicans attacked more specifically Democratic tax policies. Twenty-three of the forty-two victorious House freshmen spoke out for rapid tax reductions, though only two focused primarily on the issue. North Dakotan Otto Krueger bemoaned the "sickening feeling" engendered by Fair Deal tax levels, which Douglas Stringfellow of Utah's First District described as "pure and simple confiscation." One Maryland House candidate made Democratic tax levels bear a heavy mantle indeed, warning that there was genuine "danger of communism coming in the back door of taxes rather than the front door of invasion."[39] The exact means by which the graduated income tax would be transformed into the Marxist dialectic was left to the imagination of the voters.

Fifteen Republican candidates struck a more emotional note, inveighing against "creeping socialism," or, as New Jersey's Peter Frelinghuysen described it, the "socialistic wolf in sheep's clothing." Four even geared their campaigns to this extreme charge. One of those four, Roman Hruska of Nebraska's Second District, went the "creeping" charge one better, asserting that only the efforts of Republicans and conservative Democrats had averted "leaping socialism." Acerbic references to "parlor pinks," "left-leftists," "socialistic 'planners,'" and "the New Deal–Fair Deal–ADA crowd" abounded in the Republican campaigns. Not content to rest his case merely on the evil implications of socialist economic thought, for example, San Diego's Robert Wilson likened life in Fair Deal public housing projects to "living in a police state." Nor were Republicans modest in their own cause against the subversive influence of socialism. One victorious New York freshman, writing immediately after his election, described it as representing a "return to the American way of life," and Frank Small, in his inimitable way, depicted the campaign as one pitting "honest, true, constitutional American people against

from 1952 campaign files, copy in author's possession; Oakman in Detroit *Free Press*, Sept. 28; Warburton in Wilmington *Journal-Every Evening*, Sept. 17; Coon in *East Oregonian*, Oct. 3.

39 Krueger in Fargo *Forum*, Oct. 2; Stringfellow in Ogden *Standard-Examiner*, Sept. 19; Hyde in Washington *Post*, Oct. 1.

the socialists and pinks."[40] In all, outrage against "big government" and its consequent inflation, high taxes, and socialistic
tendencies served as key issues in the campaigns of sixteen of the
new GOP House members. By this measure, the Republican party
in 1952 was still far from total acquiescence in the New and Fair
Deals.

As in the presidential campaign, "communism-in-government"
did not play an especially salient role in these congressional contests. Not more than half of the Republican House newcomers
raised the issue to a significant extent, and only four concentrated
their campaigns on it. Alvin Bentley, of Michigan's Eighth District, had resigned his State Department post in 1950 in protest
against its "softness" and belabored the issue in his 1952 campaign. Bentley's fellow Michiganders Kit Clardy (Sixth) and
Charles Oakman (Seventeenth) echoed his sentiments, denouncing the "policy of coddling" and "the repulsive parade of Reds,
Parlor Pinks, and Communist sympathizers into high office." In
explaining the importance of the communism issue in his campaign, one successful California Republican suggested to non-
believers that "sophisticates in [the] East gravely underestimated
McCarthy's effect."[41] In most of the campaigns, however, the assessment of those 1952 "sophisticates" was probably the more
nearly correct.

Given the relatively localistic character of House campaigns,
it is not surprising that the 1952 congressional races did not re-
volve to any great extent around foreign policy considerations.
The Korean War, of course, received at least some attention from
a high proportion of the Republican candidates (twenty-six of

40 Frelinghuysen press release of Oct. 24, in author's possession; Hruska in
Omaha *Morning World-Herald*, Oct. 22; Pelly in Seattle *Daily Times*, Sept. 19;
Dawson in Ogden *Standard-Examiner*, Oct. 3; Pillion campaign pamphlet, in author's possession; Clardy in Detroit *Free Press*, Sept. 21; Wilson in San Diego *Union*,
Oct. 2; Bosch in "Why I Won, Why I Lost," *U.S. News & World Report* 33 (Nov.
14, 1952), 81; Small in Washington *Post*, Sept. 19.
41 Confidential statement on Bentley, undated and unsigned, among papers
assessing certain new Republican House members as possibilities for the Appropriations Committee, in John Taber Papers, Collection of Regional History and Univ.
Archives, Cornell Univ., Ithaca, N.Y. Clardy in Detroit *Free Press*, Sept. 14; Oakman, *ibid.*, Sept. 28; Hosmer, in *U.S. News & World Report* 33 (Nov. 14, 1952), 78.

the forty-two), but only eight focused on the war as their primary issue. Most who "used" the war did so only in negative terms, to castigate the Democrats, as exemplified by Joel Broyhill's (Virginia Tenth District) denunciation of President Truman's policies as "red-coddling, red ink and the red blood of fighting men." They also placed strong reliance on the magic to be worked by the party's presidential standard-bearer, a device typified by one Republican candidate's plea for the public to send him "to Congress to Help IKE Win the Korean War." The candor award on the war issue should have gone to John Robsion, Jr., of Kentucky's Third District. After remarking to one audience on the futility of Democratic policy in Korea, Robsion advocated instead that the United States win the war, and then concluded rather lamely, "I just don't have the answer."[42] This was equally true, even if unadmitted, of all his seat-seeking party brethren.

Related to Republicans' comments about the Korean War were their condemnations of post-1945 foreign policy as a whole. Although none of the House candidates relied upon such criticism for their main line of attack, no fewer than twenty-seven of the forty-two had unkind words for the Truman-Acheson policies which had "lost the peace" and "permitted the enslavement of hundreds of millions." The State Department, according to the prevailing Republican line, had "sold this country . . . down the river" and "bungled its way about the world leaving a mass of envious and resentful nations nominally our allies."[43]

The internationalist note sounded in the Eisenhower campaign had but few echoes among the party's House freshmen-to-be. Of those stressing foreign policy to any extent in their campaigns, only Laurence Curtis (Massachusetts Tenth District), Peter Frelinghuysen (New Jersey Fifth), and Stuyvesant Wainwright (New York First) came across as definite internationalists. Nine of the party hopefuls called directly in their campaigns for

---

[42] Broyhill in Washington *Post*, Oct. 28; Cole advertisement in St. Joseph *News-Press*, Nov. 3; Robsion in Louisville *Courier-Journal*, Oct. 21.

[43] Wampler in Bristol *Herald-Courier*, Oct. 28; Pillion campaign literature, in author's possession; Scherer in Cincinnati *Enquirer*, Oct. 7; Merrill in Evansville (Sunday) *Courier and Press*, Sept. 21.

massive reductions in foreign aid, and at least four others implied such reductions in advocating closer supervision of the program.[44]

Republican House freshmen elected in November 1952 were on the whole harshly critical of federal "encroachment" in the everyday life of individual citizens. They equated such encroachment with the New and Fair Deals—a traditional position for Republicans by the 1950s. Moreover, many of the freshmen roundly denounced the nature and scope of Truman's internationalist foreign policies. On the basis of their campaigns, there was at least some chance that the "Class of 1952" in the lower house would prove unenthusiastic about any conversion of their party to a "modern" stance inconsistent with its past.

## THE SENATE

Senate candidates, running for election in constituencies considerably less homogeneous than the typical House district, must conduct campaigns correspondingly more on the order of the presidential candidates' search for a political least common denominator. Less localistic and particularistic than House campaigns and necessarily more extensively waged, the campaigns of senatorial aspirants typically deal with the whole spectrum of national issues in a given election, especially in a presidential year. The campaigns of the nine Republicans elected to the Senate for the first time in 1952 reflect this political fact.

As a rule, the GOP senatorial candidates addressed themselves to a wider range of "major" issues than Republican House candidates.[45] Eight of the nine dwelt at some length on both the "mess in Washington" ("Trumanism") and inflation and government waste (see Table 2). Four concentrated on the former issue (Bar-

44 The nine outright opponents were Clardy, Coon, Merrill, Pelly, Rhodes, Scherer, Westland, Young, and Younger.

45 This apparent tendency may be exaggerated because senatorial races usually get much greater coverage from the press than do House contests. Since I relied almost exclusively on newspapers for this analysis, it is possible that the inequity in coverage made the Senate campaigns seem "more extensive."

Table 2  Issues in 1952 Campaigns of Republican Senate Freshmen in Eighty-Third Congress[a]

| Name and State | "Trumanism" | Inflation and Waste | Tax Levels | Communism-in-Government | Korean War | Post-1945 Foreign Policy | Information Source |
|---|---|---|---|---|---|---|---|
| Barrett, Frank (Wyo.) | ** | * | | | | | Laramie Republican and Boomerang |
| Beall, J. Glenn (Md.) | ** | * | * | | * | * | Baltimore Sun |
| Bush, Prescott (Conn.) | * | * | | * | | * | Hartford Courant |
| Cooper, John Sherman (Ky.) | ** | * | * | ** | ** | * | Louisville Courier-Journal |
| Goldwater, Barry (Ariz.) | * | * | * | * | ** | * | Phoenix Gazette |
| Griswold, Dwight (Neb.) | * | ** | | ** | * | | Omaha Morning World-Herald |
| Payne, Frederick (Maine) | * | * | | * | * | * | Bangor Daily News |
| Potter, Charles (Mich.) | ** | | | | ** | | Detroit Free Press |
| Purtell, William (Conn.) | | * | * | | * | * | Hartford Courant |
| Total References | 8 | 8 | 4 | 5 | 7 | 6 | |
| Percent | 89 | 89 | 44 | 56 | 78 | 67 | |
| Total Times Main Issue | 4 | 1 | 0 | 2 | 2 | 0 | |
| Percent | 44 | 11 | 0 | 22 | 22 | 0 | |

[a] Notations and definitions used in this table are the same as those used in Table 1.

rett, Beall, Goldwater, and Potter), and one on the latter set of issues (Payne). One of these, Arizona's Barry Goldwater, managed to subsume both into one unattractive agglomeration, characterizing the Fair Deal period as seven years "of expanding governmental bureaucracy, of increasing central authority, of economic tinkering, of government-created inflation, [and] of pyramiding confusion on crisis, and crisis on confusion . . ."[46]

Foreign policy considerations were also widely emphasized in the Senate races. Seven of the nine Republican freshmen made use of the Korean War issue, and six severely criticized post-1945 Democratic foreign policy making. Only two (Cooper and Purtell), however, made the war the central issue. The usually circumspect Cooper at one point bluntly stated that the issue in 1952 was simply "peace or war," though he had nothing more specific to offer than did Connecticut's Purtell, who keyed his election drive on the war issue by pointing to Eisenhower as the "best chance for ending the Korean bloodletting."[47]

Finally, the specter of communism-in-government received slightly greater attention from Republican Senate hopefuls than from party House candidates. Five of the nine used domestic communism as an issue, and two (Bush and Griswold) apparently focused their campaigns on it. Perhaps this stronger emphasis on Communist subversion reflected the feeling of Republican senatorial candidates that they should take a position on the activities of one of the best-known members of their party in that body, Senator Joseph R. McCarthy. Of the five who used the issue, only Maryland's J. Glenn Beall actually linked himself with the Wisconsinite, challenging one audience to "show [him] one charge that McCarthy has ever made that he's been wrong on . . . ." Several of the other first-time Senate winners, however, were also vehement in their denunciations of what they described as "soft-headed coddling of Commies" and the dominance of "pinko intellectuals" in Washington.[48]

[46] Phoenix *Gazette*, Sept. 19, 1952.

[47] Cooper in Louisville *Courier-Journal*, Oct. 30; Purtell in Hartford *Courant*, Oct. 8.

[48] Beall in Washington *Post*, Sept. 18; Goldwater in Phoenix *Gazette*, Nov. 1;

Attacks on the Truman administration, in contrast to positive proposals for change, predominated in the campaigns of victorious Republican challengers in 1952 Senate races, just as in the case of first-time House winners. Nevertheless, because Senate candidates must conduct broader campaigns, several of the nine incoming GOP senators also indicated how they felt with respect to specific policy in the major substantive areas. On the large question of accepting the "welfare state" as constructed by the New and Fair Deals, for example, six of the Republican candidates expressed fairly clear opinions. Of these six, five sounded definitely hostile to the underlying concepts of the welfare state. The common Republican attitude toward post-1932 Democratic domestic policy is apparent in the position taken by candidate Charles E. Potter, who was viewed as a middle-of-the-road Republican. The chief issue of 1952, according to Potter, was whether we "return to our Democratic [!] form of government or continue on the road toward Socialism." Another Republican candidate who pretended to accept the "gains" represented by social security, the Federal Housing Administration, the Securities and Exchange Commission, and other New Deal innovations simultaneously railed against the "alphabetical red tape . . . which spins its grasping spider web around every human activity today." Others, if not so prone to mix metaphors, were equally hostile to Democratic big government programs. Only Connecticut's Purtell seemed disposed to accept much of the New and Fair Deals.[49] Finally, four of the nine (Barrett, Bush, Cooper, Griswold) strongly advocated tax reductions, a cause which necessarily indicated opposition to existing levels of federal activity.

On the other hand, despite their strong condemnations of Democratic foreign policy after World War II, most of the new Republican senators who expressed any clear position apparently accepted Eisenhower's brand of internationalism. All five who

---

and Griswold in Omaha *Morning World-Herald*, Sept. 19. Only Cooper and Purtell were openly reluctant to support McCarthy and his methods.

[49] Description of Potter in Detroit *Free Press*, Oct. 25; his statement is from the same paper, Oct. 23; Goldwater in Phoenix *Gazette*, Sept. 19.

took definite foreign policy stands came out in favor of collective security and the continuation of foreign aid. Beall, Cooper, and Potter were the strongest such advocates, while Griswold and Payne hedged their support for foreign aid by urging the need for thrift. Wyoming's Barrett specifically condemned the reciprocal trade program, urging a return to a trade policy more protective of American interests.[50] In matters of foreign policy generally, however, the new senators avowed themselves "Eisenhower men."

## Portents in the Victory

Republican campaigns in 1952—for the Presidency and Congress alike—attacked the existing situation far more often than they proposed concrete solutions. The heavy emphasis on "Trumanism" and the exploitation of popular unrest over the Korean War evidenced the party's typically "out-party" appeal. Yet the campaigns revealed enough about the party's policy orientation to give a fairly distinct picture of what Republicanism might be expected to embrace after November 1952. Eisenhower and, to an even greater extent, the fifty-nine Republican freshmen in Congress possessed a strong distaste for the "big government" approach of the previous twenty years. This would suggest that 1952 did not witness the Republican party's tacit acceptance of the New Deal. Rather, at least in domestic policy, the Republican elephant labored furiously only to bring forth not so much a rejuvenated, more liberal offspring, but one very much like its parent.

In foreign policy, however, the campaigns of newly victorious Republicans did seem to foreshadow a change in orientation. Eisenhower himself waged a clearly internationalist campaign, and if many of the new House Republicans could not be counted as "internationalist" on the basis of their campaigns, neither were most of them strongly committed in the opposite direction.

[50] Barrett in Laramie *Republican and Boomerang*, Oct. 23.

Most of the new Republican senators, moreover, seemed disposed to accept the new President's foreign policy approach.

The 1952 campaigns of Republican newcomers to Washington revealed a good deal about the style of Republicanism which would emerge in the capital during the next two years. At least as important in shaping the party's future direction, however, were the embattled veterans—Republican congressmen and senators longer established and in most cases longer committed to particular positions. The residual force represented by these congressional veterans was the final important factor in determining Republican policy in the years of the Eighty-third Congress.

# CHAPTER TWO

# Residual Republicanism

Republican incumbents who had been re-elected to Congress in 1952 were more numerous than freshmen, and therefore perhaps more important to administration plans. To a considerable extent the new President would have to shape both his program and his tactics to fit the proclivities of these more senior, presumably less tractable legislators. The way these veterans had acted and voted during the Eighty-second Congress was therefore a crucial part of the political picture confronting the Eisenhower administration.

Quantitative analysis of voter behavior has the advantage of forcing political bombast to yield to reality. The ideological coloration of the vast majority of Republican members of the Eighty-third Congress—the returning incumbents—can therefore be described with greater accuracy than can the attitudes of Republican freshmen. For analyzing the ideological baggage which incumbent Republicans brought back with them to Washington in 1953, I have employed the Guttman scaling method.

The literature on Guttman scaling is formidable—both in quantity and in rhetorical density. Briefly, however, the technique involves examining the responses of subjects on a given set of questions which measure a single underlying attitude. Once all the subjects' responses are recorded, a scale is constructed in which the subjects are arranged in descending order according to the degree of positiveness of their attitudes on the set of questions. Individual subjects with the same response pattern (for example, two legislators who voted "no" on the same two questions and "yes" on another twelve questions) are said to be the same "scale type." Their attitude on the set of questions embraced by the scale is defined as more "positive" than that of another individual who voted "no" on more than two of the roll calls on the same scale.[1]

Guttman scaling is an appropriate tool for sorting out the various "brands" of Republicanism espoused by the thirty-nine returning GOP senators and their 171 counterparts in the House in the Eighty-third Congress,[2] but it does contain difficulties. Specifically, the ideological classifications assigned to positions on a single scale, or continuum, are relative rather than absolute. Even though the extreme "liberal" and extreme "conservative" positions on the Republican scales in this study do represent

[1] Construction of the scale also requires that the questions (roll calls) themselves be arranged so that, from left to right, they range from least popular (that is, the least number of positive responses) to most popular. For concise explanations of Guttman scaling, see Lee F. Anderson, Meredith W. Watts, Jr., and Allen R. Wilcox, *Legislative Roll Call Analysis* (Evanston: Northwestern Univ. Press, 1966), 89–121, and Duncan MacRae, Jr., *Issues and Parties in Legislative Voting: Methods of Statistical Analysis* (New York: Harper, 1970), 15–38. On the uses and particular advantages of the Guttman technique, see Aage R. Clausen, "Measurement Identity in the Longitudinal Analysis of Legislative Voting," *American Political Science Review* 41, No. 4 (Dec. 1967), 1020; George M. Belknap, "A Method for Analyzing Legislative Behavior," *Midwest Journal of Political Science* 2, No. 4 (Nov. 1958), 390, 401; and Charles D. Farris, "A Method of Determining Ideological Groupings in Congress," *Journal of Politics* 20, No. 2 (May 1958), 321–25.

[2] In addition to the 39 incumbents, two new Republican senators, J. Glenn Beall (Md.) and Charles Potter (Mich.), had also sat in the Eighty-second Congress, in the House of Representatives. Because a shift from House to Senate involves a sometimes sharp change in constituency and therefore might alter an individual legislator's voting pattern, it is more logical to treat Beall and Potter as Senate freshmen (see Ch. 1).

This analysis includes only 163 Republican House incumbents, although 171 were actually re-elected to the House of Representatives in 1952. Congressmen Merlin Hull (Wis.-9) died and Norris Poulson (Calif.-24) resigned early in 1953, so that their respective voting profiles are irrelevant to this study. The analysis also omits consideration of the records of six other re-elected Republicans who had not begun service in the Eighty-second Congress until after it was underway and thus had incomplete records: Joseph L. Carrigg (Pa.-10), Robert D. Harrison (Neb.-3), Karl C. King (Pa.-8), Clifford G. McIntire (Maine-3), Frank C. Osmers (N.J.-9), and Paul F. Schenck (Ohio-3).

strongly liberal and conservative outlooks, respectively, a legislator ranked in the middle of a Republican scale would not auto-
matically rank in the ideological center if both parties were
considered together. For example, Jacob Javits ranked at the
strongest "liberal" pole of every domestic scale (see Appendix
B) because he consistently voted the "liberal" position; he would
therefore rank as a strong liberal on any scale based on the same
roll calls, no matter who else was included in it. But since a scale
constructed for Democrats, or for both parties together, would
probably "break" differently or might even include different
roll calls, a legislator ranked in the intermediate ranges of scales
in this study might not necessarily rank the same way if Democrats had been included. But the relative positions of Republicans would remain the same; therefore the Guttman method is
quite useful for the purpose of delineating "types" within the
party itself.[3]

Scaling is used here, then, primarily to classify returning congressional Republicans according to their ideological differences.
Besides sorting out individuals, it is useful also to note how certain subgroups of Republicans felt about particular policy areas.
Specifically, did ideological "type" depend upon when the legislator first entered Congress, or where he came from (home region, and, in the case of House members, demographic type of
district)? Did the members of powerful committees or of the
party leadership incline to particular ideological positions? To
answer these questions, I have broken down the total group of
Republican incumbents in each house into subgroups defined
according to period of initial entry into Congress, region, and (for
House members) district type, and have examined the collective
profiles of GOP incumbents on leading committees and within the
party leadership.[4]

---

[3] In employing the Guttman method, it is both common and proper to construct scales separately for the two parties. See MacRae, *Issues and Parties in Legislative Voting*, 27, and the same author, *Dimensions of Congressional Voting: A
Statistical Study of the House of Representatives in the Eighty-first Congress*
(Berkeley: Univ. of California Press, 1958), 222.

[4] "Periods of entry" are defined as: Pre-New Deal (to 1932), New Deal (1932–39),

There are many ways to scale a Congress. Theoretically, the Guttman method can be used to assign every roll call in a given session to a quantitatively determined and demonstrably "unidimensional" policy area. It is also legitimate, however, to preselect issue areas, then tentatively build a scale for each based on all those roll-call votes which would seem to measure attitudes in that area. Those roll calls which prove not to "fit" the pattern of the scale thus constructed may then be discarded. The completed scale should contain no more than 10 percent "errors" (individual roll-call responses which do not fit the scale pattern —that is, a legislator responding "aye" when he or she should have voted "nay," assuming that the roll calls in the scale measure attitudes about a single subject).[5]

To define shades of differences among Republicans returning from the Eighty-second Congress, I preselected four distinct policy areas: foreign policy, fiscal and economic policy, welfare policy, and power and resource development (see Appendix A for exact roll-call composition of each scale). The foreign policy area includes measures related to foreign aid, foreign trade, and immigration; fiscal and economic policy includes questions bearing on taxation and government involvement in setting wage, price, and rent ceilings; the welfare scale includes legislation dealing with public housing and federal provisions for health and social welfare; and power and resource development com-

---

World War II (1940–45), and Postwar (1946–51). Regions are defined as: New England (Connecticut, Maine, Massachusetts, New Hampshire, Rhode Island, Vermont); Mid-Atlantic (Delaware, Maryland, New Jersey, New York, Pennsylvania); Border (Kentucky, Missouri, North Carolina, Oklahoma, Tennessee, Virginia); North Central (Illinois, Indiana, Michigan, Minnesota, Ohio, Wisconsin); Plains (Iowa, Kansas, Nebraska, North Dakota, South Dakota); and Far West (Arizona, California, Colorado, Idaho, Montana, Nevada, Oregon, Utah, Washington, Wyoming). Congressional District types are: rural, small-town, mid-urban, and metropolitan, as defined in *Congressional Quarterly Almanac*, Vol. XII (1956), 788, 790–91.

5 When this is true, the scale is said to have a reproducibility of .90 or higher. Each of my scales meets this criterion. In building the scales, I discarded any single roll call from the scale which contained 10 percent or more legislators voting "wrong" (that is, not "fitting" with other roll calls in the scale). For a discussion of these points, see MacRae, *Dimensions of Congressional Voting*, 317–18.

31

prises matters such as conservation, reclamation, and power development.

In foreign policy, the scale has been constructed to separate "internationalists" (those accepting an active world role for the United States, and therefore favoring foreign aid and opposing protectionist trade barriers and restrictive immigration policies) from "nationalists" (holding opposite viewpoints). In the three domestic areas, legislators are graduated on liberal-conservative continua, with "liberalism" denoting relative acceptance of an active federal role with respect to the particular questions involved (for example, providing public housing or social insurance of some sort, building dams, or acting assertively in the field of resource conservation) and "conservatism" implying rejection of such a role.

After constructing the scales, assignment of legislators to categories such as "strong liberal" and "moderate conservative" is necessarily a somewhat arbitrary process. I have used one of the simplest of several possible categorization methods: for each scale, I have created five classifications (categories) of legislators, including in each category—insofar as possible—an equal number of consecutive scale types. For example, if a certain scale yields fifteen separate "scale types" (designated 0 through 14), then the first three scale types (0 through 2) would be grouped as "strong liberals," the second three as "moderate liberals," the next three as "uncommitted," and so on.[6] This method does not produce categories which purport to separate attitudes, or scale types, by any absolutely equal distance, but it does accurately position the legislators along the chosen attitude continuum relative to one another.

### The Senate Incumbents

The thirty-nine returning Republican senators were a mixed ideological group, but they tended generally to nationalism and

[6] For a discussion of the methods which can be used to assign scale types to categories, see MacRae, *Issues and Parties in Legislative Voting*, 28–37.

domestic conservatism. In two of the three domestic areas and on the foreign policy scales, there were about three times as many senators adhering to those basic positions as there were on the liberal and internationalist sides. Only on power and resource development questions was the breakdown sharply different: roughly 30 percent liberal, 40 percent conservative, with the rest either uncommitted or unscalable. (Table 3 shows the exact breakdown for each policy domain.) Generally, a domestic conservative was also a nationalist in foreign policy, and conversely a liberal was more apt to take an internationalist viewpoint. Appendix B, which shows each incumbent senator's ranking in every policy area, demonstrates this relationship.

It would seem logical that members coming to Congress together at particular times might share certain ideological perspectives. For example, those coming to Washington after American involvement in World War II began might be expected to hew to internationalist lines, and those Republicans brought to power in the 1930s might share a special animus against the New Deal and related "big government" programs. In fact, however, if the incumbents are separated by period of entry into Congress (as pre–New Deal, New Deal, World War II, and postwar senators), no single group emerges as unique or atypical on all counts. New Deal–period Senate Republicans were more conservative than their colleagues in fiscal and economic matters but did not stand apart on other issues. The single other obvious departure from the norm was the World War II group's relative liberalism on welfare policy—possibly as a reflection of the wartime tendency to accept heavy government involvement in previously private sectors of the economy. There were no significant differences among the four groups on foreign policy.

Region was more clearly related to voting patterns among Republican senators than was period of entry (see Table 4). Midwestern senators (from North Central and Plains states) were most strongly nationalist, and those from the Northeast (New England and Middle Atlantic) were most inclined to internationalism. The Northeast also supplied the highest proportions

*Table 3* IDEOLOGICAL CLASSIFICATIONS OF REPUBLICAN
SENATORS RETURNING TO THE EIGHTY-THIRD CONGRESS*

| Ideological Position | Percent |
|---|---|
| *Foreign Policy* | |
| Strong internationalist | 15% |
| Moderate internationalist | 10 |
| Uncommitted | 13 |
| Moderate nationalist | 23 |
| Strong nationalist | 33 |
| Not scaled | 5 (100%=39) |
| *Fiscal and Economic Policy* | |
| Strong liberal | 8 |
| Moderate liberal | 15 |
| Uncommitted | 15 |
| Moderate conservative | 33 |
| Strong conservative | 23 |
| Not scaled | 5 (100%=39) |
| *Welfare Policy* | |
| Strong liberal | 13 |
| Moderate liberal | 8 |
| Uncommitted | 15 |
| Moderate conservative | 23 |
| Strong conservative | 36 |
| Not scaled | 5 (100%=39) |
| *Power and Resource Development* | |
| Strong liberal | 10 |
| Moderate liberal | 21 |
| Uncommitted | 13 |
| Moderate conservative | 13 |
| Strong conservative | 28 |
| Not scaled | 15 (100%=39) |

* For lists of the roll calls making up each policy area (scale), see Appendix A.
For individual senators' scale scores and ideological classifications in the four policy
areas, see Appendix B.

34

*Table 4* IDEOLOGICAL CLASSIFICATIONS OF REPUBLICAN SENATORS RETURNING TO THE EIGHTY-THIRD CONGRESS, BY PERIOD OF ENTRY AND REGION

| | FOREIGN POLICY | | | | | |
| | *Classification* | | | | | |
| *Category*\* | SI† | MI | U | MN | SN | Not Scaled |
| --- | --- | --- | --- | --- | --- | --- |
| *Total* (39) | 6 | 4 | 5 | 9 | 13 | 2 |
| *By Period of Entry* | | | | | | |
| New Deal (9) | 1 | 1 | 2 | 3 | 2 | 0 |
| World War II (13) | 2 | 1 | 2 | 3 | 4 | 1 |
| Postwar (17) | 3 | 2 | 1 | 3 | 7 | 1 |
| *By Region* | | | | | | |
| New England (6) | 2 | 2 | 0 | 2 | 0 | 0 |
| Mid-Atlantic (7) | 3 | 0 | 1 | 0 | 2 | 1 |
| North Central (9) | 0 | 2 | 0 | 3 | 4 | 0 |
| Plains (8) | 0 | 0 | 2 | 2 | 4 | 0 |
| Far West (9) | 1 | 0 | 2 | 2 | 3 | 1 |

| | FISCAL AND ECONOMIC POLICY | | | | | |
| | *Classification* | | | | | |
| *Category* | SL | ML | U | MC | SC | Not Scaled |
| --- | --- | --- | --- | --- | --- | --- |
| *Total* (39) | 3 | 6 | 6 | 13 | 9 | 2 |
| *By Period of Entry* | | | | | | |
| New Deal | 0 | 0 | 3 | 5 | 1 | 0 |
| World War II | 1 | 3 | 1 | 4 | 3 | 1 |
| Postwar | 2 | 3 | 2 | 4 | 5 | 1 |
| *By Region* | | | | | | |
| New England | 1 | 2 | 3 | 0 | 0 | 0 |
| Mid-Atlantic | 1 | 3 | 0 | 1 | 1 | 1 |
| North Central | 0 | 0 | 3 | 4 | 2 | 0 |
| Plains | 0 | 0 | 0 | 5 | 2 | 1 |
| Far West | 1 | 1 | 0 | 3 | 4 | 0 |

*Table 4* (CONTINUED)

WELFARE POLICY

| | Classification | | | | | |
|---|---|---|---|---|---|---|
| Category | SL | ML | U | MC | SC | Not Scaled |
| *Total* (39) | 5 | 3 | 6 | 9 | 14 | 2 |
| *By Period of Entry* | | | | | | |
| New Deal | 1 | 1 | 0 | 4 | 2 | 1 |
| World War II | 2 | 2 | 3 | 2 | 4 | 0 |
| Postwar | 2 | 0 | 3 | 3 | 8 | 1 |
| *By Region* | | | | | | |
| New England | 2 | 1 | 2 | 1 | 0 | 0 |
| Mid-Atlantic | 1 | 1 | 1 | 0 | 4 | 0 |
| North Central | 0 | 1 | 1 | 1 | 6 | 0 |
| Plains | 1 | 0 | 0 | 5 | 1 | 1 |
| Far West | 1 | 0 | 2 | 2 | 3 | 1 |

POWER AND RESOURCE DEVELOPMENT

| | Classification | | | | | |
|---|---|---|---|---|---|---|
| Category | SL | ML | U | MC | SC | Not Scaled |
| *Total* (39) | 4 | 8 | 5 | 5 | 11 | 6 |
| *By Period of Entry* | | | | | | |
| New Deal | 0 | 3 | 1 | 1 | 2 | 2 |
| World War II | 2 | 2 | 4 | 1 | 4 | 0 |
| Postwar | 2 | 3 | 0 | 3 | 5 | 4 |
| *By Region* | | | | | | |
| New England | 1 | 0 | 0 | 0 | 4 | 1 |
| Mid-Atlantic | 0 | 0 | 0 | 1 | 4 | 2 |
| North Central | 0 | 0 | 1 | 2 | 3 | 3 |
| Plains | 1 | 4 | 2 | 1 | 0 | 0 |
| Far West | 2 | 4 | 2 | 1 | 0 | 0 |

* Figures in parentheses refer to the total number of senators in each group.

† Abbreviations of classifications are as follows: SI and MI =strong and moderate internationalists; U =uncommitted; MN and SN =moderate and strong nationalists; SL and ML =strong and moderate liberals; MC and SC =moderate and strong conservatives.

of liberally inclined Republican senators on both economic and welfare issues, with the Plains and North Central regions again at the opposite ideological pole. Western senators occupied a generally intermediate position on these issues, but—together with the Plains group—they were the most liberal on power and resource development questions.

The ideological profiles of the chairmen and Republican members of the most powerful Senate committees are also worth investigating. Since the powers of congressional committees to shape legislation are nearly definitive,[7] much of the legislative product of the Eighty-third Congress would depend on their ideological composition.

The Foreign Relations Committee, especially, has been traditionally near-sovereign in its area of concern. So great has its influence been that it has often marked a sort of "middle ground" between the executive and legislative branches in foreign policy making.[8] While the eight Republican incumbents on the committee in 1953 could not fairly be described as predominantly internationalist-minded, they were at least slightly friendlier to the concept of internationalism than were their party colleagues: three of the eight had internationalist records, compared with 26 percent among all returning Republican senators. Significantly, the committee's new chairman, Alexander Wiley of Wisconsin, ranked on the basis of his recent voting behavior as a moderate internationalist.[9]

While other Senate committees hold less undisputed sway in their policy domains, certain of them do have pronounced au-

7 See George Goodwin, Jr., *The Little Legislatures: Committees of Congress* ([Amherst]: Univ. of Massachusetts Press, 1970), x.

8 David N. Farnsworth, *The Senate Committee on Foreign Relations*, Vol. XLIX of Illinois Studies in the Social Sciences (Urbana: Univ. of Illinois Press, 1961), 11.

9 Wiley had earlier had a rather pronouncedly isolationist reputation, which had not changed completely by 1952. See, e.g., Bernard DeVoto, "Stevenson and the Independent Voter," *Harper's Magazine* 204, No. 1223 (Apr. 1952), 63. One 1952 survey did class Wiley as a "moderate internationalist," in agreement with my findings; see George D. Blackwood, "Let's Look at the Record," *The Reporter* 7, No. 2 (July 22, 1952), 16. One explanation for Wiley's "conversion" is the influence of his second wife, the former Dorothy Kydd, whom he married in 1952. Interview with John W. Bricker, Feb. 2, 1971, Columbus, Ohio.

thority. The Finance Committee, for example, plays a key role in shaping legislation relating to taxation, tariffs, and social security. Republican incumbents on that committee in 1953 tended strongly to the conservative side on both fiscal and welfare policy (six of the eight incumbent members scaled as conservatives, compared with Senate-wide Republican totals of 56 percent conservatives in the former area and 59 percent in the latter). The committee's chairman, Eugene Millikin of Colorado, was sufficiently far to the right that one knowledgeable observer tagged him "Mr. Conservative." Millikin's influence within the party was considerable—perhaps second only to Taft's, as the Eighty-third Congress convened.[10]

The Banking and Currency Committee, chaired in 1953 by Homer Capehart of Indiana, also had great influence in the Senate, bearing responsibility for considering legislation on housing as well as on economic controls. Of the four Republican incumbents on Banking and Currency, only Irving Ives of New York was moderately liberal. The others, including chairman Capehart, ranked as conservatives on both welfare and fiscal and economic matters.

The Appropriations and Labor and Public Welfare committees also played leading roles in policy areas which became important in 1953 and 1954. Appropriations, chaired by New Hampshire's Styles Bridges, had a voice in every piece of legislation requiring allocation of federal funds, including foreign aid. Conservative in their outlook in all three domestic policy areas, the twelve incumbent Republican members of Appropriations were also less inclined to accept internationalism than were Senate Republicans generally (only two could be styled internationalists). Bridges, senior in point of Senate service among Republican members, was a moderate nationalist, uncommitted on fiscal and economic policy, and otherwise conservative on domestic matters. On the other hand, the four GOP incumbents on the Labor and Public Welfare Committee all had either non-

10 Douglass Cater, " 'Mr. Conservative'—Eugene Millikin of Colorado," *The Reporter* 8, No. 6 (Mar. 17, 1953), 26.

committal or liberal records in the areas of their committee's special competence—welfare and fiscal and economic policy. The chairman, H. Alexander Smith of New Jersey, was a moderate liberal in both areas.

Although the vaunted independence of United States senators frustrates efforts at tight partisan discipline in the upper chamber, the Senate leadership in each party does often wield considerable influence.[11] The top Republican leadership positions in the Senate (majority leader, majority whip, and chairman of the Policy Committee) were held in January 1953 by Senators Robert A. Taft of Ohio, Leverett Saltonstall of Massachusetts, and William Knowland of California, respectively. When Knowland replaced Taft as majority leader in June 1953, he was succeeded by Michigan's Homer Ferguson.

These party leaders ranged across the ideological spectrum. Only on power and resource development were they together: Taft, Saltonstall, and Ferguson were conservatives, with Knowland uncommitted. Saltonstall, an early supporter of Eisenhower for the 1952 nomination, was easily the most liberal of the four in both other domestic areas, as well as the only internationalist among them. Ferguson was strongly conservative on welfare policy as well as being a nationalist, but he was uncommitted on fiscal matters. Senator Knowland, by contrast, presented something of a *tabula rasa* on the basis of his previous voting patterns, which showed him to be uncommitted in all areas except economic policy, where he ranked as a strong conservative.

Most powerful and important of all Senate Republicans at the beginning of the Eighty-third Congress was Robert Taft. Despite having fought the good fight on behalf of congressional conservatives for the presidential nomination in 1952, Taft had an interesting and varied record which showed him to be relatively liberal on welfare measures, uncommitted in the area of fiscal and economic policy, conservative on questions of power and resource development, and only moderately nationalist in his approach

11 Donald R. Matthews, *U.S. Senators & Their World* (New York: Vintage Books, 1960), 119, 121.

to foreign policy matters. Although a fellow senator's later, post-humous tribute to Taft as "one of the great liberals of [his] generation" undoubtedly overstated the case, the Ohioan's record indicated his receptiveness to at least a somewhat "activist" Republicanism if such should prove to be the desire of the new administration.[12] Taft's mixed record, like the diverse political profiles in the leadership group, served to emphasize the ideological variety which characterized Republicanism in the Senate of the Eighty-third Congress.

## The House Incumbents

House Republicans re-elected in 1952 had a collective political profile very much like that of their counterparts in the upper house. Only in power and resource development was there more than a slight difference between the breakdown of liberals and conservatives in the two chambers: on power questions, the House incumbents were considerably more conservative (see Table 5).

As with Republican senators, the period of House members' entry into Congress accounted for some differences in their voting patterns. Where noteworthy deviations existed in the lower house, the World War II bloc stood apart. Congressmen who had begun their service in Washington between 1940 and 1945 were more apt to be internationalists in foreign policy and liberals on domestic matters than were their colleagues dating from other periods. The only other striking difference related to period of entry was on the fiscal and economic policy scale, where, as in the Senate, the New Deal group was appreciably more conservative than other House Republicans (see Table 6).

Another parallel to the situation in the Senate was that Re-

---

[12] The quote is from a speech by Senator Ralph Flanders of Vermont, entitled "The Mission of a Liberal," delivered at St. Louis, Oct. 14, 1954. A copy is in the Irving M. Ives Papers, Collection of Regional History and Univ. Archives, Cornell Univ., Ithaca, N.Y. For a description of Taft as a domestic liberal, see Marquis Childs, *Eisenhower: Captive Hero; A Critical Study of the General and the President* (New York: Harcourt, 1958), 142. See also Patterson, *Mr. Republican*, esp. 315–34, 616.

*Table 5*  COMPARISON OF IDEOLOGICAL CLASSIFICATIONS OF
RETURNING REPUBLICAN INCUMBENTS, SENATE AND HOUSE,
EIGHTY-THIRD CONGRESS

| FOREIGN POLICY | | | | | |
|---|---|---|---|---|---|
| *Classification, percent* | | | | | |
| SI* | MI | U | MN | SN | Not Scaled |
| Senate (100%=39) 15 | 10 | 13 | 23 | 33 | 5 |
| House (100%=163) 6 | 18 | 22 | 18 | 33 | 4 |

| FISCAL AND ECONOMIC POLICY | | | | | |
|---|---|---|---|---|---|
| SL | ML | U | MC | SC | Not Scaled |
| Senate (100%=39) 8 | 15 | 15 | 33 | 23 | 5 |
| House (100%=163) 10 | 13 | 13 | 17 | 43 | 4 |

| WELFARE POLICY | | | | | |
|---|---|---|---|---|---|
| SL | ML | U | MC | SC | Not Scaled |
| Senate (100%=39) 13 | 8 | 15 | 23 | 36 | 5 |
| House (100%=163) 12 | 9 | 19 | 47 | 9 | 4 |

| POWER AND RESOURCE DEVELOPMENT | | | | | |
|---|---|---|---|---|---|
| SL | ML | U | MC | SC | Not Scaled |
| Senate (100%=39) 10 | 21 | 13 | 13 | 28 | 15 |
| House (100%=163) 2 | 5 | 10 | 38 | 39 | 5 |

* Abbreviations used are the same as those in Table 4.

publican House members from the Northeast (New England and
Mid-Atlantic states) were likely to have relatively liberal records
on fiscal-economic and welfare measures and to be more strongly
internationalist than Republican congressmen from other sections of the country. Conversely, those from the Midwest (especially the Plains states) and from the Border states tended to
deviate in a conservative and nationalist direction (see Table 6).
Only in the area of power and resource development questions

*Table 6*  IDEOLOGICAL CLASSIFICATIONS OF RETURNING RE-
PUBLICAN HOUSE INCUMBENTS, EIGHTY-THIRD CONGRESS, BY
PERIOD OF ENTRY, REGION, AND DISTRICT TYPE

|  | FOREIGN POLICY | | | | | |
|---|---|---|---|---|---|---|
|  | *Classification, percent**  | | | | | |
| *Category* † | SI** | MI | U | MN | SN | Not Scaled |
| *Total* | 6% | 18% | 22% | 18% | 33% | 4% |
| *By Period of Entry* | | | | | | |
| Pre-New Deal (14) | 0 | 21 | 14 | 21 | 43 | 0 |
| New Deal (31) | 3 | 13 | 29 | 6 | 45 | 3 |
| World War II (46) | 11 | 17 | 17 | 20 | 30 | 4 |
| Postwar (72) | 4 | 19 | 24 | 21 | 28 | 4 |
| *By Region* | | | | | | |
| New England (16) | 19 | 37 | 31 | 6 | 6 | 0 |
| Mid-Atlantic (43) | 14 | 28 | 28 | 5 | 19 | 7 |
| Border (6) | 0 | 0 | 0 | [33] | [50] | [17] |
| North Central (58) | 0 | 9 | 16 | 22 | 50 | 3 |
| Plains (18) | 0 | 6 | 17 | 22 | 56 | 0 |
| Far West (22) | 0 | 23 | 32 | 32 | 14 | 0 |
| *By District Type* †† | | | | | | |
| Metropolitan (40) | 15 | 27 | 35 | 5 | 15 | 2 |
| Mid-urban (45) | 4 | 18 | 22 | 18 | 31 | 7 |
| Small-town (53) | 2 | 15 | 21 | 19 | 42 | 2 |
| Rural (24) | 0 | 4 | 4 | 37 | 50 | 4 |

did the picture alter, where—again as in the Senate—the Far West
tended toward greater acceptance of federal involvement.

The type of district from which a congressman came seems to
have accounted for much sharper differences than either period
of entry or region.[13] The more heavily urban a congressman's

[13] Several studies of congressional behavior have emphasized the impact of
constituency (or district type) on a legislator's voting patterns. See, for example,
David R. Mayhew, *Party Loyalty Among Congressmen: The Difference Between
Democrats and Republicans, 1947–1962* (Cambridge: Harvard Univ. Press, 1966),
esp. 7–8, and Lewis A. Froman, Jr., *Congressmen and Their Constituencies* (Chicago: Rand McNally, 1963), esp. 92–95. See also Warren Miller and Donald E.
Stokes, "Constituency Influence in Congress," in Angus Campbell et al., *Elections
and the Political Order* (New York: Wiley, 1966), 351–72.

*Table 6* (CONTINUED)

| | FISCAL AND ECONOMIC POLICY | | | | | |
|---|---|---|---|---|---|---|
| | *Classification, percent* | | | | | |
| Category | SL | ML | U | MC | SC | Not Scaled |
| *Total* | 10% | 13% | 13% | 17% | 43% | 4% |
| *By Period of Entry* | | | | | | |
| Pre-New Deal | 29 | 0 | 14 | 21 | 36 | 0 |
| New Deal | 10 | 0 | 10 | 23 | 52 | 6 |
| World War II | 9 | 22 | 13 | 15 | 41 | 0 |
| Postwar | 8 | 15 | 14 | 15 | 42 | 6 |
| *By Region* | | | | | | |
| New England | 37 | 12 | 25 | 6 | 6 | 12 |
| Mid-Atlantic | 14 | 26 | 21 | 19 | 19 | 2 |
| Border | 0 | [17] | [17] | 0 | [67] | 0 |
| North Central | 7 | 7 | 9 | 17 | 59 | 2 |
| Plains | 0 | 0 | 0 | 17 | 78 | 6 |
| Far West | 5 | 14 | 9 | 27 | 41 | 5 |
| *By District Type* | | | | | | |
| Metropolitan | 22 | 27 | 12 | 15 | 20 | 2 |
| Mid-urban | 11 | 13 | 18 | 18 | 40 | 0 |
| Small-town | 4 | 6 | 15 | 21 | 49 | 6 |
| Rural | 0 | 4 | 0 | 12 | 75 | 8 |

district, the more inclined he was to favor internationalism and liberal fiscal-economic and welfare policies. No perceptible relationship existed between district type and ideology on power and resource questions (see Table 6).

House committees are at least as important as Senate committees in shaping particular pieces of legislation. In fact, the nature of its organization and responsibilities causes the lower house to be dominated by a handful of its committees: Rules, Ways and Means, and Appropriations. So important are these three that they are the only ones whose members are prohibited from serving on any other committee.[14]

14 See Nicholas A. Masters, "Committee Assignments in the House of Representatives," *American Political Science Review* 55, No. 2 (June 1961), 351; and Goodwin, *Little Legislatures,* 76, 114.

*Table 6* (CONTINUED)

| | WELFARE POLICY | | | | | |
|---|---|---|---|---|---|---|
| | *Classification, percent* | | | | | |
| Category | SL | ML | U | MC | SC | Not Scaled |
| *Total* | 12% | 9% | 19% | 47% | 9% | 4% |
| *By Period of Entry* | | | | | | |
| Pre-New Deal | 14 | 7 | 29 | 29 | 21 | 0 |
| New Deal | 10 | 6 | 19 | 48 | 10 | 6 |
| World War II | 24 | 7 | 15 | 43 | 7 | 4 |
| Postwar | 6 | 12 | 19 | 51 | 8 | 3 |
| *By Region* | | | | | | |
| New England | 6 | 19 | 31 | 31 | 6 | 6 |
| Mid-Atlantic | 26 | 14 | 23 | 28 | 7 | 2 |
| Border | 0 | [17] | [17] | [67] | 0 | 0 |
| North Central | 9 | 7 | 14 | 53 | 14 | 3 |
| Plains | 0 | 6 | 6 | 83 | 6 | 0 |
| Far West | 14 | 0 | 27 | 41 | 9 | 9 |
| *By District Type* | | | | | | |
| Metropolitan | 25 | 15 | 17 | 32 | 5 | 5 |
| Mid-urban | 7 | 9 | 22 | 44 | 11 | 7 |
| Small-town | 11 | 6 | 15 | 57 | 9 | 2 |
| Rural | 0 | 8 | 25 | 54 | 12 | 0 |

Of these three powerful bodies, the Rules Committee, with authority for setting the ground rules for consideration of every bill to come before the House, is perhaps most important to any administration's legislative plans. On the basis of their past voting behavior, Republican incumbents on the Rules Committee in the Eighty-third Congress seemed likely to exercise their influence in a strongly conservative direction. On the foreign policy scale, one of its eight Republican members, Hugh Scott of Pennsylvania, had an internationalist record, while half of the members were nationalists—a division fairly consistent with the overall division among House Republicans. Rules members were slightly more conservative than House Republicans generally on fiscal and economic policy, and even more strongly so on welfare mea-

*Table 6* (CONTINUED)

POWER AND RESOURCE DEVELOPMENT

| Category | Classification, percent | | | | | |
|---|---|---|---|---|---|---|
| | SL | ML | U | MC | SC | Not Scaled |
| *Total* | 2% | 5% | 10% | 38% | 39% | 5% |
| *By Period of Entry* | | | | | | |
| Pre-New Deal | 7 | 0 | 7 | 36 | 43 | 7 |
| New Deal | 3 | 3 | 3 | 29 | 52 | 10 |
| World War II | 2 | 9 | 13 | 30 | 39 | 7 |
| Postwar | 1 | 4 | 12 | 47 | 33 | 1 |
| *By Region* | | | | | | |
| New England | 0 | 0 | 0 | 37 | 56 | 6 |
| Mid-Atlantic | 2 | 0 | 5 | 26 | 58 | 9 |
| Border | 0 | 0 | [33] | [50] | [17] | 0 |
| North Central | 3 | 2 | 9 | 50 | 34 | 2 |
| Plains | 6 | 6 | 11 | 33 | 39 | 6 |
| Far West | 0 | 27 | 27 | 32 | 9 | 5 |
| *By District Type* | | | | | | |
| Metropolitan | 2 | 2 | 0 | 40 | 47 | 7 |
| Mid-urban | 0 | 7 | 7 | 47 | 36 | 4 |
| Small-town | 4 | 6 | 13 | 36 | 38 | 4 |
| Rural | 4 | 4 | 29 | 25 | 33 | 4 |

\* Percentages are summed across rows.

\*\* Abbreviations used are the same as those in preceding tables.

† Figures in parentheses refer to the total number in each group.

†† Does not include one at-large representative (George Bender of Ohio), whose district was not classified by *Congressional Quarterly*.

sures; on power policy, Republican members and nonmembers were equally strongly conservative. Rules chairman Leo Allen of Illinois was about as conservative on all issues as any on his committee. He was also "a straight party-line man who [could] be depended upon to route legislation the way the party leaders want it."[15]

Republican incumbents on the other two key House committees were not quite as politically intransigent as those on the

[15] "The Republican 83rd," *Time* 60, No. 20 (Nov. 17, 1952), 27. See Appendix B for Allen's voting profile.

Rules Committee. Ways and Means Committee members, with primary responsibility for tax measures, were disposed in about the same proportions as other House Republicans on fiscal and economic matters (23 percent liberals and 62 percent conservatives, as against total House GOP figures of 23 and 60 percent). Since Ways and Means also had control over trade legislation, the strongly nationalist orientation of its Republican members toward foreign policy questions was also significant. Only two of the committee incumbents scaled as internationalists, while eight were nationalists.

Republican incumbents on the powerful Appropriations Committee were barely to the internationalist side of nonmembers (only one-fourth of the committee Republicans rated an internationalist label), and otherwise differed significantly from other House Republicans only on welfare matters: 12 percent of the committee's Republican holdovers were liberals and 62 percent were conservatives on such matters, compared with the overall party figures of 21 and 56 percent.

The collective attitudes of the very powerful Ways and Means and Appropriations committees were heavily colored by the outlooks of the men who in 1953 became their chairmen, New Yorkers Daniel A. Reed and John Taber. Reed and Taber were both strong nationalists in foreign policy matters and conservatives in each of the major domestic policy areas (see Appendix B). Because of their seniority and influence among Republicans both inside and outside their committees, the degree of tractability exhibited by the two New York congressmen in the Eighty-third Congress would be of major importance to the fate of the Republican legislative program.

In addition to the three major House committees, the Foreign Affairs and Banking and Currency committees had important roles to play in the Eighty-third Congress. Foreign Affairs members were more inclined to internationalism than other House Republicans (over half its incumbents were internationalists, and only one-fifth nationalists). The committee's chairman, Robert Chiperfield of Illinois, scaled as uncommitted on foreign policy questions, but the group's "chieftain in fact," John M. Vorys of Ohio, was a moderate internationalist.[16] The Banking and Currency Committee, influential in housing, government controls, and other economic matters, had a strongly conservative Republican membership. In fiscal and economic matters, only one of its eleven incumbent members was a liberal, while nine were conservatives; on welfare measures, the division was two and eight, respectively. Chairman Jesse Wolcott of Michigan fitted in well with other members, exercising a generally conservative influence.

The Republican House leadership was on the whole more conservative than that of the Senate. Speaker Joseph Martin of Massachusetts, Floor Leader Charles Halleck of Indiana, and Whip Leslie Arends of Illinois did not have a liberal rating among them on any of the four scales. Martin's record, however, was noncommittal in all areas except that of power and resource development, where his record was so erratic that he could not be scaled. Floor Leader Halleck scaled as uncommitted on the foreign policy and welfare scales but as a conservative on other domestic questions. Arends, who had held the position of whip since 1943, was the most conservative of the three, scaling as such in each of the three domestic areas and as a strong nationalist on questions of foreign policy. Arends's conservatism was also reflected in the political complexion of his GOP whip organization, whose fifteen members he appointed. Of the thirteen assistant whips who were incumbents, only two were internationalists, one scaled as a liberal in both fiscal and welfare policy (Horace Seely-Brown of Connecticut), and none was a liberal on the power and resource development scale.[17]

16 On the roles of Chiperfield and Vorys in committee, see Goodwin, *Little Legislatures*, 94, 142; Holbert N. Carroll, *The House of Representatives and Foreign Affairs* (Pittsburgh: Univ. of Pittsburgh Press, 1958), 95–96; and H. Bradford Westerfield, *Foreign Policy and Party Politics: Pearl Harbor to Korea* (New Haven: Yale Univ. Press, 1955), 101, 104. For voting records, see Appendix B.

17 In the 83rd Congress, two of the 15 assistant whips were freshmen (Holt and Mailliard, Calif.). Arends's three regional deputy whips were Ralph Gamble (N.Y.), Charles Hoeven (Iowa), and Wesley D'Ewart (Mont.); the 10 incumbent assistants were William Bates (Mass.), C. W. "Runt" Bishop (Ill.), Leon Gavin (Pa.), Ralph

In general, leading Republicans in the House mirrored the predominantly conservative and nationalist sentiment of the party in that chamber. The Rules Committee, with a finger in every legislative pie, was strongly predisposed to the right in all areas; the elected party leaders who would guide administration programs on the floor were only slightly less conservative and nationalist; and if the Foreign Affairs Committee was internationally oriented, that tendency was countered for purposes of foreign policy legislation by the nationalist-dominated Appropriations and Ways and Means committees, which also had strong roles in foreign aid and trade legislation. The Old Guard was far from dead in January 1953, and the state of the party in the House—even more than in the Senate—bore solemn witness to the fact.

## The Outlook

The overall tenor of Republicanism in the Eighty-third Congress was undeniably nationalist and conservative, but—as Eisenhower later pointed out—individual party members "displayed a wide variety of political and philosophic views."[18] Senate Republicans, particularly, presented a diverse picture. In the three domestic policy areas, a consistent 20 to 30 percent of the Republican incumbents were liberals, with another 20 percent either uncommitted or too erratic in their voting to be classified. On foreign policy matters, just over one-fourth (ten of thirty-nine) were internationalists, and another 18 percent either uncommitted or unclassifiable. Such a group in itself offered the new President at least a chance to lead Senate Republicans in a liberal and/or internationalist direction, if he so desired. The addition of nine freshmen who were relatively unknown political quanti-

Harvey (Ind.), Harold Lovre (S.Dak.), Harry McGregor (Ohio), Walter Norblad (Ore.), Katharine St. George (N.Y.), Horace Seely-Brown, Jr. (Conn.), and William Van Pelt (Wis.). List taken from a memorandum, Homer Gruenther to Wilton Persons, Mar. 10, 1954, in OF 101–B–1 (3), Dwight D. Eisenhower Papers, Dwight D. Eisenhower Library, Abilene, Kans.

18 Eisenhower, *Mandate for Change*, 192.

ties in January 1953 only increased this potential for administration leadership.

In the House, Republicans seemed somewhat less diverse and perhaps less tractable. The eighty-three nationalists (51 percent of the incumbents), however, were nearly balanced by the thirty-eight internationalists and forty-two uncommitted or unscalable —not to mention the bumper crop of fifty Republican freshmen who might feel especially prone to follow their President's lead. On domestic matters, as well, the newcomers represented the possibility of countering Old Guard influence among House veterans. In fiscal and economic policy and on welfare questions, even if all the conservatives held firm to their convictions, the combination of incoming freshmen and uncommitted returnees could theoretically tip the balance among House Republicans in a liberal direction. Conservatism seemed certain to prevail among GOP members only on power and resource development questions.

Notwithstanding the general conservatism of the Republican leadership (especially in the major committees) with whom the new administration would have to work, then, the potential for change existed in the congressional wing of the Republican party in January 1953. Given the thinness of Republican majorities in both houses, Eisenhower would without doubt need Democratic votes to pass his programs, whether liberal or conservative, internationalist or nationalist; and the inherent divisions in the Democratic party, regional and otherwise, assured those votes. The real question at the outset of the Eighty-third Congress was not whether the first Republican President in twenty years would be able to secure passage for his program; the "honeymoon" effect, the certainty of Democratic support of one stripe or another (Southern conservatives or Northern liberals, depending on the policy), and the awareness among Republicans that they dared not buck their own administration too frequently all augured the enactment of a good deal of the Eisenhower program. But there were some important questions remaining: What would the nature of that program be? What would the "Eisen-

49

hower" brand of Republicanism mean, for the ultimate direction of the party? And how well would the party-in-Congress, presumably hostile as a whole to their own President's nomination in July 1952, respond to his leadership?

# CHAPTER THREE

# President Versus Party: Whose Foreign Policy?

$S$ince the days of Franklin D. Roosevelt, Republicans in Congress had chafed at the growth of executive influence and the concomitant increase in secrecy in the conduct of American foreign policy. While even the rabid Republican critics of Yalta, Potsdam, and other instances of presidential "usurpation" trusted Dwight Eisenhower far more than they had trusted either of his two Democratic predecessors, a large number of them continued to resent the executive branch's domination of American foreign relations. This bloc consisted almost entirely of Republicans identifiable as nationalists on foreign policy issues.[1]

To fight successfully against opposition to his internationalist programs, Eisenhower had to overcome congressional challenges to his authority in foreign policy making. This he did on three separate occasions in 1953–1954—by blocking enactment of the Yalta Resolution, securing confirmation of Charles Bohlen as ambassador to the Soviet Union, and fighting off passage of the Bricker amendment.

---

[1] On a Guttman scale constructed especially to show the attitudes of Republican senators to questions bearing on executive control of foreign policy during the 82nd Congress, all internationalists ranked as pro–executive control, and all nationalists as anti–executive control. Those who scaled as uncommitted (or were unscalable) on foreign policy issues were either uncommitted or anti–executive control on the special scale. See Appendix C for individual senators' scale scores on the foreign policy control scale and a list of the roll calls included in it.

The three cases demonstrated the diversity of White House techniques for congressional "crisis management." In the conflict over the Yalta Resolution, the administration failed to get the kind of draft declaration it wanted, and so forestalled debate on any. In securing Bohlen's confirmation, the President succeeded by obtaining the support of the Republican Senate leadership (particularly Senator Taft), and capitalized on his own reputation as one who understood the workings of the Cold War better than anyone else. Against proponents of the Bricker amendment, the White House victory was more limited. On the final roll calls, the administration barely prevailed, and then more because of Democratic votes than Republican. Although Eisenhower won over only one nationalist GOP senator in his fight against Senator John W. Bricker's proposed amendment "relative to the making of treaties and executive agreements," he did gain the support of several Republicans who had initially favored the measure. In this battle, perhaps more than on any other occasion during the life of the Eighty-third Congress, strong White House lobbying efforts were responsible for victory. Together, the three controversies help to illuminate the nature and limits of Eisenhower's influence within his party. Their outcomes, moreover, ensured that the executive would continue to dominate foreign policy for the duration of the Eisenhower Presidency.

The so-called Yalta (or "Enslavement of Peoples") Resolution was never enacted by the Eighty-third Congress. Yet Republicans had criticized the Yalta settlement almost from the time it was drawn up in early 1945, charging that its vague provisions for "democratic" regimes in East European countries then under the physical control of the Soviet Union amounted to underwriting the forceful subjugation of those peoples. As the Cold War intensified, so did partisan criticisms, with the result that the 1952 Republican platform included a pledge to repudiate any and all secret agreements which had helped to produce or justify Communist "enslavement" of unwilling peoples. Yalta was named specifically.

Early indications were that the new administration would follow through on the platform pledge. Secretary of State–designate John Foster Dulles, testifying in hearings on his confirmation in January 1953, stated that he fully supported the party platform statements on foreign policy, implying approval of the anti-Yalta section. Eisenhower, in his 1953 State of the Union message delivered shortly thereafter, announced that he would later ask for "an appropriate resolution" dealing with secret agreements.[2] By late February, the President became more specific about what he meant by "appropriate," as he forwarded a draft resolution to Congress for its consideration.

The administration draft, embodied in a measure (H.J. Res. 200) introduced by Representative John Vorys on February 23, disappointed nationalist Republicans who favored outright repudiation of the Yalta settlement. Declaring that the American government would not recognize any previous agreement which tended to legitimize Communist enslavement, the resolution criticized the Soviet Union for violating the "intent" of the Yalta accords. In thus failing to condemn the substance of the agreement itself, the declaration mirrored the political dilemma confronting the White House. Eisenhower understood that to imply guilt or willful deceit on the part of Presidents Roosevelt or Truman would alienate the bulk of congressional Democrats, many of whom might otherwise support his foreign policy.[3] The administration strategy, therefore, was to emphasize the future-mindedness of its draft declaration. "The past is controversial," Dulles told the Senate Foreign Relations Committee during hearings on the measure. "The resolution which President Eisenhower has proposed would avoid this realm of controversy. It

---

[2] Athan Theoharis, *The Yalta Myths: An Issue in U.S. Politics, 1945–1955* (Columbia: Univ. of Missouri Press, 1970), 155–56. See 1953 State of the Union Message, in *Public Papers of the Presidents of the United States: Dwight D. Eisenhower, 1953* (Washington: Government Printing Office, 1960), 13–14.

[3] Robert J. Donovan, *Eisenhower: The Inside Story* (New York: Harper, 1956), 48; Theoharis, *Yalta Myths*, 158–59; William S. White, *The Taft Story* (New York: Harper, 1954), 244.

validates nothing that is invalid. . . . What the President seeks is a solemn act of dedication for the future."[4]

Deadlock ensued almost immediately. After defeating a number of amendments offered by nationalist Representative Lawrence Smith (Wisconsin), the House Foreign Affairs Committee followed Vorys's lead and approved the resolution, 22–0.[5] But the White House wanted virtual unanimity behind the resolution, and this could not be presumed once it got to the House floor. On the Senate side, meanwhile, the declaration could not even get out of committee. Within the Foreign Relations Committee, Republicans Taft and Hickenlooper, dissatisfied with the failure of the draft to disown the Yalta accords *in toto*, proposed a reservation to the effect that its "adoption . . . does not constitute any determination by the Congress as to the validity or invalidity of any of the provisions of the said agreements or understandings."[6] Democrats on the committee understandably opposed such a statement, which, by Taft's admission, "raise[d] a doubt as to the validity of the Yalta and other agreements." Therefore, though the committee voted to report the amended resolution, the danger of a divisive floor struggle led the Republican leadership to delay publicizing the results of the group's deliberations pending further discussion.[7]

The Yalta resolution was laid to rest after the death of Joseph Stalin on March 5, 1953. Citing the unsettled world conditions resulting from the dictator's passing, the administration took the initiative in consigning the resolution to limbo. H. Alexander Smith of the Senate Foreign Relations Committee, who worked hard to come up with a compromise resolution through March

4 Undated copy of Dulles statement before the committee, H. Alexander Smith Papers, Princeton Univ. Library, Princeton, N.J.

5 See mimeographed copy, "Amendments proposed by Mr. [Lawrence] Smith," dated Feb. 27, 1953, with handwritten tallies of the committee votes on each amendment, John M. Vorys Papers, Ohio Historical Society, Columbus.

6 Theoharis, *Yalta Myths*, 160.

7 Undated handwritten memorandum by Robert Taft, and letter from Senator Alexander Smith to members of the Foreign Relations Committee, Mar. 7, 1953, Taft Papers.

7, recorded that "After talking with Dulles over [the] phone it was decided to postpone the matter at least for a few days," and Representative Vorys simultaneously agreed to postpone any further action in the House.[8] On March 10, the Foreign Relations Committee voted to table H.J. Res. 200 "without prejudice," and—although Senator Smith briefly considered reviving it—the Yalta Resolution did not re-emerge as an issue during the Eighty-third Congress.[9]

The shelving of the Yalta declaration represented an administration triumph, rather than a victory for Senator Taft and other opponents of the White House draft. Taft, in fact, was somewhat disgruntled, writing later that "it was a mistake to propose any kind of resolution if we weren't going to go through with the one which was promised."[10] It was true that the Eisenhower administration's draft was much milder than the strong "anti-Yalta" plank in the 1952 platform had promised. When nationalist leaders within the GOP inevitably balked at the President's version, he managed to have the matter quietly put aside rather than accepting a resolution sure to offend congressional Democrats and to impair his working relationship with them. Stalin's death provided a rationale for abandoning the resolution, but the White House probably would have reached the same decision sooner or later on tactical grounds. Throughout the period of political maneuver, the cooperation and leadership of Senator Smith and Representative Vorys were indispensable to the President's success.

Charles Bohlen's confirmation represented a more clear-cut triumph for the Eisenhower administration. Again Yalta entered the picture, as Bohlen, a career diplomatic official, had served as an interpreter at the 1945 conference. Although Bohlen was

---

8 See unsigned memorandum dated Mar. 7, 1953, Smith Papers.

9 See copy of Smith's letter to fellow Foreign Relations Committee members, dated Apr. 21, 1953, but unsent, and Walter George to Smith, Apr. 25, 1953, Smith Papers.

10 For the view that the outcome was a Taft victory, see White, *The Taft Story*, 251. The quote is from Robert Taft to Vernon Romney, Mar. 18, 1953, Taft Papers.

eminently qualified for the ambassadorial post, the same nationalist faction that supported a specific and vindictive Yalta declaration tended to oppose his appointment. In winning confirmation for him in late March 1953, however, the administration ultimately enjoyed the support of several of these nationalists, including some of the most powerful Republicans in the Senate.

Republican members of the Senate Foreign Relations Committee waged a formidable battle against Bohlen's appointment, but President Eisenhower never wavered from his position.[11] Within the committee, Senator Homer Ferguson was the ringleader of Republican forces arrayed against Bohlen. Ferguson's aim may have been more to condemn Democratic foreign policy generally than to imply that Bohlen bore direct responsibility for it, but his efforts had the latter effect. When the hearings opened on March 2, Ferguson, along with H. Alexander Smith and Knowland, did most of the questioning, while Senator Taft remained conspicuously silent. Bohlen, despite the urgings of his inquisitors, steadfastly refused to denounce either the Yalta agreement or President Roosevelt's motives in making it. Moreover, although Dulles had asked the diplomat to claim that he had been only an interpreter at the wartime conference, Bohlen insisted on admitting his advisory role there.[12]

By March 10, there were indications that the nomination would run into trouble from the Republican right wing. Citing rumors that a routine FBI check had shown Bohlen to be a possible security risk, Senators Bridges, Knowland, and McCarthy spoke out critically about the nomination.[13] In response to these criticisms, Secretary Dulles appeared before the committee on March 18 and, in an unprecedented move, personally testified as to the nature of the FBI report, holding that it indicated nothing

[11] See Eisenhower, *Mandate for Change*, 212; Charles E. Bohlen, with the editorial assistance of Robert H. Phelps, *Witness to History, 1929–1969* (New York: Norton, 1973), 322–23, 328.

[12] Farnsworth, *The Senate Foreign Relations Committee*, 51; James N. Rosenau, *The Nomination of "Chip" Bohlen*, Case 1 in Eagleton Institute Cases in Practical Politics ([New York]: McGraw-Hill, 1960), 7; and Bohlen, *Witness to History*, 313–14.

[13] Bohlen, *Witness to History*, 321–22, 324.

of the sort.[14] Following Dulles's testimony, the Foreign Relations Committee voted 15–0 for Bohlen's confirmation.

The unanimous vote of so prestigious a committee—including as it did affirmative votes by Senators Ferguson, Hickenlooper, Knowland, and Taft—helped to undermine Senate opposition to the appointment. Several prominent Republican senators, however, remained unconvinced, among them McCarthy and the powerful Styles Bridges. The floor debate, which lasted from March 23 to 27, was bitter and heated. The issue was finally settled only after Senators Taft and John Sparkman, a Democrat, were delegated by the Senate to appraise the questionable FBI report and returned with a verdict upholding Secretary Dulles's earlier testimony. A number of Republicans opposed to the nomination engaged in verbal catharsis during the debate, but once Senator Taft's prestige was thrown into the balance, it was obvious that most party members would support the President by voting for confirmation.

The administration triumphed resoundingly on March 27. The final vote for Bohlen was 74–13, with Republicans dividing 37–11 in his favor. All ten internationalists and six of the seven Republican senators who ranked as uncommitted or unscalable on foreign policy in the previous Congress voted aye, as did nine of the ten Republican freshmen.[15] Most significantly, twelve of twenty-one nationalists voted for Bohlen's confirmation. The "converts" included Senators Bennett, Hugh Butler, Capehart, Case, Ferguson, Langer, Martin, Margaret Chase Smith, Taft, Watkins, Williams, and Young; remaining in opposition were Bricker, Bridges, Dirksen, Dworshak, Hickenlooper, Malone, McCarthy, Schoeppel, and Welker.

The heavy vote confirming Charles Bohlen's nomination owed a great deal to Senator Taft. Having announced his intention to support the appointment before the Foreign Relations Committee reached its decision, the majority leader supported Eisen-

---

[14] *Ibid.*, 321–22, 324–25; Rosenau, *Nomination of "Chip" Bohlen,* 9.

[15] Among the uncommitted, the lone dissenter was Karl Mundt, and among freshmen, Barry Goldwater.

hower unstintingly in the ensuing debate. Taft was motivated by a desire to avoid a party split so early during the new administration, as well as by his belief that the President was exercising a legitimate prerogative in making the appointment; moreover, he thought the ambassadorial position insufficiently important "to make an issue of."[16] The question of executive prerogative probably decided the issue for a number of other senators as well, but there were other underlying forces at work, such as opposition to congressional examination of FBI files and nascent resentments of Senator McCarthy's use of the Bohlen case to attack the administration.[17]

After the Senate had voted confirmation, Taft stated that in supporting the nomination he "didn't believe [it] involved foreign policy—it related to past policy instead of future policy."[18] This was a spurious distinction, however. Even more directly than the Yalta declaration, the controversy over the Bohlen nomination involved the basic question of what the spirit of American foreign policy would be in the 1950s.

The protracted struggle over the Bricker amendment overshadowed all other Republican intraparty disagreements on foreign policy during 1953–1954. Again the White House won an important victory, though only by the thinnest of margins. On the crucial roll calls, taken in the Senate in February 1954, only one previously nationalist Republican senator (Ferguson) sided with the President by voting against the amendment, and the bulk of administration support came from Democrats. Yet, of forty-five GOP senators originally included among the measure's sponsors, eight ultimately voted against it. The fact that seven of these (Aiken, Duff, Flanders, Ives, Saltonstall, H. Alexander Smith, and Thye) were internationalists prior to 1953 should not obscure the very real achievement that this massive conversion represented.

16 White, *The Taft Story*, 234; Donovan, *The Inside Story*, 89; Patterson, *Mr. Republican*, 596.

17 Theoharis, *Yalta Myths*, 171.

18 Taft's statement of Mar. 27, 1953, quoted in Rosenau, *Nomination of "Chip" Bohlen*, 30.

Basically, Senator Bricker's proposal, introduced as S.J. Res. 1 on January 7, 1953, would have increased congressional authority over foreign policy making by limiting the power of the executive branch to enter into treaties and other international agreements. The Judiciary Committee revised the original proposal so that it actually resembled more closely a measure presented by Senator Arthur Watkins of Utah, but it continued to bear the name of Bricker, who had advocated such an amendment since 1951. Proponents of the measure argued primarily from the states' rights principle, specifically depicting the amendment as a preventative against treaties or executive agreements which might effect changes in "internal" (domestic) law in areas not delegated to the federal government in the Constitution. More likely, however, they were motivated by two other forces: opposition to Roosevelt's actions at Yalta and other wartime conferences and a desire to ensure that no President could ever again act with such autonomy; and fear that a President might irrevocably commit the United States to a United Nations convention on human rights (racial and sexual), which would upset patterns of segregation and discrimination prevalent in a number of the states.[19]

From the outset, Senator Bricker emphasized his desire to work "in close cooperation with the new Administration so that there [would be] no danger of hamstringing the President in the conduct of the Nation's foreign policy."[20] Soon, however, the administration moved into opposition against the key provision in the proposal—that no treaty could become effective as "internal law" except through "appropriate legislation" by Congress. In reporting the resolution on June 15, 1953, the Judiciary Committee transformed the original wording into the controversial "which clause": "A treaty shall become effective as internal law in the United States only through legislation which would be valid in the absence of a treaty." Even more restrictive

[19] See Herman Phleger Oral History Transcript, Dulles Project, Princeton Univ., 17; Theoharis, *Yalta Myths*, 181.

[20] Bricker to Dulles and Bricker to Brownell, Jan. 7, 1953, John W. Bricker Papers, Ohio Historical Society, Columbus.

than Bricker's wording, the "which clause" promised to curtail drastically the treaty-making power of the executive. Another section of the committee version, giving Congress the "power to regulate all executive and other agreements with any foreign power or international organization," proved equally unacceptable to the Eisenhower administration.

The White House support anticipated by Bricker never materialized, despite the fact that the 1952 Republican platform had seemed to point to some such amendment. By February 1953, both Secretary Dulles and Attorney General Brownell were advising Eisenhower to oppose the amendment, and in April both testified against it in the Judiciary Committee hearings.[21] Bricker was surprised that Eisenhower failed to support the measure, but evidently the President decided quite early to oppose it, believing that it would "just put us right back in the confederation of 1783."[22] In fact, Eisenhower played a crucial role in formulating the administration strategy, rejecting Dulles's advice to fight the amendment on the grounds that the executive branch should be free of such congressional restraints in foreign relations. Wisely, the President urged instead the ultimately successful strategy: arguing to Congress that the exigencies of the Cold War required the nation as a whole—and therefore the President, as its spokesman—to have greater maneuvering room in foreign policy making than the amendment would permit.[23]

Bricker soon despaired of the attitude in the executive branch. With some prescience, he wrote to Brownell in April 1953 of "the dangers in an all-out Administration attack on my position." He continued: "There is too much support for this amendment to

---

[21] On the early opposition of Dulles and Brownell, see Dulles to Sherman Adams, Jan. 2, 1953, and Brownell to Eisenhower, Feb. 13, 1953, OF 116–H–4 (1), Eisenhower Papers. By March, the Secretary of State was advising the Cabinet that even a revised version of the amendment was unacceptable.

[22] Dwight Eisenhower Oral History Transcript, Dulles Project, Princeton Univ., 17.

[23] Louis Gerson, *John Foster Dulles*, Vol. XVII of *The American Secretaries of State and Their Diplomacy*, ed. Robert H. Ferrell (New York: Cooper Square Publishers, 1967), 121; Herbert Parmet, *Eisenhower and the American Crusades* (New York: Macmillan, 1972), 309.

pass it off. A year's delay would make it seem to be a real attack upon the Administration and to show a lack of confidence in it. There is no such overtone at this time."[24]

While the administration decided early to oppose the Bricker amendment, it maintained a conciliatory tone and gave little active support to outright opponents of the measure. Senator Wiley, chairman of the Foreign Relations Committee, who took a public stand against the amendment or any compromise version thereof, received no White House encouragement whatever.[25]

The President's restrained opposition apparently had a strong impact on certain Republicans who were among the amendment's co-sponsors, however. In mid-April, Frank E. Holman of the American Bar Association wrote to Senator Bricker expressing concern that "one or two Senators now for the 'Bricker' Amendment had indicated . . . that since the Dulles et al [*sic*] testimony the issue had become 'politically hot' and that instead of voting for the Amendment and opposing the State Department they might merely absent themselves when the vote is taken." A few weeks later, one of those Republican waverers substantiated Holman's fears in a letter to Bricker. "I think you will recall that when I joined you in this resolution it was because I approve heartily of the importance of your bringing to the attention of the country at this time the possible abuses of the treaty making power," H. Alexander Smith wrote in early May 1953. "I was not sure then, and I am not sure now that we need an amendment to the Constitution." The next month, Smith's fellow New Jerseyite, Senator Robert Hendrickson, confided to one White House official that he, too, wanted "out" on S.J. Res. 1, and that he no longer felt obligated to support it as a co-sponsor because the Judiciary Committee version differed from the original.[26]

24 Bricker to Brownell, Apr. 2, 1953, Bricker Papers.

25 By late April 1953, Wiley was engaged in a "propaganda war" with Bricker, wherein each was sending fellow senators material regarding the amendment. See copies of letters from Wiley, dated Apr. 28, 1953, and Bricker, dated Apr. 30, to all senators, Bricker Papers.

26 Holman to Bricker, Apr. 13, 1953, and Smith to Bricker, May 4, 1953, Bricker Papers; Hendrickson to Bernard Shanley, June 16, 1953; and Shanley to Hendrickson, June 11, 1953, in OF 116–H–4 (3), Eisenhower Papers.

61

Negotiations proceeded sporadically throughout the first session of the Eighty-third Congress. At various times during the spring of 1953, Vice President Nixon and Cabinet members Herbert Brownell, George Humphrey, and Sinclair Weeks were each delegated to try to get Bricker to settle for establishment of a commission headed by himself to study the problem. For a time, the Ohio senator seemed disposed to compromise, writing in late May that it "would be very much in the public interest" to avert "an all-out fight" on the matter. After a mid-June conference at the White House, however, it was apparent that neither Bricker nor the President was willing to compromise on the essential "which clause." When the Senator notified the White House on June 23 that he would not concede the point, Eisenhower decided that "there was nothing else to do but get ready for a fight to the end."[27]

Both sides continued to act as if they believed that agreement was possible. "Whatever may be the Administration's ultimate position on this question," wrote Bricker to *Time* publisher Henry Luce in July, "I cannot regard the proposed amendment as an anti-Administration measure."[28] In the same month, the White House attempted, through the vehicle of a substitute sponsored by Majority Leader Knowland, to get the Senate to accept a formula which would require "appropriate legislation" to put a treaty into effect as "internal law" only if the Senate should so stipulate in its ratification vote. Although the President announced that the Knowland substitute had his "unqualified support," Bricker judged it unacceptable, as did many of his rank-and-file supporters. "This trashy Substitute," one such irate constituent wrote of the Knowland proposal, "sounds Stassony [*sic*], Dullesish, and reeks of the old tactics of the State Department."[29] The Senate took no action on the amendment before the first session ended.

27 Bricker to H. Alexander Smith, May 29, 1953, Bricker Papers; Eisenhower, *Mandate for Change*, 283.
28 Bricker to Luce, July 10, 1953, Bricker Papers.
29 Constituent letter to Bricker, Aug. 18, 1953, Bricker Papers.

Further unsuccessful compromise efforts occupied succeeding months. They reached a peak in December and January, when, according to Bricker, "at least fifty drafts of a compromise text" were produced.[30] During this time the Republican Policy Committee, and especially its chairman, Senator Ferguson, took a leading part in negotiations between the Brickerites and the administration; the committee held no fewer than twelve meetings on the amendment in June–July 1953 and January–February 1954.[31] These last efforts, probably doomed in any case by the fundamental differences separating the two sides, were also hampered by the administration's handling of Senator Bricker. Eisenhower and his advisers seem to have completely misread the Ohioan's motives, believing that what Bricker wanted was "something big in public with his name on it."[32] The Senator was treated accordingly. In one "negotiating" session, held on January 8, 1954, Bricker reported being presented with "practically an ultimatum" and said he felt as if he were being subjected to "brain washing."[33] This session seems to have ended even the pretense of negotiating, for immediately afterward Senator Bricker determined to "go to work on all . . . contacts and supporters throughout the country," in preparation for a showdown. He also renewed on a grand scale his propaganda efforts within the Senate itself, especially with those still undecided on the amendment. While Senators Saltonstall, Millikin, and Knowland pressed Eisenhower to continue negotiations with Bricker, Senator Wiley, on behalf of the congressional forces opposed to the measure, urged the President to stand firm against the amend-

[30] Bricker to Senator Karl Mundt, Feb. 1, 1954, Bricker Papers.

[31] Jewell, *Senatorial Politics and Foreign Policy*, 93; Bone, *Party Committees and National Politics*, 190.

[32] Hughes, *Ordeal of Power*, 143.

[33] Bricker had apparently held out little hope for the Jan. 8 session beforehand, writing the day before to White House aide I. Jack Martin that "agreement . . . now seems improbable." Letter dated Jan. 7, 1954, in possession of Mrs. I. Jack Martin, Kensington, Md. For a detailed description of the Jan. 8 meeting, based on Bricker's own summary, see Frank Holman to Clarence Manion and other members of the ABA Committee on Peace and Law Through the United Nations, Jan. 9, 1954; also see Bricker's letter to senators not definitely opposed to S. J. Res. 1, dated Jan. 20, 1954, both in Bricker Papers.

ment. "It seems apparent to me that you cannot agree to any language that would limit your authority," wrote Wiley, since "our [world] leadership will depend, in large measure, upon your ability to act decisively when the situation requires it."[34]

The month of January was decisive for the fate of the amendment. For a time early in the month, Eisenhower considered accepting a slightly watered-down version that would have met Bricker's main objective: requiring legislation before a treaty could have "internal effect." An exchange of letters with his old friend John J. McCloy, however, steeled the President in his opposition. Responding to Eisenhower's request for his opinion, McCloy reinforced the President's own early feelings, arguing against any amendment at all. At a time when the Cold War demanded firm American response, he argued in a letter to the President on January 18, "the constitutionally elected executive of this country should be armed with weapons of the temper and form necessary to enable him to maintain the leadership of the free nations . . . ."[35] On January 25, President Eisenhower publicly announced that he opposed the Bricker amendment "unalterably."[36]

As a showdown neared, neither side felt entirely confident of its chances for success. Bricker, however, believed that the public was behind him: "I am sorry that the influence of the one-worlders at the White House exceeds mine," he wrote to one concerned citizen in mid-January 1954, "but glad that their influence on Main Street is negligible." Of the outcome in the Senate, he was more dubious. Although he told a sympathetic Republican congressman that he thought the measure would pass, Bricker admitted that it was "impossible . . . to judge the

---

[34] Wiley to Eisenhower, Jan. 8, 1954, in possession of Mrs. I. Jack Martin, Kensington, Md.

[35] Eisenhower to McCloy, Jan. 13, 1954, and McCloy to Eisenhower, Jan. 18, 1954, copies in possession of John W. Bricker, Columbus, Ohio.

[36] Eisenhower to William F. Knowland, OF 116–H–4, Eisenhower Papers. See also the President's press conference remarks of Feb. 3, 1954, in *Public Papers . . . 1954*, 225.

effect of an all-out attack by the President."[37] Administration insiders, meanwhile, foresaw a clear-cut defeat for any measure which included the "which clause." In the interests of harmony, they urged a "substitute . . . agreeable to [a] bipartisan group."[38] Meanwhile, attrition continued to reduce the number of Republican senators supporting the amendment. According to Senator Flanders, by late January a number of "the liberal Senators" backing the amendment intended "to make individual withdrawals from commitment."[39] In the face of such news, White House optimism grew.

Most of February was consumed by the maneuvering of the Brickerites, administration forces, and moderate amendment advocates who coalesced around a substitute offered by Democrat Walter George. On February 4, Bricker tried to merge his forces with supporters of the George substitute, which provided that only international agreements other than treaties would require congressional legislation in order to become "internal law." Bricker's new version substituted George's wording for the controversial "which clause" but provided that treaties, too, require congressional implementation, unless the Senate waived the requirement by a two-thirds vote. Senator George was not amenable, remarking that any further attempts to compromise would be futile. Meanwhile, as debate proceeded on the Senate floor, a number of modifying amendments were successfully pressed by Senators Ferguson, Knowland, Millikin, and Saltonstall on behalf of the administration. The Republican leaders' amendments considerably weakened the provisions of S.J. Res. 1. One of Ferguson's amendments, for example, deleted the "which clause"

[37] Bricker to Edmond Lincoln, Jan. 18, 1954, and Bricker to Rep. Lawrence Smith (Wis.), same date, Bricker Papers.

[38] Homer Gruenther memorandum to Wilton Persons, Gerald Morgan, and I. Jack Martin, Jan. 23, 1954, Box 2, A67–19 Accessions, Gerald Morgan Records, Eisenhower Papers.

[39] Flanders to Paul G. Hoffman, Jan. 27, 1954, Ralph E. Flanders Papers, George Arents Research Library, Syracuse Univ., Syracuse, N.Y. For evidence of lessening Republican support, see Prescott Bush to Bricker, Jan. 19, 1954, and Bricker reply, Jan. 21, Bricker Papers.

and provided that treaties were to become "the supreme law of the land" so long as they were "made in pursuance of [the] Constitution." Another administration-backed change stipulated that international agreements could take effect if they did not "conflict with" the Constitution. Over the space of eleven days (February 15 through 25), the Senate accepted a number of these administration-supported amendments, by widely varying margins. Attention then turned to the two crucial votes: on Bricker's amended version of February 4 and the substitute offered by Senator George.

In a sense, the administration's success in staving off both the Bricker and George proposals owed comparatively little to Senate Republicans. The 42–50 defeat of Bricker's revised measure saw only eighteen Republicans vote for the President's position (against the amendment), while twenty-eight voted with Bricker. Republicans gave even less help to the administration on the George substitute. On a roll call taken to decide whether the Georgia Democrat's wording should be substituted for the original S.J. Res. 1 (a matter requiring only a simply majority in favor), the vote was 61–30, with Republicans voting 30–17 for it, despite the President's opposition. In the end, however, the administration won a narrow victory. On the final roll call, to decide whether the measure (now consisting of the George substitute) should be submitted to the states for ratification, the Senate divided 60–31, falling short by one vote of the two-thirds majority required for approval of a constitutional amendment. Still, on that final test, only fifteen of forty-seven voting Republican senators voted nay.

Taking into consideration all three of the crucial roll calls held on S.J. Res. 1, President Eisenhower enjoyed full support from relatively few Republican senators. Only thirteen, including four freshmen (Bush, Cooper, Purtell, and Robert Upton, who had replaced the late Charles Tobey in the Senate) voted for the administration position every time. Of the nine non-freshmen who did so, only Policy Committee chairman Homer Ferguson was a nationalist on foreign policy matters; the eight others

(Aiken, Duff, Ives, Morse, Saltonstall, H. Alexander Smith, Thye, and Wiley) were internationalists. Aside from Ferguson, every Republican nationalist (twenty in all) voted against the administration on all three roll calls. More diverse was the response of the uncommitted and unscalable Republicans: three (Hendrickson, Knowland, and Millikin) voted with the administration twice, one (Carlson) did so on one of the roll calls, and three (John Butler, Cordon, and Mundt) voted against it all three times. Yet even though President Eisenhower made little headway with party nationalists in the Bricker amendment controversy, he did what he had to do. By regaining the support of internationalists like Ralph Flanders and H. Alexander Smith, he avoided defeat.

Nearly two decades after the climactic roll calls, John Bricker stated that his constitutional amendment failed to pass because of "Dwight Eisenhower—nobody else!" Although Bricker was uncertain whether actual pressure from the administration or the mere fact of its opposition had caused the shifts, he claimed that the White House was responsible for the opposition of a number of senators who had originally supported the proposal, among whom he listed Senators Bush, Duff, Ferguson, Purtell, H. Alexander Smith, and Wiley.[40] Eisenhower admitted later that he "used all the powers he could" against the Bricker amendment,[41] and this included putting pressure on individuals. One undated list in the Eisenhower Papers shows that for the last, important roll calls, the White House assigned a personal "contact" to each Republican senator. Then, according to Bricker, when the final votes were actually taken, "two or three" administration emissaries were hard at work in the Senate cloakrooms.[42] Testi-

---

40 Interview with Bricker, Feb. 2, 1971, Columbus, Ohio. He was probably incorrect in including Wiley in this group, since the Wisconsin senator did not co-sponsor S.J. Res. 1 and was more intransigent throughout than the President.

41 Nov. 23, 1961, CBS television program, "Eisenhower on the Presidency—II," summarized in the *New York Times*, Nov. 24, 1961.

42 See list of senators, with probable "yeas" and "nays" recorded, and names of individual liaison men assigned to them (issue unspecified, but filed in folder marked "Secret Pacts and Executive Agreements 1954"), in OF 116–H–4, Eisenhower Papers. Bricker interview, Feb. 2, 1971, Columbus, Ohio.

mony given by one consistent opponent of the amendment most likely held true for others: "Actually, to support Eisenhower, I voted against it on the floor," said Leverett Saltonstall years later, "although I hated to do it."[43]

The battles over the Yalta Resolution, the Bohlen nomination, and the Bricker amendment all ended without defeat for the Eisenhower administration. None of the controversies revolved around a question of specific policy favored by the new President, but each represented a challenge to his control of the machinery by which foreign policy was made and implemented. If the nationalists in Congress had been able to muster enough votes to defeat Eisenhower on any one of the three issues, they might have sought other victories. Moreover, such an outcome might have produced attrition among the supporters of specific administration programs in foreign policy (such as foreign aid, reciprocal trade, and revision of immigration restrictions). Through compromise, patience, and painstaking effort, the Eisenhower administration managed to hold off the forces of opposition. In so doing, it conserved its offensive energies for the substantive measures which together formed the "internationalist" program of 1953–1954.

[43] Saltonstall Oral History Transcript, Eisenhower Project, Eisenhower Library, 150.

# CHAPTER FOUR

# The "Internationalizing" of the GOP

According to several who knew him well, Dwight Eisenhower believed more deeply in the cause of collective security than in any other single policy goal, foreign or domestic. In fact, it may have been this concern alone which led him to challenge Robert Taft for the 1952 nomination.[1] As President, consequently, he worked hard to ensure adoption of collective security policies by the Republican-controlled Eighty-third Congress. Eisenhower believed the question to be as simple as it was basic: "whether or not the United States was willing to accept the leadership of world democracy . . . ."[2]

The period 1945–1952 produced an unprecedented degree of peacetime bipartisan cooperation on issues such as the United Nations, the Marshall Plan, and the North Atlantic Treaty Organization, all of which epitomized an "internationalist" approach in United States foreign policy. Even if this postwar bipartisanship fell short of achieving perfect harmony,[3] Repub-

---

[1] Arthur Larson, *Eisenhower: The President Nobody Knew* (New York: Scribner's, 1968), 68. Roper says that this same commitment could have brought Eisenhower into one or the other party race in 1948, had either nominated an isolationist (*You and Your Leaders*, 235). See also Donovan, *The Inside Story*, 147; Hughes, *Ordeal of Power*, 81; and Bernard DeVoto, "Preliminary Forecast," *Harper's Magazine* 206, No. 1232 (Jan. 1953), 53.

[2] Adams, *Firsthand Report*, 104.

[3] Cecil V. Crabb, Jr., *Bipartisan Foreign Policy: Myth or Reality?* (Evanston: Row, Peterson, 1957), 2.

lican support for such programs nevertheless testified that, as Eisenhower said during the 1952 campaign, "isolationism" was a dead issue. Yet the period also witnessed increasingly sharp rhetorical conflict—between and within the parties—on fundamental questions about the proper extent and nature of United States involvement in world affairs. "Nationalists," desirous of a reduced American role in global matters, resided primarily in the Republican party. On the basis of voting in the Eighty-second Congress, between 50 and 60 percent of all Republicans returning to Congress in 1953 held this viewpoint.

While Republican nationalists occasionally differed on questions of specific policy, such as the relative importance of European and Asian problems, nearly all shared a desire to cut the amount of foreign aid favored by Democrats and "internationalists" in their own party. Ending this international "give-away" became one of their primary objectives. Many of these nationalists looked with suspicion upon their new President, fearing that he would continue to overextend the nation's resources in the pursuit of collective security, through lenient trade policies as well as foreign aid. Such intraparty differences, Walter Lippmann wrote, presaged "a very stormy Administration."[4]

In his 1953 State of the Union message, President Eisenhower proclaimed the onset of a "new, positive foreign policy." Over the next two years this new policy came to include requests for new foreign aid appropriations totaling nearly $9 billion, successive requests for extension of the reciprocal trade program, and a bill to liberalize immigration restrictions, as well as a number of more specific programs bearing on the disposal of surplus farm commodities. In the end, though he had to agree to reductions and alterations in nearly all these programs, Eisenhower succeeded in getting a majority of Republicans in both houses to support his foreign policy measures. The building of this "internationalist" majority within his party demonstrated the

[4] Lippmann, "Responsibility and the Republicans," Washington *Post*, Oct. 23, 1952.

strength of the President's leadership on matters which concerned him deeply.

Realizing the difficult situation in the Republican party, Eisenhower launched his internationalist program with caution. Therefore, he used the rhetoric of economy in requesting $5.8 billion in new funds for the mutual security (foreign aid) program in fiscal 1954. "Unequivocally," the President announced in his foreign aid message of May 5, 1953, "I can state that this amount of money judiciously spent abroad will add much more to our Nation's ultimate security in the world than would an even greater amount spent merely to increase the size of our own military forces . . . ."[5] Leading congressional Republicans, including Senators Taft, Bridges, Dirksen, and Millikin, and Representatives Robert Chiperfield and John Taber, chairmen of the House committees (Foreign Affairs and Appropriations, respectively) with primary jurisdiction over foreign aid authorization and appropriations, reacted negatively to the presidential message.[6] Shortly thereafter, the White House sliced another $354 million from the original figure, citing "savings" from the previous year.

On June 16, after hearing testimony from several high-level administration officials, the House Foreign Affairs Committee introduced an authorization measure calling for approximately $500 million less than the President had asked. The bill also included a provision withholding half of all authorized military aid from any European nation failing to ratify the European Defense Community (EDC) pact. The administration opposed the EDC stipulation but followed the advice of Representative John Vorys, chief White House spokesman on the Foreign Affairs Committee. Vorys warned Dulles and Mutual Security Agency director Harold Stassen that advocates of the provision would

---

5 Message in *Public Papers . . . 1953*, 256–59. See also, e.g., Dulles statement of Apr. 3, 1953, in *New York Times*, Apr. 4.

6 See *ibid.*, Mar. 22, Apr. 30, May 1, May 2, May 3, May 15, and *Washington Post*, May 6, all 1953.

"quote me and they may quote you" in a floor debate, and in any case the Senate was not considering such a rider, so that a conference might be expected to drop it.[7] The EDC provision therefore remained in the bill, and after two days of rather acrimonious debate, the authorization measure passed by a vote of 280–108, with House Republicans voting for it by 119–81. In the Senate, the authorization bill had somewhat smoother sailing, passing by voice vote on July 1. The conference then compromised the EDC provision, stipulating that all European military aid could be contracted for, but only half could be delivered unless the EDC were ratified. In its final form, the act authorized just over $5.1 billion in foreign aid for fiscal 1954.

Traditionally, the appropriations half of the process is the more damaging to executive foreign aid measures; 1953 was no exception. The House Appropriations Committee, given first crack at the total, reported out a bill calling for only $4.4 billion —this following the assiduous wooing of chairman John Taber by the White House.[8] Although Eisenhower publicly criticized the committee cuts as "too heavy" on July 22, one day later the House voted by 289–115 (Republicans dividing 129–82) to uphold the $4.4 billion figure.[9]

The President announced almost immediately after the House action that the foreign aid program could manage, after all, on the $4.4 billion, despite his earlier description of $5.4 billion as an irreducible minimum. Administration spokesmen in the Senate were reportedly asked only to "hold the line" against further cuts, but the White House conducted a fairly energetic campaign to persuade Republican senators to vote to restore some of the cuts. On July 24, for example, Eisenhower's chief liaison official, General Wilton Persons, received a "reminder" from one of his staff members to "apply [his] remarkable wiles to Senator McCarthy in regard to the MSA appropriations." The memo continued: "The pitch is to ask that the Senate restore some [$700 million]

---

[7] Vorys Oral History Transcript, Dulles Project, Princeton Univ., 25.
[8] *New York Times*, July 16, 1953.
[9] Press conference statement on July 22, 1953, in *Public Papers . . . 1953*, 508.

of the House cut . . . ."[10] Senate performance fell short of White House hopes, but its bill provided an appropriation of $4.56 billion—or a restoration of about $150 million. Thirty-two of the forty-one Republican senators answering the final roll call voted for the appropriation. Remaining in opposition were eight of the party's staunchest nationalists (Bricker, Capehart, Dworshak, Jenner, Langer, Malone, Welker, and Young) and freshman Barry Goldwater. After conference, the appropriation stood at slightly over $4.53 billion. Thus, the President had to accept a reduction in his original request nearly as great as the 24 percent cut accepted by Truman in 1952.[11]

Administration spokesmen talked of a much-reduced aid program for fiscal 1955. Even Harold Stassen, head of the agency which handled the program and an enthusiastic proponent of foreign aid, declared in December 1953 that the following year would see "more trade and less aid."[12] A month later, in his 1954 State of the Union message, the President promised reductions at least in economic aid because of "gratifying evidence that its objectives are being achieved."[13] He then confirmed earlier indications by asking in the budget message only for approximately $3.5 billion for the 1955 foreign aid program. The requested amount, Eisenhower told Congress in a later special message, was "minuscule compared to the cost of a global war which these programs help to prevent."[14] As the President had predicted earlier, the bulk of the $3.5 billion represented military aid. The administration proposal also mollified some of its Republican critics by shifting the emphasis from Europe to Asia, with nearly one-third going for support of "anti-Communist forces in Indo-China."[15]

[10] Report in *New York Times*, July 27, 1953; memorandum, Bryce Harlow to Wilton Persons, July 24, 1953, Eisenhower Papers.

[11] Parmet, *Eisenhower and the American Crusades*, 286.

[12] *New York Times*, Dec. 22, 1953.

[13] *Public Papers . . . 1954*, 9–10. See also predictions of reductions by Sens. Carlson and Ferguson, *New York Times*, Dec. 24, 1953, and Jan. 12, 1954.

[14] Special Message on Mutual Security, June 23, 1954, in *Public Papers . . . 1954*, 592.

[15] *New York Times*, Apr. 7, 1954.

The White House paid close attention to House action on its foreign aid request. In order to head off the attempts of nationalists on the Foreign Affairs Committee (led by Marguerite Stitt Church of Illinois) to impose severe restrictions on implementation of the program, President Eisenhower sent a special message to Congress urging that no further cuts or restrictions be effected on his proposal. Within hours of his appeal, in an action described by Vorys as "unprecedented," the committee voted out a bill only $7 million shy of the $3.5 billion request.[16] The administration's strong interest in the measure was obvious when Speaker Martin scheduled for June 28 the first Republican party caucus ever called on a foreign aid bill. After being assured by colleagues that "the line could be held," Martin canceled the projected caucus, but the message undoubtedly got through to Republican House members who were still on the fence.[17] Following an energetic floor debate, the lower house voted an authorization of $3.37 billion. On the final vote, Republicans divided about as they had in the first session, favoring the bill by 118–79. Twenty-one of seventy-five nationalists (28 percent) voted for it, as did thirty-one of forty-one (76 percent) of the voting Republicans who were uncommitted on foreign policy prior to 1953. Important "converts" included Rules Committee chairman Leo Allen, Republican whip Leslie Arends, and Taber. The administration also gained the support of thirty-three of forty-eight (69 percent) of the voting freshmen.

Because the Senate was bogged down on other matters, the House proceeded to take up the appropriations stage before the authorization bill cleared the upper chamber. Once again the Appropriations Committee carved up the proposal, recommending only $2.9 billion in new funds. Taber, by this time apparently sympathetic to the administration, explained that "the problem was how to avoid deeper cuts in the full committee."[18] As an indication of the committee's mood, its report sharply

---

16 *Ibid.*, June 24, and Washington *Post*, June 24, 1954.
17 *New York Times*, June 28, June 29, 1954.
18 Washington *Post*, July 25, 1954.

criticized Stassen and the Foreign Operations Administration for "fiscal irresponsibility." [19] The full House put its imprimatur to mood and measure alike, accepting the $2.9 billion figure by a vote of 266–128 (Republicans supported it, 121–85) on July 28.

The Senate acted on both authorization and appropriation bills in the space of two weeks. The Foreign Relations Committee set an authorization figure of $3.1 billion, about halfway between the $3.3 billion authorization and $2.9 billion appropriation voted by the House. In the face of a lackluster Republican floor defense of the President's program, Democrat Russell Long of Louisiana secured adoption of an amendment cutting the authorization by another half-billion dollars. Much of the sentiment for such a cut grew out of opposition to continued military and economic aid for Indochina, now that a cease-fire had been achieved there. Dulles's plea that "the armistice does not diminish the need for these funds" failed to overcome that sentiment. [20] Significantly, Senate Republicans stuck by the President, however, opposing the Long amendment by 26–19. Though most of the nationalists voted for it, the President was supported by a number of "converts" whom he was coming to rely upon on foreign policy questions; these included Bridges, Dirksen, Ferguson, Hickenlooper, Edward Martin, and Margaret Chase Smith.

During the floor debate on the authorization bill, defense of the administration's program was neither altruistic nor idealistic. Appealing to the hardheaded nationalism of their party colleagues, Senator Wiley described the aid program as "probably the single most anti-Communist program we have," and H. Alexander Smith advised the Senate to face the fact that mutual security was "a program to save our own lives . . . ." [21] The Senate passed the reduced authorization easily, with Republicans supporting it by 30–15.

The President tried his best to be accommodating in the face

---

19 *New York Times,* July 25, 1954.

20 See Dulles statement in a letter read on the floor by Sen. Wiley, *Congressional Record,* Vol. c, Part 10, 83d Cong., 2d Sess., 13025.

21 *Ibid.,* Part 9, 83d Cong., 2d Sess., 12326.

of congressional frugality. On August 4, he told his press conference that although the Senate cut was "too deep," he now believed that the House figure (the $2.9 billion appropriation) was "as good a guess as ours." At almost the same time, Senator Smith guessed privately that after conference the authorization would be about $3 billion, "which will probably be okay."[22] Smith's estimate of the outcome of the conference was correct, as the final authorization was $3.05 billion. When the Senate took up the appropriation bill, however, it reduced the amount by another $200 million, adopting a Democratic amendment limiting the funds available for military aid in Indochina. In a show of support for Eisenhower's foreign policy, Republicans unsuccessfully opposed the cut by 12–27. Three freshmen supported the cut (Barrett, Goldwater, and Potter); of the other nine who supported it, all but Karl Mundt were nationalists (Case, Dworshak, Jenner, Langer, Schoeppel, Watkins, Williams, and Young). After Senate passage, the conferees then settled on a final appropriation of $2.78 billion.

Although the foreign aid allotment for fiscal 1955 fell $700 million short of President Eisenhower's original request, the result did not represent a defeat for the administration. Senator Smith, after conferring with Dulles, privately described as "okay" the $3 billion authorization—a figure only $200 million higher than the final appropriation ($2.78 billion).[23] Moreover, the White House succeeded, through the direct intercession of Dulles, in persuading the Senate Foreign Relations Committee to reject the EDC stipulation which the House had adopted, thereby keeping the rider out of the 1954 bill. Most important as an indicator of the President's leadership, a majority of Republicans in House and Senate alike supported him on nearly every crucial roll call. Included among the previously noninternationalist senators who fully backed the program were such influentials as Dirksen, Ferguson, Knowland, and Millikin.

22 Press conference remarks in *Public Papers . . . 1954*, 685. Smith comment in his 1954 Diary, Smith Papers, 311 (Aug. 4).
23 *Ibid.*, 312–13 (Aug. 5, 1954).

Eisenhower could take a major share of the credit for the Republican response. In part, of course, it reflected the general respect which congressional party members felt for his expertise in foreign affairs. A second important reason for success, however, was the administration's willingness to accept gracefully congressional reductions in its original requests. Such grace was possibly only because the Eisenhower administration, notwithstanding its denials, repeated the Truman tactic of asking for more funds than it needed. Finally, the White House pursued a course of argument designed to win over Republicans who did not sympathize with the principle of foreign aid. Appeals to American self-interest and national security were combined with the rhetoric of economy. The new administration, said Senator Wiley at one point during the 1954 authorization debate, was "getting away from the idea of spend, spend, spend" and moving toward a "philosophy . . . of save, save, save."[24] These tactics could not, of course, produce unanimous Republican support for foreign aid, but Eisenhower's construction of a party majority in favor of the internationalist program was a notable achievement.

In some respects, President Eisenhower met with less success in selling his trade policies to fellow Republicans than he did with foreign aid. Faced with strong opposition in both sessions of the Eighty-third Congress, the President had to settle for consecutive one-year, "as is" extensions of the Trade Agreements Act, although he originally wanted more. In part this was because the reciprocal trade program flew in the face of traditional Republicanism even more than did foreign aid. The mutual security program, after all, dated only from the end of World War II and was billed by its proponents as a merely temporary expedient. Moreover, the spirit of bipartisanship in Congress after 1945 had produced a certain degree of Republican cooperation on the program from the outset. Reciprocal trade, on the other hand, had prevailed as an instrument of American public policy since

24 *Congressional Record*, Vol. c, Part 9, 83d Cong., 2d Sess., 12332. See Parmet, *Eisenhower and the American Crusades*, 284, 286–87.

Franklin D. Roosevelt had signed it into law in 1934. Between then and 1953, successive renewals of the Trade Agreements Act lowered United States tariff rates by approximately 50 percent. To a Republican party long committed to restrictive tariff policies, the program seemed a Democratic-inspired subversion of the nation's economic well-being. When Eisenhower persuaded a majority of his party to support even one-year extensions of the program in 1953 and 1954, therefore, he scored an impressive victory.

The new President attached great importance to a liberal trade policy. Although the Republican platform had treated the subject cautiously in 1952, the candidate had repeatedly emphasized the importance of an increased trade flow for the United States. The administration recognized, however, the political pitfalls standing in the way of such a policy: one official warned during the pre-inaugural planning period that those who espoused "traditional Republican" attitudes on the tariff question were bound to launch "unconstructive efforts" against any executive moves toward trade liberalization.[25]

Despite such warnings, the President resolved to press forward, even if gradually, with his plans. In a special message to Congress in April 1953, Eisenhower requested one-year extension and establishment of a commission to conduct a "thorough and comprehensive reexamination" of the nation's foreign economic policy. Even in offering so circumspect a measure, he emphasized national security, stressing the need for "cooperative action among the free nations" and the "vital" role of trade policy in any effort to establish true collective security.[26]

Although "as is" renewal implied retention of the Republican-favored "peril point" and escape clause amendments to the original Trade Agreements Act,[27] many Republican congressmen

[25] Unsigned memorandum to Budget Bureau Director-designate Joseph Dodge, Dec. 17, 1952, OF 99, Eisenhower Papers.

[26] *Public Papers . . . 1953*, 163–65.

[27] These two provisions were protectionist in spirit. The former enpowered the Tariff Commission to notify the President whenever a given tariff fell so low as to

had been hoping (and plotting) for a return to a more protective tariff policy altogether. Chief among these high-tariff advocates was Representative Richard Simpson of Pennsylvania, third-ranking majority member on the House Ways and Means Committee. It was primarily with Simpson that the administration had to deal on trade matters in 1953 and 1954. Also playing an important role was Daniel Reed, the stubborn septuagenarian chairman of Ways and Means.

The 1953 trade struggle began inauspiciously for the President. Instead of holding hearings on the administration bill, sponsored by Representative Kenneth Keating of New York, Reed chose to focus on a strongly protectionist measure presented by Simpson. The Pennsylvanian's bill proposed to raise existing tariff levels, set import quotas, expand the Tariff Commission by one member (thereby assuring a Republican majority rather than a partisan balance), and require the President to heed the commission's advice in "peril point" situations. Eisenhower found it repugnant, believing that it would make him a "messenger boy" in trade negotiations.[28]

Administration officials testified in an unenthusiastic fashion throughout the committee hearings. Dulles, though he opposed the bill, assured the Ways and Means members that he had "no preconceived ideas and no policies to which he was committed," and Secretary of Commerce Sinclair Weeks remarked that he could see both "some good and some bad" in the Simpson bill.[29] Weeks's ambivalence no doubt stemmed from his own traditional protectionist sentiments, but Dulles's unconvincing performance seems to have been rooted in his personality. Dulles's then-assistant, Thruston B. Morton, explained later that the Secretary "hated" to appear before congressional committees on

"imperil" the competitive position of a domestic industry, and the latter permitted any industry to be dropped from the terms of a reciprocal agreement found to be causing it "damage."

28 Eisenhower, *Mandate for Change*, 209.

29 Joe R. Wilkinson, *Politics and Trade Policy* (Washington: Public Affairs Press, 1960), 74–75; *New York Times*, May 6, 1953.

"economic matters." "When he got over into this question of trade," Morton explained, "then he felt a little bit uncertain of his own background . . . ."[30]

Eisenhower himself also gave signs of wavering, stating that he "wouldn't say . . . that [he was] not ready to accept any amendment whatsoever."[31] In fact, the basis for a deal with Simpson had already been worked out. The earliest public indication of what such a deal might involve had come from the Pennsylvania congressman, who had said on April 5 that he would yield on a number of points if he could be "assured of a Tariff Commission that would be 'fair' to domestic industries." The President already knew this, for on April 2 White House aide Gerald Morgan had sent him a memorandum indicating that Simpson would "go along with" one-year extension "if something could be done about the membership of the Tariff Commission."[32] Then, in late April, Simpson renounced his insistence on the "mandatory peril points" provision in his bill, claiming that he was "persuaded in talks with Administration leaders, that such a limitation . . . was not necessary."[33] The long-rumored compromise took shape on June 2, when the congressman dropped his bill and introduced two others: one containing most of the protectionist features of his original bill (H.R. 5496, which was later recommitted by the House), and another (H.R. 5495) which embodied Eisenhower's request for one-year extension and a study commission, but called simultaneously for enlargement of the Tariff Commission. The administration then managed to gain Daniel Reed's cooperation by assuring him on June 4 that no attempt would be made in the Senate to tack a rider onto the trade bill to extend the excess profits tax, which Reed opposed.[34]

[30] Morton Oral History Transcript, Dulles Project, Princeton Univ., 25.

[31] Press conference remarks of Apr. 23, 1953, in *Public Papers . . . 1953*, 197.

[32] Simpson statement in *New York Times*, Apr. 6, 1953; memorandum in Box 6, A67–19 Accessions, Morgan Records, Eisenhower Papers. Two weeks later, Morgan assured the Cabinet that Simpson would be cooperative on the matter.

[33] *New York Times*, Apr. 28, 1953.

[34] Unsigned memorandum, dated June 4, Daniel A. Reed Papers, Collection of Regional History and Univ. Archives, Cornell Univ., Ithaca, N.Y. On the excess profits tax struggle, see Ch. 5, below.

Once out of Ways and Means, the new trade bill fared well. Reed did join other protectionists in attacking it on the floor, but it passed the House unamended, with Republican members voting for it by 179–25. In the Senate, the Finance Committee held no public hearings and reported the bill without the Tariff Commission clause supported by Simpson. The upper chamber then accepted it by voice vote. A month-long conference deadlock which ensued over the question of enlarging the commission was finally broken in a manner which revealed the nature of the rapprochement between Simpson and the White House: on July 31, a high-tariff advocate from Maryland was appointed to the Tariff Commission, thereby balancing "high" and "low" tariff interests on that board. Within a week, the conference committee finalized the bill. It dropped the idea of enlarging the commission and provided instead that tie votes on "peril point" and "escape clause" cases would require that the President decide the question (previously a majority vote had been necessary to send a case to the White House). Simpson's conditions were thus met, and the bill became law in early August.

The study commission set up by the bill (named after its chairman, Inland Steel Company president Clarence B. Randall) kept alive the controversy over trade policy. Performing the bulk of its work during the last months of 1953, the Randall Commission issued its report in January 1954. As high-tariff Republicans had feared, the report advocated an internationalist (pro–reciprocal trade) position, recommending that the President's authority under the Trade Agreements Act be enlarged and extended for at least another three years.

The three high-tariff congressional members of the Randall Commission countered immediately with criticisms of varying intensity. Reed characterized the report as "an amateurish, inadequate and incompetent" document which reflected "a very considerable preconceived bias," and he and Simpson together drew up their own ten-point foreign economic policy proposal for 1954.[35] Senator Millikin, the third congressional protectionist

35 Reed to Vice President Nixon, Senator Millikin, and Simpson, Jan. 8, 1954,

on the panel, issued a milder protest, but his criticisms were perhaps the more damaging because he was less closely identified
with the rabidly protectionist wing of the Republican party and
was highly respected in the Senate. Moreover, his objections
came as a surprise to Randall and the administration, since certain features—such as retention of the peril point and escape
clause provisions and the placing of strict limitations on the level
of tariff reductions permissible in any one year—had been written
into the report largely to ensure his support.[36]

If the aim of establishing the study commission had been to
create goodwill and a consensus in favor of a long-term, liberalized trade program, it did not entirely succeed. Even commission
member John Vorys, who signed the majority report, was critical
of the group's work, writing in mid-1954 that he had "become
allergic to advisory boards, based on [his] experience and observation on the Randall Commission . . . .These boards," he continued, "tend to be mere sounding boards for the person they
are supposed to advise."[37]

Despite such indications of division and in the face of less than
enthusiastic support from Millikin, Knowland, and Representative Halleck, Eisenhower moved ahead with his plans. In a message to Congress on March 30, 1954, the President asked for most
of the points recommended by the Randall Commission report,
including three-year extension of the Trade Agreements Act and
gradual but steady reduction of certain existing tariff schedules.[38]
Difficulties arose immediately in the House. Congressman Robert
Kean of New Jersey, fourth-ranking Republican on Ways and
Means, was the senior member of his party on that committee
willing to sponsor the administration bill; within the commit-

Reed Papers. The story of the struggle within the Randall Commission between
its authoritarian chairman and Reed, Simpson, and Millikin is told in Raymond A.
Bauer, Ithiel deSola Pool, and Lewis A. Dexter, *American Business and Public
Policy: The Politics of Foreign Trade* (New York: Atherton, 1963), 42–49.

36 *Ibid.*, 45–46.

37 Vorys to Sen. Prescott Bush (also a member of the Randall Commission),
July 31, 1954, Vorys Papers.

38 Message on Foreign Economic Policy, in *Public Papers . . . 1954*, 352–64,
especially 353–55.

tee, Reed displayed clear opposition to it.[39] Before long the lack of Republican support led to a reappraisal in the White House. Speaking of his trade proposal on May 5, Eisenhower declared that he would not "be horribly disappointed if they [Congress] don't do it my way. Some of these things have to be done quickly and some slowly."[40]

On May 20, the President officially altered his trade request. In an open letter to Chicago businessman Charles Percy, cleared more than two weeks earlier with Reed and probably with others, Eisenhower announced that he was dropping his proposals for three-year extension and gradual tariff reductions and would ask instead for another simple one-year extension in order to allow Congress time to study the Randall Commission report.[41] Amid false rumors that the administration had promised Reed not to use its negotiating authority under the one-year extension,[42] the Ways and Means Committee reported out a revised bill calling for simple "as is" extension.

Once the administration had capitulated, Congress acted rapidly. In the House, Reed defended the bill on the floor as a measure to "preserve the status quo until a sound tariff policy can be developed." Receiving support from what has been aptly described as a "rather strange status quo coalition" of both friends and foes of reciprocal trade, the measure passed the lower house resoundingly (281–53), with Republicans voting for it 126–39.[43] Obviously, nationalist sentiment was closely related to opposition to the President's watered-down request. Among the Republicans voting against the bill were twenty-nine with records in foreign policy from the previous Congress: twenty-one were nationalists,

[39] Unsigned memorandum dated Apr. 13, 1954, in Box 3, A67–19 Accessions, Morgan Records, Eisenhower Papers.

[40] Press conference remarks, in *Public Papers . . . 1954*, 458.

[41] Eisenhower to Percy, *ibid.*, 503–504; Eisenhower to Daniel Reed, May 4, 1954, Box 3, A67–19 Accessions, Morgan Records, Eisenhower Papers.

[42] In fact, Dulles wrote Reed on June 8 that the administration deemed essential a new reciprocal trade agreement with Japan, though he added that no other agreements were "in contemplation." Dulles to Reed, Reed Papers.

[43] Quote from Wilkinson, *Politics and Trade Policy*, 90; Reed speech in *Congressional Record*, Vol. c, Part 6, 83d Cong., 2d Sess., 8077.

six were uncommitted or unscalable, and only two ranked as moderately internationalist. It seems unlikely, therefore, that many Republican House members voted against the 1954 trade bill because they believed it did not go far enough in an internationalist direction.

Senate action was somewhat more dramatic, even if the outcome was never in doubt. In an interesting turn-about, Senate Democrats, led by Tennessee's Albert Gore, attempted to transform the bill into President Eisenhower's original request for three-year renewal. As a final note of irony to the two-year trade struggle, the White House characterized Gore's amendment as "political gunplay" and urged party loyalists to defeat the move and approve only the one-year extension. Senate Republicans responded by voting against the Gore proposal 39–0 and then supporting the bill by 37–2.[44] The dominant mood of Republicans was typified in the remarks of Senator Millikin, leader of the floor fight for the administration. "If we say, 'Boys, we will give you a year longer to come up with something,' " said Millikin, "that is not at all unreasonable."[45]

The two-year contest over trade policy represented a victory for Eisenhower's internationalism, even if in moderate form. The administration had to make concessions to the protectionist-nationalist element among congressional Republicans, but it did succeed in keeping the Trade Agreements Act alive during 1953–1954. In 1955, the Democratic-controlled Eighty-fourth Congress would finally grant the President's request for three-year extension. In the meantime, Republican support for "as is" extension of reciprocal trade during the Eighty-third Congress gave tribute to President Eisenhower's patience and ability to win converts through compromise.

[44] Republican voting on the Gore amendment presents problems for quantification. *Congressional Quarterly Almanac* for 1954 maintains that a vote for the amendment was a vote for the original Eisenhower program, and was therefore a "pro-Eisenhower" vote. Of all the roll calls designated by *CQA* as "Eisenhower issues," this is the single instance where I disagree with its interpretation. In the interests of consistency, however, I have, in the quantitative analysis of Republican voting in this chapter, accepted *CQA*'s interpretation of the vote.

[45] *Congressional Record*, Vol. c, Part 7, 83d Cong., 2d Sess., 8720.

None of the other foreign policy roll-call votes in the Eighty-third Congress was marked by the drama or extended controversy which characterized the aid and trade struggles. Both houses quickly approved the President's request of June 10, 1953, that Congress empower the Commodity Credit Corporation to provide famine-stricken Pakistan with one million tons of wheat. The Senate cleared the bill by voice vote, with no significant Republican opposition. In the House, Republicans voted for the bill, 164–29, and it passed easily. The GOP opposition came almost exclusively from nationalists, as only two of the twenty-nine were internationalists (another two, including one freshman, were unclassified on foreign policy matters). Among the diehards opposing the wheat bill were both Daniel Reed and John Taber.

Congress also easily adopted a similar but more general measure granting the President authority to use up to $100 million worth of CCC surplus in order to relieve conditions of need in "friendly" nations. The Senate again gave its approval by voice vote, as GOP floor leader Knowland and Agriculture Committee chairman George Aiken shepherded the bill through. In the House, their counterparts—Charles Halleck and Clifford Hope, respectively—met with equal success, beating back a motion sponsored by a Southern Democrat to recommit the measure. Only ten of 204 Republicans—again mostly nationalists—opposed the President's position by voting for recommittal. Both these bills had generally internationalist overtones, but in a time of mounting farm surpluses both also seemed to provide a relatively cheap and convenient way to score propaganda points abroad. This fact, rather than particularly strong pressure from the White House, was probably decisive.

Other important foreign policy roll calls involved immigration, which can be described as a foreign policy issue because it touches on the question of how far the nation's world responsibilities obligate it to accept aliens pressing for admittance. Although President Eisenhower did not take any steps in 1953 toward redeeming his campaign pledges to seek revision of the restrictive McCarran-Walter immigration quota law, he did throw his influence behind a proposal to issue special visas to 240,000 non-quota refugee immigrants. In this instance, the administration had less trouble with the House than with the Senate. The House Rules Committee did put up short-lived resistance to granting a rule on the bill,[46] but eventually the lower house passed a rather generous bill. It allowed for admittance of 247,000 refugees over a twenty-nine-month period (rather than the twenty-four-month authority the President had asked for). House Republicans supported the bill by 132–74; only two internationalists voted against it (W. Sterling Cole of New York and Oregon's Walter Norblad), with the bulk of the opposition coming from Midwestern congressmen.

The refugee immigration bill ran into considerable opposition in the Senate. The Republican chairman of the Judiciary Subcommittee on Immigration, Arthur Watkins, worked hard on behalf of the measure, but he had to cope with the obstinate Pat McCarran, top-ranking Democrat on the full committee. Senator McCarran was assisted in his obstructionism by Republican committee members William Jenner and John Marshall Butler. Together they ensured that the Senate hearings dragged on for nearly two months. McCarran was at first unreceptive to White House overtures: Eisenhower personally met with the Nevada Democrat on at least one occasion, but felt he "made about as much impression . . . as beating an anvil with a sponge."[47] With Watkins serving as mediator, however, McCarran finally capitulated in late July. The Judiciary Committee then reported, and the Senate passed, a bill granting only 209,000 refugee visas and adding certain screening and sponsorship restrictions. Republican senators supported the bill by 39–8, after a debate in which Senators Watkins, Irving Ives, and Homer Ferguson led the administration forces.

On the refugee immigration bill, as on aid and trade legisla-

---

[46] Rep. John Heselton to Sherman Adams, July 28, 1953, in OF 99, Eisenhower Papers.

[47] Eisenhower, *Mandate for Change*, 217.

tion, long-time nationalists provided the opposition within the GOP. Among the bill's opponents in the House, the tendency was clear: forty-eight were nationalists, eight were uncommitted or unscalable, and only two were internationalists (sixteen were new House members). Of the eight Senate Republicans opposing the bill, all but Guy Cordon of Oregon, who was unscalable on foreign policy questions, were strong nationalists: Bricker, Capehart, Dworshak, Jenner, Malone, Welker, and Williams.

Although the final version of the Refugee Relief Act after conference increased the Senate figure to 217,000 special visas, the total still fell nearly 10 percent below the President's request. Moreover, administration forces frankly admitted to favoring a halfway measure: "By including protective features of the [McCarran-Walter] Act in this new legislation," wrote Charles Halleck to a Democratic colleague, "we tended to reaffirm the principles of the . . . Act at the same time that we cut a lot of ground from beneath those who would like to see the whole program wrecked."[48] The full cost of the administration's limited victory was revealed two months later, when the *New York Times* ferreted out the reason for McCarran's reversal, and possibly for the strong Republican support for the bill on the Senate floor. As a result of a "compromise," the *Times* reported, revisions of the McCarran-Walter Act had been "ruled out" for the duration of the Eighty-third Congress.[49] Significantly, there were no further administration initiatives on immigration revision during the next year.

Eisenhower's effective leadership on foreign policy questions is obvious from the response of Republicans in the Eighty-third Congress. The President took a definite position on thirty-eight such roll calls in 1953–1954; at least half of the voting Republicans supported him on thirty-one of those occasions. Supporting the President meant, in every case, taking an internationalist

[48] Halleck to Rep. Brady Gentry of Texas, Aug. 26, 1953, Charles A. Halleck Papers, Lilly Library, Indiana Univ., Bloomington, Ind.
[49] *New York Times*, Sept. 24, 1953.

position.[50] In both houses, many more Republicans voted consistently "pro-Eisenhower" (internationalist) than "anti-Eisenhower": of Republican legislators whose voting records could be tabulated, 57.4 percent in the House and 62.2 percent in the Senate ranked as pro-Eisenhower. By contrast, only 22.7 percent in the House and 24.4 percent in the Senate voted consistently anti-Eisenhower.[51]

In keeping with pre-1953 Republican voting patterns, the least internationalist—and therefore least strongly pro-Eisenhower—legislators in both houses came from the Midwest. As Table 7 shows, this disparity was much more obvious in the House, where only 27.6 percent of the Republican members from the Plains and North Central states were Eisenhower supporters on foreign policy, while 40.2 percent were "antis" (nationalists). Leading Midwestern opponents of administration foreign policy in the Senate included Midwesterners John Bricker, Homer Capehart, William Jenner, William Langer, Joseph McCarthy, Andrew Schoeppel, and Milton Young. In the House, anti-Eisenhower legislators formed large parts of the state delegations from Illinois, Iowa, Michigan, Minnesota, and Wisconsin. Likewise, the internationalist bias of Republicans from the Northeast continued to prevail in the Eighty-third Congress.

Many of those who supported Eisenhower's internationalism were converted from previously nationalist or noncommittal attitudes. The President won over 39.1 percent (fifty) of the 128 non-internationalist returnees in the House and 44.4 percent of such Republican senators in the Eighty-third Congress. These conversions took place especially among legislators from the Mid-Atlantic and Western states, and least frequently among those

[50] For a complete list of the thirty-eight "Eisenhower issue" roll calls in foreign policy during the 83rd Congress, see Appendix D.

[51] Throughout this study, the terms "pro-Eisenhower" and "anti-Eisenhower" refer to the level of support which a legislator gave to the President's position in 1953–1954. Support for Eisenhower on 80 percent or more of the roll calls in a policy area classifies a legislator as "strongly pro-Eisenhower"; on 60 to 79 percent, as "moderately pro-Eisenhower"; on 40 to 59 percent, as a "waverer"; on 20 to 39 percent, as "moderately anti-Eisenhower"; and on 0 to 19 percent, as "strongly anti-Eisenhower."

| Category | Level of Support † | | | | |
|---|---|---|---|---|---|
| | .80–1.00 | .60–.79 | .40–.59 | .20–.39 | .00–.19 |
| SENATE | | | | | |
| *Region* | | | | | |
| New England | 5 | 3 | 0 | 0 | 0 |
| Mid-Atlantic | 3 | 2 | 2 | 1 | 0 |
| Border | 1 | 0 | 0 | 0 | 0 |
| North Central | 2 | 3 | 0 | 3 | 1 |
| Plains | 1 | 2 | 2 | 2 | 0 |
| Far West | 4 | 2 | 2 | 2 | 2 |
| *Previous Scale Type* | | | | | |
| Strong internat'st | 4 | 1 | 0 | 0 | 0 |
| Moderate internat'st | 4 | 0 | 0 | 0 | 0 |
| Uncommitted, not scaled | 4 | 1 | 2 | 0 | 0 |
| Moderate nationalist | 0 | 6 | 1 | 1 | 0 |
| Strong nationalist | 0 | 1 | 2 | 6 | 3 |
| (Freshmen) | 4 | 3 | 1 | 1 | 0 |
| TOTAL** | 16 | 12 | 6 | 8 | 3 |

* For roll calls, see Appendix D; for individual scores, Appendix K.

† Classifications: strongly pro-Eisenhower (.80–1.00), moderately pro-Eisenhower (.60–.79), waverer (.40–.59), moderately anti-Eisenhower (.20–.39), strongly anti-Eisenhower (.00–.19).

** Excludes Sens. Butler and Griswold (Neb.), Taft (Ohio), and Tobey (N.H.), who responded on fewer than half the foreign policy roll calls studied in 1953–1954.

from the Midwest.[52] Often, a "convert" was of more value to the administration than a long-time internationalist. For example, on the House Foreign Affairs Committee, where chairman Chiperfield exercised very minor influence, the "convert" John Vorys was more useful in persuading others to support Eisenhower's program than was Jacob Javits, an outspoken internationalist. As one pro-administration congressman put it during the 1953 foreign aid appropriations debate, "With all due respect to Jake

[52] These totals do not include House and Senate returnees whose voting records were incomplete on foreign policy questions in 1953–1954.

*Table 7* (CONTINUED)

| | HOUSE | | | | |
|---|---|---|---|---|---|
| *Region* | | | | | |
| New England | 15 | 0 | 1 | 2 | 0 |
| Mid-Atlantic | 30 | 21 | 5 | 3 | 1 |
| Border | 1 | 6 | 3 | 2 | 2 |
| North Central | 14 | 6 | 18 | 22 | 7 |
| Plains | 3 | 1 | 10 | 4 | 2 |
| Far West | 18 | 9 | 6 | 3 | 1 |
| *Previous Scale Type* | | | | | |
| Strong internat'st | 9 | 0 | 0 | 0 | 0 |
| Moderate internat'st | 21 | 7 | 1 | 0 | 0 |
| Uncommitted, not scaled | 20 | 13 | 11 | 3 | 0 |
| Moderate nationalist | 3 | 6 | 8 | 10 | 1 |
| Strong nationalist | 3 | 5 | 16 | 18 | 11 |
| (Freshmen) | 25 | 12 | 7 | 5 | 1 |
| TOTAL‡ | 81 | 43 | 43 | 36 | 13 |

‡ Excludes Reps. Dolliver (Iowa), Lipscomb (Calif.), and O'Hara (Minn.), who responded on fewer than half the foreign policy roll calls, and Speaker Joseph Martin, who did not participate in House roll calls.

Javits, he just cannot lead . . . a fight in behalf of the Administration without losing votes en route."[53] Similarly, long-standing internationalists in the Senate—like Irving Ives and Leverett Saltonstall—did not have the sort of credibility among their party colleagues that was enjoyed by converts such as Styles Bridges and Everett Dirksen.

Obviously, not every conversion of a congressional Republican resulted from direct administration pressure. Eisenhower's prestige and reputed expertise in foreign policy matters very likely exercised an indirect pull on previously noninternationalist Republican congressmen and senators to "go along" on internationalist programs like foreign aid and reciprocal trade. On the other hand, the administration—and sometimes the President

[53] Rep. John Heselton to Sherman Adams, July 24, 1953, OF 99, Eisenhower Papers.

himself—did on occasion take direct action. The memorandum advising Persons to apply pressure to Senator McCarthy on the 1953 mutual security bill, as well as Eisenhower's timely meetings with Congressmen Reed and Simpson during the reciprocal trade battles, implied a healthy presidential interest in winning party support for his internationalist programs of 1953–1954.[54]

An interesting pattern characterized "conversions" among congressional Republicans. While the administration enjoyed an exceptional conversion rate among senior Republicans in both houses (fourteen of thirty-six from the pre–New Deal and New Deal periods in the House; four of six in the Senate), it met with a less favorable response from relative newcomers, especially in the Senate. In the upper house, only two of twelve previously noninternationalist postwar-period Republican senators (Bennett of Utah and Hendrickson of New Jersey) switched to become "pro-Eisenhowerites" on foreign policy. Five who remained opposed to the President's internationalist views were members of the strongly conservative "Class of 1946" (the Eightieth Congress): Bricker, Jenner, Malone, McCarthy, and Williams. The greater success experienced by the Eisenhower administration in converting older, more senior Republicans to an internationalist position in part reflects the President's own preferences and methods of congressional leadership. Eisenhower often appeared to prefer and to work more closely with the older members of his party. It is also possible, however, that the high conversion rate among these most senior senators and House members was a function of their positions of leadership in Congress, which made them feel particularly obligated to go along with the President.

If Eisenhower did well on foreign policy matters among the oldest hands in the congressional wing of his party, he did even better with Republican members of the Class of 1952. Thirty-seven of the fifty House freshmen and seven of the nine Senate

---

[54] See *New York Times*, Apr. 3, 1953, and Washington *Post*, June 3, 1953; also Eisenhower, *Mandate for Change*, 215, and Parmet, *Eisenhower and the American Crusades*, 286–87.

newcomers ranked as internationalists (pro-Eisenhower) in the Eighty-third Congress. Twenty-five of the former and four of the latter supported the President at least 80 percent of the time on foreign policy questions.[55] This was not especially surprising in the case of the new senators, whose 1952 campaigns had reflected a collectively high degree of receptiveness to an active United States role in world affairs, but such had not been the case with House freshmen. It may be, however, that the support given Eisenhower by Republican freshmen—in foreign policy as on other matters—reflected the efforts of loyal party leaders in the two houses more than the President's concern for the junior legislators; criticisms of White House inattention to rank-and-file Republicans in Congress were frequent, both in the press and in private.[56]

The Republican House and Senate leadership played a large part in helping President Eisenhower to "internationalize" his party in 1953–1954. Individual party leaders and members on the leading committees (both Appropriations committees, Senate Foreign Relations and Finance, House Foreign Affairs, Ways and Means, and Rules) demonstrated relatively strong support for the President's foreign policy views. In the Senate, eight of the twelve Republicans on the Appropriations Committee, five of the six on Foreign Relations, and four of the seven on Finance ranked as internationalists on the basis of their roll-call responses in the Eighty-third Congress. Chairmen Styles Bridges, Alexander Wiley, and Eugene Millikin, respectively, had support scores of .79, .91, and .87, which put them near the front ranks of pro-Eisenhower sentiment on foreign policy. Likewise, the three Republican party leaders in the upper house (after the death of

[55] Regional variations existed within freshman ranks, too. All sixteen House freshmen and the four Senate newcomers from New England and the Mid-Atlantic states were internationalists during the 83rd Congress. By contrast, among the twelve first-term members of the two houses from the North Central and Plains regions, only four could be called "pro-Eisenhower" on foreign policy.

[56] See, e.g., *New York Times*, July 24, 1953; also letters from Rep. John Heselton to Sherman Adams, July 16, 1953; Rep. T. Millet Hand to Adams, Jan. 20, 1954; and Rep. Joseph Holt to Adams, May 11, 1954, all in OF 99, Eisenhower Papers.

Robert Taft in July 1953)—William Knowland, Homer Ferguson, and Leverett Saltonstall—all ranked as internationalists; of
these, only Saltonstall had been an internationalist in the previous Congress.

In the lower house, Republicans on the most important foreign
policy–related committees were not so solidly behind the President, though their chairmen responded well. Only Foreign Affairs had a preponderantly internationalist GOP membership,
twelve of its sixteen Republicans ranking as "pro-Eisenhower."
On the other committees which played leading roles in legislation
affecting aid, trade, and other foreign policy questions, the proportion of internationalist Republicans declined sharply: three
of eight on Rules, seven of fifteen on Ways and Means, and eleven
of thirty on Appropriations. On the other hand, chairmen John
Taber (Appropriations), Leo Allen (Rules), and Robert Chiperfield (Foreign Affairs) were all converted to internationalism in
the Eighty-third Congress. In fact, of the major committee chairmen, only Daniel Reed failed to respond to the President's lead,
supporting him on only one-third of the foreign policy roll calls.
Nine of the seventeen who made up the formal Republican leadership in the House were "pro-Eisenhower" in foreign policy
matters, including Floor Leader Charles Halleck and Chief Whip
Leslie Arends, both "converts" with scores of .87.

High support scores sometimes masked very real limitations
on the willingness of given individuals to "fall in." On foreign
policy questions in 1953–1954, Halleck, Allen, Chiperfield, Saltonstall, and Wiley seem never to have caused the President head-
aches of any sort. On the other hand, despite records of seemingly
strong support, Senators Bridges and Knowland (on foreign aid)
and Millikin (on reciprocal trade) all had less than supportive
things to say on occasion, both in public and on the floor of the
Senate.

Congressman Taber's sometimes equivocal role makes his influence especially hard to gauge. Although the Appropriations
Committee made deep cuts in Eisenhower's foreign aid requests

in both 1953 and 1954, the President and others who should have known considered its chairman a loyal and valuable ally.[57] But grounds for doubt exist. Taber quarreled openly with FOA director Stassen throughout the latter months of 1953, and in December he released a statement to the editor of a national news magazine in which he said that "Foreign Aid . . . must go down very sharply this coming year."[58] A few months later, Taber was thinking in more specific terms, writing to a constituent that he hoped aid funds could be cut by 40 percent in 1954.[59] Perhaps the New Yorker's high support score (.80) in foreign policy and his work on the President's behalf within the Appropriations Committee should be interpreted as the result of the administration's flexibility in scaling down the size of its foreign aid programs in both sessions of the Eighty-third Congress. Whatever Taber's motives, however, his support on House roll calls was important to the administration.

Since Republicans had criticized the Truman administration most severely for its foreign policy failures in Asia, it is interesting to examine the reaction of the so-called "Asia-first" group in 1953–1954. The response of congressional Republicans to President Eisenhower's programs sheds some limited light on the matter. Three Senate roll calls in 1953—one amendment to the foreign aid authorization bill and two amendments to the foreign aid appropriation—together provided an opportunity for legislators to demonstrate "Asia-first" predilections.[60] Eleven Republi-

57 See letters from Eisenhower to Taber, Aug. 8, 1953, and July 6, 1954, Taber Papers; also John Heselton to Sherman Adams, July 30, 1953, OF 99, Eisenhower Papers.

58 Taber to Carson F. Lyman of *U.S. News & World Report*, Dec. 14, 1953; on the quarrel, see Taber to Stassen, Aug. 13, 1953, and Taber to Homer Gruenther, Sept. 8. That Taber's suspicions of the FOA continued into the next year is evident in his letter to Eisenhower, July 7, 1954. Taber Papers.

59 Taber to Eric V. Howell, Mar. 10, 1954, Taber Papers.

60 The roll calls: Ellender (D) amendment to reduce the appropriation for European military aid by $500 million; Ellender amendment to reduce the appropriation for European economic aid by $71.8 million; and Dirksen amendment to authorize up to $25 million in surplus agricultural commodities for the use of Asia Pacific countries (see Appendix D for the full Senate vote). Affirmative responses on all three questions would suggest a general preference for Asian nations in the distribution of American largesse.

94

cans had response patterns on the three votes which classified them as possible Asia-firsters (Barrett, Dworshak, Goldwater, Hickenlooper, Langer, Martin, Morse, Mundt, Margaret Chase Smith, Welker, Young), and six others qualified on the basis of their response on two of the roll calls but were not recorded on the third (Bricker, Capehart, Jenner, McCarthy, Malone, Schoeppel).[61] Among the seventeen, only six ranked as pro-Eisenhower (internationalist) on foreign policy during 1953–1954, while an equal number scored as nationalists. This breakdown was markedly less favorable to the White House than that among Republican senators as a whole (see Table 7). It is possible, then, that Eisenhower's general success in internationalizing congressional Republicans obscured his failure to overcome the resentment of the Asia-first bloc to foreign policies which its members regarded as European-dominated.

Overall, however, the degree of Republican support for Dwight Eisenhower's consistently internationalist position on matters of foreign policy represents something of a watershed within the party in 1953–1954. Even though foreign aid appropriations wound up lower than the President wanted, it was noteworthy that a majority of Republicans voted in favor of any mutual security appropriations, in light of the party's previous performance and its excoriations of the later Truman aid program. Moreover, despite the administration's failure to secure all of its desired liberalizations in the area of foreign trade from the Eighty-third Congress, the early Eisenhower years did see the end of Republican high-tariff "solidarity."[62] If Speaker Martin was correct in assuming that "probably two-thirds of the Republicans in the House" still opposed the reciprocal trade program

[61] Since an affirmative vote on the Dirksen amendment could also indicate a legislator's interest in the farm surplus problem, it is conceivable that the performances of the four farm-state senators listed (Hickenlooper, Langer, Mundt, Young) reflected general opposition to existing foreign aid levels combined with pro-agriculture leanings.

[62] See Wilkinson, *Politics and Trade Policy*, 121. For the view that this change resulted from economic gains after World War II, see Richard Watson, "The Tariff Revolution: A Study of Shifting Party Attitudes," *Journal of Politics* 18, No. 4 (Nov. 1956), 699.

in 1953–1954, Eisenhower's achievement in getting so many party members to support his foreign trade policy was substantial.[63]

The President's accomplishment was built on compromise. Not only did Eisenhower have to accept downward revisions in most of his foreign policy proposals, but he had to stress fiscal economy and businesslike efficiency as much as the principle of collective security in trying to sell his programs at all. This approach made of foreign aid that "most rare" program: "the standard saluted with equal respect by those most preoccupied with foreign policy and those most obsessed with domestic economy."[64] Actually, this emphasis may have been agreeable to Eisenhower anyway, as it came through in private discussions as well as in public.[65]

It is difficult to evaluate Dwight Eisenhower's total impact on his party's foreign policy approach. That he had considerable influence is evident in the high proportion of "conversions" among congressional Republicans to an internationalist posture during 1953–1954. For leading the party from domination by its nationalist wing to general acceptance of an extended world role for the United States, Eisenhower was praised by liberals and moderates in the 1950s and 1960s who thought his views appropriate in the Cold War era. Only in the years since 1968, when many members of the Cold War political establishment have come to question the propriety of such a national role, has the value of Eisenhower's achievement come into question. There is no debating, however, the fact of the accomplishment: by the end of the Eighty-third Congress, the internationalist President had succeeded in altering considerably the foreign policy stance of his party.

63 Joseph W. Martin, as told to Robert J. Donovan, *My First Fifty Years in Politics* (New York: McGraw-Hill, 1960), 229.

64 Hughes, *Ordeal of Power*, 81; see also Parmet, *Eisenhower and the American Crusades*, 285.

65 Donovan, *The Inside Story*, 147.

# CHAPTER FIVE

# Republicans and Revenue

Republicans campaigning for election in 1952 dwelt with considerable vehemence on the fiscal iniquities of the New and Fair Deals. Dwight Eisenhower himself, while avoiding pie-in-the-sky promises of instant tax reduction, repeatedly denounced the interrelated evils of excessive federal spending, high tax levels, and inflation. Republican congressional candidates also scored Democratic fiscal practices and were often less circumspect than their party's presidential candidate in promising quick remedies.[1] Since the record of Republicans returning from the previous Congress also reflected strong opposition to Democratic spending and taxing levels, fiscal policy appeared to be an area where the new President and his congressional majority would be in substantial agreement.

The matter of fiscal priorities, however, caused dissension among Republicans. Confronted with a Truman budget for fiscal 1954 which estimated a deficit of $9.9 billion, President Eisenhower and his leading economic advisers (Treasury Secretary George Humphrey and Budget Director Joseph Dodge) were determined from the outset to balance the budget before attempting any tax reductions. The President explicitly set forth these priorities in his 1953 State of the Union message. Listing a balanced

[1] See Ch. 1, especially Tables 1 and 2.

budget as the "first order of business," he consigned tax reduction to fifth place among the necessities for a stable economic policy under Republican direction. "Reduction of taxes," he told Congress, "will be justified only as we show we can succeed in bringing the budget under control . . . . Until we can determine the extent to which expenditures can be reduced, it would not be wise to reduce our revenues." Treasury Secretary Humphrey echoed this sentiment somewhat more succinctly a few weeks later, announcing that "deficits should be avoided like the plague."[2]

To many congressional Republicans, the President's failure to espouse immediate tax cuts was heresy. Consequently, there ensued a struggle between Republican advocates of instant tax reductions and an administration which believed in the principle of such reductions, but wanted to reduce spending first. The battle consumed a major part of the energy of both sides throughout the first session of the Eighty-third Congress. Ultimately the Eisenhower administration made peace with those who disagreed with the President's fiscal priorities, with the result that in 1954 the omnibus tax bill received the overwhelming support of congressional Republicans. Along the way, Eisenhower found it expedient to compromise. While taxes were reduced on three separate occasions (through the scheduled expiration of the income tax surcharge on January 1, 1954, the excise tax revisions of March 1954, and the omnibus tax bill), the Republican administration ran budget deficits of $3.1 billion in fiscal 1954 and $4.2 billion in 1955.

The President's flexible strategy cost him little. Deeply committed to the broad Republican goals of reduced spending and lower taxes, he was eventually able to make progress on both fronts: in both 1956 and 1957, the budget showed a surplus of approximately $1.6 billion. By compromising during the first

[2] State of the Union Message, *Public Papers . . . 1953*, 19–21; Humphrey speech of Apr. 1, 1953, in Nathaniel R. Howard, ed., *The Basic Papers of George M. Humphrey, Secretary of the Treasury, 1953–1957* (Cleveland: Western Reserve Historical Society, 1965), 46.

two years of his Presidency, moreover, Eisenhower ensured that the Republican party would remain unified on an aspect of domestic policy which had served it as a central unifying force since the New Deal. Despite the controversy over tax policy which marked the first several months of the new administration, the net result of the Eisenhower fiscal program of 1953–1954 was to revive and enforce Republican orthodoxy.

Immediately following the 1952 elections, the President-elect and his advisers were apprised by outgoing Democratic Treasury officials of the fiscal task ahead. "In the tax field," stated a Treasury memorandum prepared for the occasion, "the immediate problem will relate to a number of defense tax increases . . . which are due to expire between June 20, 1953, and March 31, 1954. The new Administration will have to formulate a tax program for recommendation to the Congress to meet this situation." The report then underscored the difficulties facing the new President, pointing out that the "importance of the tax problem is indicated by the fact that the government is operating at a deficit . . . ."[3] The newly elected President barely had time to ponder the implications before an initiative was launched by a number of congressional Republicans who had long chafed at Democratic tax levels.

The Republican tax-cutters began their drive on the first day of the new Congress, even before Eisenhower took office. Daniel Reed, the new chairman of the Ways and Means Committee, introduced a bill to speed up expiration of an 11 percent income tax surcharge from the scheduled date of January 1, 1954, to July 1, 1953. As a measure of the importance of both Reed and his bill, it was numbered H.R. 1. Despite Reed's claim that "practically everybody" favored his bill, however, several leading congressional Republicans refused to support it before receiving a fiscal policy statement from the President. Speaker Martin, House Floor Leader Halleck, and Senate Finance Committee chairman Millikin all responded coolly to Reed's proposal. Undaunted,

---

[3] Quoted in Donovan, *The Inside Story*, 14.

Reed announced that he "intended to get the bill passed, no matter what Eisenhower, or Humphrey, or anyone else had to say about it."[4]

The President soon made his position known, clearly laying out his "budget-first" priorities in the State of the Union message on February 2. A week later Eisenhower reiterated this theme to a legislative leadership meeting, and he drove the point home again in a February 17 press conference.[5]

Others also began to speak for the President. Secretary Humphrey, in his statements, was diplomatic and cautious. At a private dinner with the Republican members of the Ways and Means Committee on February 11, the Treasury Secretary said only that the White House was "not yet ready to take a stand" on Reed's bill, but repeated the Presidential warning against "precipitous action." Then in a public address six days later, Humphrey spoke somewhat—but only somewhat—less guardedly. Putting the administration on record as favoring a tax reduction, the Secretary said it was "a problem of precedence . . . a problem of timing."[6] Senator Frank Carlson, an Eisenhower intimate since before the 1952 campaign, muddied the water further by telling the upper house near the end of February that there was still hope for tax reduction in 1953. Although protesting that he was speaking solely for himself, Carlson admitted that he had "discussed the problem" with the President.[7]

In this atmosphere proponents of H.R. 1 pushed ahead. On February 16, the Ways and Means Committee reported the measure out by a vote of 21–4, without holding any hearings. In its report the group denied the need for balancing the budget first,

[4] Joseph and Stewart Alsop, "Who's Boss?" New York *Herald Tribune*, Jan. 30, 1953, clipping in Reed Papers. For Martin, Halleck, and Millikin statements, see *New York Times*, Jan. 28, 1953.

[5] Donovan, *The Inside Story*, 60; Eisenhower's press conference remarks in *Public Papers . . . 1953*, 47–48.

[6] *New York Times*, Feb. 12, 1953. Eisenhower had warned against "precipitous action" in economic matters in his State of the Union message. See Humphrey's speech to the Cleveland Chamber of Commerce, Feb. 17, 1953, in Howard, ed., *Papers of George M. Humphrey*, 39–40.

[7] *New York Times*, Feb. 28, 1953.

arguing that "a tax reduction now" would provide "strong inducement for the elimination of unnecessary expenditures."[8] In contrast to the administration's tepid public statements, the response of Republican House leaders at this point demonstrated that the White House strongly opposed the bill. Acting at the behest of Speaker Martin, chairman Leo Allen of the Rules Committee announced that he would keep H.R. 1 from coming to the floor for at least two months; Martin, like Floor Leader Halleck, was "personally converted" to such a position by the President.[9] Reed at first demonstrated no particular pique at this action, writing to Carlson in late February that it was the "New Deal press" which was trying "to create a rift in the Republican Party." His patience waned, however, as time wore on.[10]

In early March 1953, Reed renewed his request to Leo Allen that the Rules Committee give prompt consideration to H.R. 1. He received in return from the Illinois Republican a clear expression of the administration position. Allen would not release the bill for House consideration, he explained, because it was not his "purpose to thwart or hinder the objectives, plans, or programs of the chosen leaders of the Congress of the United States or President Eisenhower."[11] Allen's control over the Rules group, on behalf of the administration, was clearly quite strong, as Reed could not even persuade a fellow New Yorker on the committee, Henry J. Latham, to help him. Failing in his efforts to get around Allen through Latham, Reed sent the latter an angry telegram which foreshadowed his mood for the duration of the 1953 tax-reduction struggle: "It is most embarrassing to me to have you refuse to provide a hearing for a rule on H.R. no. 1," he scolded Latham. "I am wondering how long I shall have to remain in Congress [Reed was senior Republican in the House, with thirty-four years of service] to receive cooperation

---

8 *Ibid.*, Feb. 19, 1953.

9 Charles Murphy, "The Eisenhower Shift," Part 2 of four parts, *Fortune* 53, No. 2 (Feb. 1956), 232. See also Halleck to Edward L. Morgan, Mar. 16, 1953, Halleck Papers.

10 Reed to Carlson, Feb. 28, 1953, Reed Papers.

11 Allen to Reed, Mar. 10, 1953, Notebook No. 41, Reed Papers.

from a member of my New York delegation. Is there no reciprocity between us?"[12]

On March 20, Reed publicly announced that he had "not capitulated" and would work to secure the necessary signatures on a petition to discharge H.R. 1 from the Rules Committee, but he never really had a chance to win the fight.[13] By the end of the session, he had managed to get only 115 of the required 218 signatures, so that the bill never came before the full House for consideration. The measure's fate was probably sealed on May 10, when the staff of the Joint Committee on Internal Revenue Taxation issued a prediction that revenues for fiscal 1954 would fall $5.9 billion short of Truman's estimate. Such a likelihood made Reed's proposed reduction untimely, to say the least.[14]

Unable to speed up scheduled tax reductions through legislation of his own, Reed was determined to block any attempts to increase or extend the existing war-inspired tax rates. Specifically, he girded himself to fight against extension of the excess profits tax (EPT). Enacted in 1950, this tax amounted to a 30 percent levy on all profits exceeding 83 percent of a corporation's "normal profits," computed as the average of its three best years during the period 1946–1949. Although the EPT was scheduled to expire on June 30, 1953, President Eisenhower gave indications early that he might call for its extension. Asked in his February 17 press conference whether he would make such a request, the President refused to answer "in exact terms," but said that if the EPT were dropped, "a substitute of some kind in that same area" would be needed. This comment produced immediate outcries from a number of Republican congressmen dedicated to reducing taxes, including Reed and Richard Simpson of Pennsylvania, who, according to the *New York Times*, was Speaker Martin's virtual guide on tax matters.[15]

[12] Telegram dated Mar. 14, 1953, Reed Papers.

[13] *New York Times*, Mar. 20, 1953. See Reed's press release of the same date, Notebook No. 41, Reed Papers.

[14] *New York Times*, May 11, 1953.

[15] Press conference remarks in *Public Papers . . . 1953*, 49; *New York Times*, Feb. 19, 1953.

The administration did not bring up the issue again during the next few months, but by May there were rumors that Eisenhower would request extension of the tax until January 1, 1954. Republican congressional leaders waited in vain during early May to be told the President's wishes. Senator Taft's angry comment following the May 12 leadership meeting at the White House typified their growing restlessness: "The Administration is going to have to decide what they [*sic*] want," he snapped to inquiring reporters. "I haven't been able to get even a hint of what they will recommend."[16]

After notifying the Republican leadership earlier in the day, President Eisenhower finally made his intentions clear in a televised speech on May 19, asking for extension of the EPT for an additional six months. The following day he transmitted the formal request to Congress. For the most part, GOP leaders responded gamely. Speaker Martin remarked that under the circumstances, extension of the tax seemed "to be the only possible thing to do," and Senators Taft and Millikin predicted congressional cooperation with the President's request. Reed, however, now had his chance for retaliation. "When I fight," he told newsmen, "I fight."[17]

Martin immediately applied personal pressure to Reed and, following a long private conference between House leaders and Republicans on the Ways and Means Committee, announced that Reed had agreed to begin hearings on EPT extension about June 1. The Speaker did not claim that Reed had made any promises, but said that he was "prayerfully hoping" a bill would emerge.

Prayer seemed appropriate. Earlier in the year all fifteen Ways and Means Republicans had publicly declared their opposition to extension of the tax, and by late May only six seemed likely to reverse their positions.[18] At the very least it appeared that the administration would have to permit some sort of "relief" to cor-

---

16 *Ibid.*, May 13, 1953.
17 *Ibid.*, May 20, 1953.
18 *Ibid.*, May 21, May 31, 1953.

porations in any extension of the tax, probably by raising the $25,000 ceiling above which profits were to be taxed as "excess."

Hearings on the proposal opened as scheduled on June 1. In his testimony, Secretary Humphrey provided fuel for the tax-cutters' arguments by referring to the EPT as "a bad tax" even while recommending its continuance until a total revision of the tax codes could be worked out in 1954. The Secretary came under considerable fire from the committee. He had urged neutrality on representatives of both the United States Chamber of Commerce and the National Association of Manufacturers, and even though both organizations ultimately opposed the administration's position, Reed and other committee members suggested that Humphrey might have engaged in illegal lobbying activities. After listening to a string of unfavorable witnesses, Reed finally closed the hearings on June 13, declaring that the administration had "failed to make its case." Asked when he might call his committee together to vote on the proposal, the chairman replied, "We're mighty busy." [19]

Sensing that Reed's procrastination might know no bounds, Republican House leaders Martin and Halleck began to make plans to skirt the Ways and Means Committee entirely, if necessary. The tentative strategy involved the loyal Rules Committee, which, according to a little-used House precedent, could grant a rule on a bill without that bill's having been referred by another committee. The party leaders did not act at once, however, delaying their maneuvers while President Eisenhower tried to deal personally with the obstinate Reed. Eisenhower met with the chairman on June 20, and telephoned him three days later. But when White House efforts failed, the leadership decided to press for an extension bill which included the kind of "relief" that several of Reed's followers had been demanding. Consequently, on June 23, the administration swung its support from a bill calling for simple six-month extension (sponsored by Representative Robert Kean of New Jersey) to one proposed by Representative Antoni Sadlak (Connecticut) which raised the tax

[19] *Ibid.*, June 14, 1953.

credit (ceiling before profits were "excess") from $25,000 to $100,000 for an individual corporation. Reed remained unmoved, while Martin and Halleck prepared for action.

Since a poll of the Ways and Means membership showed that it would be impossible to secure the signatures of a majority on the committee to call a meeting without Reed's consent, administration forces had to turn to their contingency plan. On June 25, after hearing Halleck and Reed argue the two sides of the question, the Rules Committee adopted a rule to bypass Ways and Means on the EPT extension bill. Chairman Allen took the precaution of calling for a voice vote in order to ensure secrecy, but administration forces credited Tennessee Republican B. Carroll Reece with casting the crucial vote within the committee.[20] Eisenhower reacted gratefully, asking his top congressional liaison aide to tell Reece that the administration was looking "for a good place to appoint some fine individual from Tennessee."[21]

Even after obtaining the Rules Committee resolution, the party leadership chose not to use it for a time, in order to give the Ways and Means Committee more time to act on its own. The Speaker predicted that at least 195 of the 220 House Republicans would support the Rules Committee resolution on the floor, but he and the other Republican leaders were not eager for such a showdown.[22] Working largely through Congressman Simpson and others on Ways and Means who shared the belief that the precedent of the "bypass rule" would be a dangerous one, Martin and Halleck obtained assurances that the committee would meet on July 8, ostensibly for business other than consideration of the EPT.[23] Accordingly, Halleck told the House on June 29 that he would not call the bypass rule up for floor action.

The issue was all but settled. In a "stormy" and "uncomfort-

[20] See Charles Halleck Oral History Transcript, Eisenhower Project, Eisenhower Library, 26; and Henry Scheele, *Charlie Halleck: A Political Biography* (New York: Exposition Press, 1966), 149.
[21] Eisenhower to Wilton Persons, June 26, 1953, OF 99–D (1), Eisenhower Papers.
[22] *New York Times,* June 28, 1953.
[23] *Ibid.,* July 8, 1953.

able" session on July 8, the Ways and Means Committee voted down its chairman and reported out by 16–9 the simple EPT extension bill (the administration revived its support for Kean's bill, since it had gained nothing by offering to back Sadlak's measure, with its "tax relief" provision). In the committee, Reed was joined in opposition to the bill by three Democrats as well as fellow Republicans John Byrnes, Thomas Curtis, Thomas Jenkins, Noah Mason, and James Utt; seven Democrats and nine Republicans (Howard Baker, Carl Curtis, Angier Goodwin, Hal Holmes, Kean, Victor Knox, Thomas Martin, Sadlak, and Simpson) voted to report it. The lines of division were not completely clear, but four of eight fiscal conservatives on the committee voted against the EPT extension bill, while four of five liberal or uncommitted congressmen backed the President. Representative Simpson evidently led the administration forces within the committee.[24] Floor action in the House was foreordained but surprisingly lopsided. The bill passed by a 325–77 roll-call vote on July 10, with Republicans voting for it by 169–38; nearly all opponents of the measure were fiscal conservatives.[25]

There was never any doubt that the Senate would vote to extend the excess profits tax. Senator Millikin, chairman of the controlling Finance Committee, favored the bill, as did rank-and-file sentiment in the upper chamber. On July 14, without hearings, the Finance Committee reported the measure favorably to the Senate, which passed it the next day by voice vote. The lone challenge was Delaware Republican John Williams's amendment to increase the tax credit to $100,000, as the abandoned Sadlak bill had provided. Millikin countered by saying that the President opposed any amendments, a tactic which caused Senator Robert Hendrickson to drop his co-sponsorship of Williams's amendment and probably helped to switch a number of Republican votes on the amendment. In one of his more graphic phrases,

[24] Memorandum from Gerald Morgan to Eisenhower, July 11, 1953, Box 34, Morgan Records, Eisenhower Papers.

[25] Twenty-eight of those Republicans who voted against passage of the bill were scaled on fiscal policy in the previous Congress: twenty-two were strong conservatives, three were moderate conservatives, and only three scaled as liberals.

Millikin pleaded against appending any amendments whatever, since the bill would then have to go back to the House; this he likened to "passing a kidney stone,"[26] Williams's amendment failed by 34–52, with only nine Republicans voting for it and thirty-six opposing, and the Senate fight was over.

Extension of the excess profits tax represented a victory for the administration against uphill odds, given the strong opposition to it among Ways and Means Republicans. But the battle took its toll in party harmony. Reed's intransigence throughout the spring had caused many of his fellow House Republicans to take rigid positions early in the controversy. In addition, some powerful party figures were openly critical of Reed,[27] though he did retain a number of supporters, especially after the effort to undercut his committee's authority through the "bypass rule." The number of those offended by such tampering with customary procedure evidently far surpassed the thirty-eight Republicans who ultimately voted against EPT extension on the floor. Reporting the prevailing mood among his party colleagues on the eve of the July 8 Ways and Means Committee meeting, Representative Heselton wrote to Sherman Adams that "in the minds of a number of very reasonable Republicans who, incidentally, were not consulted in any way, it [the excess profits tax fight] was a tremendous fiasco, with the Administration suffering a very bad tactical defeat."[28]

Reed, however, quickly reconciled himself to his failure. The President moved to conciliate the New Yorker immediately after the fight was decided in the House, giving both him and Congressman Simpson places of honor at a July 11 White House luncheon. But apparently Eisenhower's talents for personal di-

---

[26] *Congressional Record*, Vol. xcix, Part 7, 83d Cong., 1st Sess., 8852; *New York Times*, July 16, 1953. Millikin had reported at the July 14 leadership conference that the Senate was likely to accept such an amendment; Secretary of the Treasury Humphrey's expressed fear that one amendment could produce a flood of others was perhaps decisive in shaping Millikin's position in the floor debate.

[27] See John Taber to Hubert Laube, July 1, 1953, and Taber to Reed, June 30, 1953, Taber Papers; also memorandum from Gerald Morgan to Eisenhower, June 30, 1953, Box 35, Morgan Records, Eisenhower Papers.

[28] Heselton to Adams, July 7, 1953, OF 99, Eisenhower Papers.

plomacy and his genuine respect for congressional prerogative had kept Reed from feeling any bitterness toward him even during the struggle. As soon as House action on the bill was ended, the Ways and Means chairman described the clash as "a good fight" and "a hard fight." More significant was his statement in a personal letter at the height of the controversy that although he and the President differed "on the policy involved in the field of taxation, I respect him very highly and feel that he means to give the country a very fine Administration."[29] The President's retention of Reed's friendship was crucially important for the future of other administration programs before the Eighty-third Congress.

As the second session opened, the Republican party seemed to be pointing toward greater harmony on tax matters than that characterizing the early months of 1953. When President Eisenhower, in his 1954 State of the Union message, requested that Congress delay the scheduled April 1 expiration of yet another pair of wartime tax measures, the 52 percent corporate tax rate and a number of special excise taxes imposed in 1952, Congressman Reed promised that his committee would promptly consider both recommendations. Two weeks later came evidence from the administration that it, too, was willing to compromise. The President, in his Budget Message of January 21, and Secretary Humphrey and Budget Director Dodge in news conferences the same day, indicated that an absolutely balanced budget, though still desirable, would no longer be considered a prerequisite for further tax cuts.[30] This apparent shift in White House strategy not only suggested that the administration would work with the "tax-cutters" on the excise and corporate rate extensions, but also hinted at tax relief in the forthcoming omnibus revenue bill.

Republicans on the Ways and Means Committee set to work immediately on a compromise package of excise reductions. The

[29] *New York Times*, July 10, 1953; Reed to Walter H. Edson, July 3, 1953, Reed Papers.

[30] *New York Times*, Jan. 8, Jan. 22, 1954.

package, announced on January 28, 1954, was largely the work of Reed and Simpson. It provided for the reduction of nearly all excises on "luxury" items from 20 to 10 percent, and retained—as Eisenhower had requested—the surtaxes on liquor, gasoline, tobacco, and automobiles. In contrast to the $3 billion loss in revenue which the scheduled April 1 expirations would have entailed, the compromise package (which included implicit agreement that the existing corporate rates would be extended) anticipated a federal income reduction of only about $1 billion.

Secretary of the Treasury Humphrey continued to oppose the measure both publicly and within the administration, but even before the House began to move on the Reed-Simpson package bill, some of Eisenhower's other advisers were urging him to accept such a compromise.[31] Given the "pro-business" charges being leveled by Democrats at Eisenhower's omnibus tax revision bill, also due for House action in March 1954, excise reductions began to look politically appealing, if not necessary.

Congress acted quickly. The House passed the excise reduction bill on March 10 by the overwhelming margin of 411–3, with all 211 voting Republicans favoring it. Republican members also voted unanimously against a Democratic amendment aimed at reducing excise revenues still further by ending the tax on admissions of less than 50 cents. Secretary Humphrey had met several times with Senator Millikin during the first week in March to discuss strategy for holding the excise level at 15 percent in the Senate (compared with the 10 percent levels adopted by the House), but Millikin indicated that he would not try to influence the Finance Committee in its consideration of the bill. Since several Republican senators were talking of reductions to rates even lower than 10 percent, Millikin's reaction all but ensured that the Senate version would be at least as extreme as that passed by the House. The sharp reductions were politically attractive because they could serve to increase consumption,

[31] *Ibid.*, Mar. 1, 1954; and memorandum from Gabriel Hauge to Eisenhower, Mar. 3, 1954, in Box 1, Gabriel Hauge Records, Eisenhower Papers.

thereby reducing accumulated inventories and stimulating employment.[32]

Left to its own devices, the upper chamber not only accepted the 10 percent House figure for nearly all excise rates, but also voted to exempt all admissions costing 60 cents or less and further reduced the excise on household appliances to only 5 percent. The latter floor action, sponsored by Senator Homer Capehart, was supported by twenty-nine Republicans and opposed by only fifteen. Actually, even though Capehart's amendment went against the administration's original wishes, it was primarily aimed at blocking a Democratic attempt to erase entirely the excise on household appliances.

As it emerged from conference and came to Eisenhower for his signature, the excise bill was closer to the Senate than the House version, entailing an estimated revenue loss of $999 million. The administration's impotent position in the face of this congressional action was well characterized in the Budget Bureau's formal report to the President on the acceptability of the act: "The bill fails to carry out the full measure of the Administration's recommendations," the report summarized, but "while this is true, it is also true that if the bill is not approved there will be more of a revenue loss to the Treasury [through the automatic April 1 expiration]."[33] Eisenhower signed the reductions into law on March 31.

All the while the excise reduction struggle had been unfolding, preparations were under way to bring a mammoth tax revision bill to the floor of the House. During the taxation clashes in 1953, the White House had consistently maintained that all needed revisions in the tax structure should be made at one time. Accordingly, throughout the first session, administration officials worked on the details of a major tax revision package for 1954. In his Budget Message of January 21, 1954, President Eisenhower

---

[32] *New York Times,* Mar. 8, 1954.
[33] Roger W. Jones, report to Eisenhower, Mar. 31, 1954, Box 17, Reports to the President on Pending Legislation, Eisenhower Papers.

presented the result, a twenty-five-point plan for changing the nation's tax codes.

On March 9, after working behind closed doors throughout January and February, the Ways and Means Committee reported out a bill (H.R. 8300) which followed closely the President's recommendations. Heralded by Reed and administration spokesmen as a measure to end "inequities" in the tax structure, the bill proposed (in accordance with the earlier Reed-Simpson compromise plan) to retain the existing rates of corporate taxation, but it established a more lenient formula for businesses to write off depreciation costs and eliminated a large part of the tax on corporate dividends. It also provided a number of specific benefits for individual taxpayers, including liberalized deductions for medical expenses, child care, and charitable contributions, and increased tax credits for those on fixed retirement incomes.

Congressional Republicans solidly supported the proposed tax revision program, but Democrats leveled heavy criticism on two points: the bill's reduction of taxes on unearned dividend income and its failure to increase the personal exemption, which Democrats wanted to raise from $600 to $700. Republican leaders in both houses believed for a time that the administration would have to make at least some concession on the exemption increase, but Eisenhower remained adamant in his opposition. On March 14, Speaker Martin and Floor Leader Halleck revealed that the President would probably veto his own tax reform bill if it included such a provision, though Eisenhower himself avoided threatening a veto. The next evening the President delivered a televised speech in support of the tax revision bill in which he spoke out explicitly against the Democratic-sponsored move for an exemption increase, citing the $2.5 billion revenue loss it would entail. This loss, added to the $1.4 billion reduction already incorporated in the bill, Eisenhower argued, would be excessive.

In addition to the White House public relations effort, House leaders worked hard to ensure party loyalty on the tax reform measure. To vote for the Democratic amendment, they said, would be to "vote against Ike." On March 16, Representatives Daniel Reed and Richard Simpson joined administration loyalists Martin, Arends, and Vorys in urging party unity on the bill before a well-attended meeting of the Republican House Conference.[34] In the end, after a bitter floor fight, House Republicans voted 201–10 for the White House position against the Democratic-sponsored amendment, and 208–5 for final passage of the bill (figures for the whole House were 210–204 and 339–80 respectively). Nearly all the Republicans voting against the administration in both cases were either liberals or uncommitted on fiscal policy.

The administration received a large share of credit for House passage of the tax bill. One commentator characterized the Eisenhower White House staff as "the smoothest-working machine Capitol Hill has seen in years" and charged that it had freely "promised jobs and campaign funds" for the 1954 elections to those who voted "right" on the omnibus measure.[35] This observation may have overstated the degree of arm-twisting and favoritism necessary for passage, since it underestimated the breadth of agreement among Republicans on the principles underlying the tax bill. There is no doubt, however, that Eisenhower was more than eager for the bill's adoption. Whether or not he exerted extraordinary pressure on Congress, strong leadership by the party chiefs certainly marked the progress of the bill through the House, where, as Daniel Reed wrote the President, "the Party has been welded into an effective unit for further contests."[36] Reed's great helpfulness throughout the fight for H.R. 8300 was ample repayment for the administration's tactful handling of him after the EPT struggle and its graceful acquiescence to the compromise excise reductions bill of March 1954.

The omnibus tax revision bill did not come before the Senate

---

34 *New York Times*, Mar. 19, 1954; also see Minutes of the Republican Conference, Mar. 16, 1954, Halleck Papers.

35 Drew Pearson, Washington *Post*, Mar. 24, 1954.

36 Reed to Eisenhower, Mar. 19, 1954, PPF 866, Eisenhower Papers.

until mid-June 1954, by which time Secretary of the Treasury Humphrey had invited all but three senators to lunch in order to explain the details of the plan.[37] Once again, in the Senate, the dividends provision and the individual exemption increase drew the greatest opposition to the administration bill. Trying to head off Democratic efforts to remove the dividend tax credit, Senator Millikin—probably with the administration's blessing—secured a compromise reduction in the credit which had been included in the House version. His reduced credit provision was then blasted from the Senate bill the next day by a 71–13 vote. Republicans voted to drop it by 34–10; most of the ten who stood by the dividend credit were from the party's conservative wing on fiscal questions. In all likelihood, Senate leaders relaxed party discipline on the dividend provision in order to concentrate their energies on defeating the drive for the $700 individual exemption, which the administration had viewed all along as the greater threat to its program. The George amendment providing for such an increase was narrowly defeated (49–46) in a nearly straight party-line vote: forty-five Republican senators opposed it, while only three (Langer, Morse, and Young) voted for it.

Despite Daniel Reed's announced intention to "get the House version [especially with regard to dividend credits] or not have a bill," the conference committee restored only part of the originally scheduled relief for stockholders.[38] Overall, however, the tax bill closely approximated the President's recommendations, and after Republicans again held off strong Democratic efforts to amend the conference report, H.R. 8300 became law on August 16, 1954. The bill which Eisenhower had described as a "cornerstone" of his program was thus set in place very much intact, as the two-year tax imbroglio ended on a happy note for the administration.[39]

Other fiscal and economic legislation during the Eighty-third

[37] Merlo J. Pusey, *Eisenhower the President* (New York: Macmillan, 1956), 212.
[38] *New York Times*, July 4, 1954.
[39] See the favorable report submitted to Eisenhower by Roger W. Jones of the Bureau of the Budget, Aug. 9, 1954, Box 32, Reports to the President on Pending Legislation, Eisenhower Papers.

Congress involved much less intraparty maneuvering than the various tax measures. On the matter of dropping wage and price controls, for example, Republicans were in almost complete agreement. Having stated publicly his opposition to continuing the Korean War–inspired controls past their scheduled expiration date of April 30, 1953, President Eisenhower assigned a task force to study the problem in January of that year. On the basis of its report, he issued a series of executive orders which brought the last of such controls to an end by March 17 (even though the fighting in Korea had not ended—and would not, until late July).

Several Republican senators, led by Homer Capehart, attempted on their own to give the President stand-by authority to impose ninety-day controls in cases of emergency. Eisenhower was largely uninterested in such authority, however, and within the Senate Robert Taft firmly opposed it.[40] As a result, though the stand-by provision was added to the Defense Production Act Amendments of 1953, its use was limited by amendment to situations of declared war or national emergency. Senate Republicans, following Taft's lead, backed the limiting amendment overwhelmingly (thirty-four to thirteen). Opponents of the limitation included a number of the more liberal Republicans, such as Prescott Bush, James Duff, Ralph Flanders, Irving Ives, William Langer, Leverett Saltonstall, H. Alexander Smith, Charles W. Tobey, and Alexander Wiley. Eventually, all of Capehart's unsolicited efforts came to naught, when House conferees insisted that the stand-by authority be removed from the bill. The President's orthodox Republican belief in minimal federal interference in the economy was thus sustained by the Eighty-third Congress.

The administration also succeeded ultimately in getting an increase in the national debt ceiling. In late July 1953, Eisenhower asked Congress for a $15 billion boost in the ceiling to a level of $290 billion. The Ways and Means Committee quickly reported out a suitable bill, although Daniel Reed grumbled privately that the request merely showed "the spenders" still controlled

40 *New York Times*, May 20, 1953.

the government.[41] The full House then voted for the increase by 239–158, with Republicans supporting it by 169–33. Apart from six freshmen (Clardy, Fino, Krueger, Laird, Pillion, Poff) and those who were unscalable, all but one opponent of the measure (Coudert) were fiscal conservatives.

Complications soon set in on the debt ceiling bill, however. Some Republican House members felt they had been "put over the barrel" in being asked to vote for the increase, especially after the Senate failed to act on the request at all before the first session ended.[42] Neither Majority Leader Knowland nor Senator Millikin, who would have had to direct the measure on the Senate floor, was at all eager to take the debt bill to the upper chamber in the waning days of the session.[43] Consequently, Millikin's Finance Committee tabled the proposal by a vote of eleven to four. Although Secretary Humphrey expressed initial displeasure, he soon indicated that the administration could probably get by under the existing ceiling until 1954. Finally, when the White House revived its request for Senate action late in the second session, Millikin gave the matter his lukewarm support. The Finance Committee then voted a temporary increase in the ceiling to $281 billion, which the Senate approved by voice vote. Again the President's wishes prevailed.

Given the extended, sometimes bitter squabbling and the compromises that characterized Eisenhower's achievements in the area of fiscal and economic legislation, the voting record of congressional Republicans is slightly surprising. In Senate and House alike, well over 90 percent of the Republican members taking a position on at least half of the "Eisenhower issue" roll calls in fiscal policy had pro-Eisenhower records. In the House, 209 of 219 Republicans took the President's position 80 percent of the time or more; none were anti-Eisenhower. In the upper house, the figures were less overwhelming but nonetheless re-

---

[41] Daniel Reed to W. P. Oakes, July 20, 1953, Reed Papers.

[42] John Heselton to Sherman Adams, Aug. 6, 1953, OF 99, Eisenhower Papers.

[43] Unsigned, undated memorandum in Box 2, A67–19 Accessions, Morgan Records, Eisenhower Papers.

vealed strong party support for the White House: forty-three of forty-seven Senate Republicans with relatively complete records ranked as pro-Eisenhower, though only ten had support scores of .80 or higher. Only William Langer (.39) and Wayne Morse (.11) had anti-Eisenhower records.

In their roll-call behavior, Republican congressional leaders and members of key committees likewise ranked as strongly pro-Eisenhower. In the House, Halleck, Reed, and Rules chairman Leo Allen had scores of 1.00, .91, and 1.00 respectively, and neither the Ways and Means Committee nor the Rules Committee included a single Republican whose support score was lower than .60. On the Senate side, Floor Leader Knowland scored .71 and Finance chairman Millikin .65, both within the moderately pro-Eisenhower range. Of the seven Republican members of the Finance Committee with near-complete records, only one fell below a score of .60 (Delaware conservative John Williams, who scored .56).

Since nearly all Republicans supported the administration's fiscal proposals as they came before Congress, little information is gained by comparing the voting behavior of previously committed fiscal conservatives and liberals, respectively. As Table 8 shows, Republican House and Senate veterans with liberal records on fiscal and economic matters were neither more nor less likely than their conservative colleagues to support the administration. All Republican freshmen in both houses ranked as pro-Eisenhower, but in doing so they were little different from their senior brethren. No other variable (period of entry, region, or district type) seems to have affected voting patterns in either house.

The administration's strongly traditional Republican approach to fiscal and economic questions gained it strong support from party members in Congress. Notwithstanding the dramatic clashes over tax reduction in 1953, Eisenhower approached fiscal policy much as any Republican administration might have been expected to. The President believed deeply in the traditional Republican economic tenets of a balanced budget, minimal tax

*Table 8*  "Eisenhower Support" by Republicans in the Eighty-Third Congress, Fiscal and Economic Policy*

| Previous Scale Type | Level of Support | | | | |
|---|---|---|---|---|---|
| | .80–1.00 | .60–.79 | .40–.59 | .20–.39 | .00–.19 |
| SENATE | | | | | |
| Strong liberal | 0 | 2 | 0 | 0 | 1 |
| Moderate liberal | 1 | 5 | 0 | 0 | 0 |
| Uncommitted, not scaled | 2 | 3 | 0 | 1 | 0 |
| Moderate conservative | 2 | 11 | 0 | 0 | 0 |
| Strong conservative | 0 | 6 | 2 | 0 | 0 |
| (Freshmen) | 5 | 6 | 0 | 0 | 0 |
| TOTAL† | 10 | 33 | 2 | 1 | 1 |
| HOUSE | | | | | |
| Strong liberal | 16 | 0 | 1 | 0 | 0 |
| Moderate liberal | 19 | 2 | 0 | 0 | 0 |
| Uncommitted, not scaled | 31 | 0 | 1 | 0 | 0 |
| Moderate conservative | 26 | 1 | 1 | 0 | 0 |
| Strong conservative | 67 | 3 | 0 | 0 | 0 |
| (Freshmen) | 50 | 1 | 0 | 0 | 0 |
| TOTAL‡ | 209 | 7 | 3 | 0 | 0 |

* For roll calls used, see Appendix E; for individual scores, Appendix K.

† Excludes six senators with responses on fewer than half the roll calls in fiscal-economic policy in 1953–54: Hugh Butler, Bowring, and Reynolds (all Neb.), Crippa (Wyo.), Taft (Ohio), and Tobey (N.H.).

‡ Excludes Speaker Joseph Martin, who did not participate in House roll calls.

levels, and the encouragement of private initiative.[44] So long as his commitment to such goals came through clearly, disagreement over priorities alone (budget balancing versus tax reductions) could not drive a permanent wedge between Eisenhower and other members of his party. The administration's strategy of reducing its commitment to the budget-first priority in early 1954, of course, helped to ensure party unity on the tax program in the second session. Finally, the Eisenhower administration also agreed with congressional Republicans on the way the tax load

[44] Adams, *Firsthand Report*, 154; Murphy, "The Eisenhower Shift," *Fortune* 53, No. 2, 11.

should be allocated. This was especially evident in the 1954 tax revision bill, which was heavily weighted in the direction of providing relief to business interests.[45]

President Eisenhower's devotion to traditional Republican dogma did more than ensure a high degree of cooperation from congressional Republicans on administration fiscal and economic policies. It also indicated that the word "Eisenhower," when used to modify "Republicanism," was a very subtle sort of modifier indeed.

[45] *Congressional Quarterly* estimated that the tax revision bill granted corporations $536 million in tax relief and individuals $827 million. Of the latter figure, however, $204 million resulted from the dividend tax credit, a "pro-business" provision (*Congressional Quarterly Almanac*, Vol. x [1954], 478).

# CHAPTER SIX

# The Needs of a Nation

W hen it comes down to dealing with the relationship between the human in this country and his Government," President Eisenhower remarked to reporters in early 1954, "the people in this administration believe in being what I think we would normally call liberal; and when we deal with the economic affairs of this country, we believe in being conservative."[1] Widely quoted—albeit in mercifully abridged form—this statement epitomized many of the internal inconsistencies in the early Eisenhower program. Nowhere were such inconsistencies more apparent than in the social welfare policies of the new administration.

In housing, health, and worker security, Eisenhower launched programs representative of the "middle way" he had advocated during the 1952 campaign. A strong current of traditional Republican ideology ran through nearly every such program, however. Whether focusing on housing, health insurance, workers' social security, or labor-management relations, Eisenhower's "middle way" in welfare matters emphasized federal noninterventionism and private initiative. Still, his programs were ideologically ambiguous enough that they frequently brought on confusion and discord within the Republican party and created

---

[1] Press conference remarks of Jan. 27, 1954, in *Public Papers . . . 1954*, 210–11.

unorthodox, and usually powerful, coalitions in opposition. Aside from his social security revision program, none of the President's major social welfare measures won complete victories in Congress, and on a few such issues he suffered serious rebuffs. Just as he succeeded in foreign policy because he believed deeply in what he was doing, perhaps Eisenhower's failure to lead his party on welfare-related matters reflected his basic lack of commitment to such programs.

In dealing with the problem of housing, Eisenhower and congressional Republicans came into some conflict. In 1949, Congress had passed a housing law calling for federal construction of 810,000 public housing units over the next six years. But by 1953, fewer than one-fourth of those units had actually been built—in part because President Truman, faced with economic pressures growing out of the Korean conflict, had never requested authority to build more than 75,000 new units in any one year. In March 1953 Eisenhower's new Housing and Home Finance administrator, former Nebraska congressman Albert M. Cole, a long-standing foe of the public housing program, exceeded Truman's parsimony by requesting on behalf of the new administration an appropriation sufficient for 35,000 new housing starts in fiscal 1954. This request was included in the Independent Offices Appropriation bill, the first money measure to come before the Eighty-third Congress.

The public housing proposal provoked strong Republican opposition in the House. Michigan's Jesse Wolcott, powerful chairman of the House Banking and Currency Committee (which did not have jurisdiction over the appropriations bill, but did have control over substantive housing legislation), had already publicly promised that "the Government [was] going to get out of the home-building business" and leave it to private enterprise.[2] Before long it was apparent that other highly placed Republicans agreed. In reporting out the appropriations bill on April 17, the House Appropriations Committee deleted all funds for new

[2] Speech to American Bankers' Association, Mar. 4, 1953, in *New York Times*, Mar. 5, 1953.

housing starts, arguing that "continuation of [the] program is not justified and is not in accord with the program for economy and a balanced budget."[3]

On the House floor, the burden of defending the President's request fell largely to Democrats. Republican congressmen T. Millet Hand and Charles Wolverton of New Jersey, Jacob Javits of New York, and Hugh Scott of Pennsylvania (all liberals on welfare policy) were the only members of their party to speak out for restoration of the public housing funds. In the course of the debate, Floor Leader Halleck surprised some by observing calmly that the administration was "not at this time taking . . . any position either one way or the other on the fundamental issue as to whether public housing is or is not a responsibility of the Federal Government," and went on to oppose restoration of the 35,000-unit provision. California Republican John Phillips, chairman of the Appropriations subcommittee on Independent Offices and therefore floor manager for the bill, and Norris Cotton of New Hampshire were most outspoken against the public housing program. Cotton denounced it as "the most monstrous, un-American, uneconomical, socialistic, and expensive legislation ever written by any Congress in our history"; he concluded by assuring his House colleagues that it would not "offend" Eisenhower if the program were scuttled.[4] The House then defeated the Democratic-sponsored amendment to restore the housing authorization to the bill, with Republicans voting against it, 176–34. Eisenhower's reaction bore out the statements of Halleck and Cotton. Denying that the House action was a rebuff, the President told reporters that he had never claimed to favor continuing the public housing program. "The matter of principle," he explained, "was not involved."[5]

The Senate version of the appropriations measure restored the full 35,000 housing units without a roll-call vote, but the lack of enthusiasm in the administration led the conferees to ignore

---

[3] *Ibid.*, Apr. 18, 1953.
[4] *Congressional Record*, Vol. XCIX, Part 3, 83d Cong., 1st Sess., 3497, 3510–11.
[5] Press conference remarks of Apr. 23, 1953, in *Public Papers . . . 1953*, 203.

the Senate lead. Instead, the conference report established a maximum of 20,000 new public housing starts in fiscal 1954, which the lower house then accepted by a vote of 239–161. The authorization included a stipulation proposed by Representative Phillips that the government could not contract for any new units without the specific approval of Congress. This meant that construction could begin in fiscal 1954 on a maximum of 20,000 public housing units already contracted for (of which there were already approximately 30,000), but no new contracts might be included among the 20,000 starts.

House Republicans voted for the 20,000-unit compromise by 173–36. The nature of the opposition, however, revealed that the nominally pro-Eisenhower settlement was fought primarily by those members of the President's party who were most liberal on welfare questions generally: of the thirty-six Republicans voting against the compromise report, twenty-six had previously liberal records on welfare matters. Included in this minority were Hand, Javits, Scott, and Wolverton, as well as a number of other congressmen from urban districts.[6]

Following this more-or-less denial of his 1953 housing requests, Eisenhower set machinery in motion to draw up a thorough program for the second session. In September he appointed a twenty-one-member Advisory Commission on Government Housing Policies and Programs, with HHFA head Cole as chairman. Although Democrats charged that the commission was "loaded with representatives of [interests] . . . whose lobbies have fought" public housing, the group did not advocate the end of the public housing program in its report to the President three months later.[7] Rather, it limited its specific recommendations to several measures designed to stimulate home building and the renovation of older homes through liberalized federal guarantees to private developers. While giving implicit support to the prin-

---

[6] Fourteen of the thirty-six (39 percent) were from metropolitan districts, and nine others (25 percent) came from mid-urban constituencies.

[7] The charge was made by Sen. Estes Kefauver (D.-Tenn.); see *New York Times*, Oct. 1, 1953.

ciple of public housing, the report left "the size of the program and the method of financing to the Administration and to Congress."[8]

Eisenhower first presented his 1954 housing proposals to party leaders at the White House conference for legislative planning in December 1953. The administration plan, modeled on the commission's report, included a request for four-year continuance of the federal public housing program. Some of the more conservative leaders present sharply criticized the plan, but the President defended it as essential to fulfilling "one of the basic needs of the people."[9]

Statements by leading Republicans during the next few weeks indicated that Eisenhower could expect some trouble from his party in securing passage of the housing package, especially the public housing portion. Homer Capehart, chairman of the Senate Banking and Currency Committee, predicted that 1954 would bring the "most constructive housing program the nation has ever seen," but he added suggestively that it would be a "joint venture" based on the President's recommendations and the "experiences" of congressional Republicans. A few weeks later, Speaker Martin told a Philadelphia audience that the Republican housing program would be so successful "that public housing soon will become only a memory of the unlamented days of the managed economy."[10]

Undaunted, President Eisenhower sent a housing message to Congress on January 25, 1954, in which he requested 140,000 new public housing units, to be constructed at the rate of 35,000 per year over a four-year period. The total program, according to the administration, would "assure construction of more than 1,000,000 housing units during 1954" and would therefore act "as a sustaining force for the entire economy."[11] The Eisenhower housing program was a mixed bag. It included sections dealing

[8] Commission recommendations listed *ibid.*, Dec. 16, 1953.
[9] Donovan, *The Inside Story*, 224.
[10] *New York Times*, Dec. 20, 1953, Jan. 24, 1954.
[11] *Ibid.*, Feb. 8, 1954.

with mortgage insurance for old and new homes, grants and loans for home renovation and rehabilitation, and slum clearance and urban renewal. Certain of its provisions were aimed at helping low-income groups—such as federal insurance for private credit used in rehabilitating homes in "decaying" neighborhoods, and lowering the down-payment requirements on FHA-insured loans for low-income housing. Like other features of the program, however, these points involved *indirect* government participation, through private lending agencies. The public housing provisions in the President's request, by comparison, looked to conservatives to be federal "interventionism."

From the outset, it was obvious that the public housing section would be the most divisive issue for Republicans. Although Martin, Halleck, and a few other party leaders initially praised the omnibus housing package, Representative Wolcott was less encouraging. In February, the Michigan congressman predicted that the public housing provision would be scrapped entirely, stating flatly that such action would "in no way" undermine the President's program.[12]

Prior to House consideration of the 1954 housing bill, conservatives in that chamber tried to deal a deathblow to the public housing program by altering the 1954 Independent Offices appropriation measure. In an effort to end the program entirely by fiscal 1957, the Appropriations Committee wrote the bill so as to permit the completion of all previously contracted units, not to exceed 35,000, over the next two fiscal years, with the proviso "that this be the end of the program."[13] Believing the Appropriations Committee too lenient in allowing the program to linger even for two more years, however, conservative members of the Rules Committee, led by Ohio Republican Clarence Brown, secured a rule on the Independent Offices bill which permitted points of order to be raised against it from the floor. When conservative Democrat Howard W. Smith then objected during floor consideration that the public housing proviso was "legislation

12 *Ibid.*, Feb. 12, 1954.
13 *Ibid.*, Mar. 27, 1954.

in an appropriation bill," he was sustained by the Speaker. The anti-housing forces were jubilant, certain that their success ended all executive authority for further federal construction of low-rent housing. As evidence, they cited the ban on "new" public housing commitments contained in the previous year's Independent Offices bill. They thought their triumph the more certain since the omnibus housing bill, due to come before the House a few days later, itself was "devoid of such authority."[14]

But the administration was prepared. By March 30, the General Accounting Office had "called Mr. Taber, Mr. Phillips, and Mr. Halleck and . . . given them the information that if the 20,000 limit is removed from the pending [Independent Offices] bill the Public Housing Administration will go back to the 35,000 limit under the 1953 appropriation act. . . ." According to the GAO, the ban on "new" commitments in the 1953 appropriation did not apply to any units already contracted for. Armed with this ruling, Halleck announced on the House floor that since the Appropriations Committee's housing proviso had been ruled out of order in the current bill, the administration was now free to go ahead with all of the contracted units in fiscal 1955. The President was reported to be "delighted at the outcome."[15] The strategic victory seemed to give momentum to the administration forces in the House just at the time the omnibus housing bill came to the floor.

The House Banking and Currency Committee reported its version of the administration's 1954 housing program on March 27. The bill fulfilled Representative Wolcott's predictions in that it included no public housing provisions, but otherwise retained virtually all of President Eisenhower's recommendations. A Democratic-sponsored move on the House floor to restore the four-year, 140,000-unit authorization produced a debate reminiscent of that a year earlier and ended in similar fashion: the

14 *Ibid.*, Mar. 30, 1954; the Banking and Currency Committee had removed the public housing section from the omnibus bill (see below).

15 Unsigned memorandum, dated Mar. 30, 1954, in Box 4, A67–19 Accessions, Morgan Records, Eisenhower Papers; *New York Times*, Mar. 31, Apr. 1, 1954.

amendment failed, 176–211, with Republicans voting 48–150 against it. Thirty-three of the thirty-six who had voted against the reduced 20,000-unit appropriation compromise of 1953 voted this time for the Democratic amendment; fifteen other Republicans (including Halleck, but no other House leaders) now joined in support of the President's position. After the failure of that amendment, Republican William Widnall of New Jersey offered a compromise which would have provided one-year authority for construction of 35,000 new units "to be occupied only by families displaced from dwellings in slum clearance projects." This amendment also failed, on a teller vote of 72–164, but evidently gained greater Republican support than the amendment for 140,000 units.[16] The housing bill, thus shorn of any public housing authorization, then passed by 353–36, with Republicans dividing 189 to 9 for the bill. Two of the nine opponents (Gordon Canfield and Javits) were strong liberals on welfare matters; the others—except the generally conservative Noah Mason, who was unscalable on welfare—were conservatives.

The administration looked to the Senate to restore its original four-year public housing request and received a prompt response. Public housing advocates in that body's Banking and Currency Committee, led by Democrat Burnet Maybank of South Carolina, wrote into the bill an even more liberal provision: in effect, it revived the authorization of the original 1949 act for 810,000 units spread over six years, or a rate of 135,000 units per year. Such a provision might have produced an interesting battle on the Senate floor and, ultimately, a dramatic confrontation in conference.

But at this point the civil rights issue was injected into the housing debate. On May 24, 1954—just ten days after the celebrated *Brown* v. *Topeka Board of Education* decision—the Supreme Court ruled against the practice of racial segregation in public housing projects.[17] Immediately, Senator Maybank and

16 *Ibid.*, Apr. 3, 1954.
17 The Court refused an appeal by the San Francisco Housing Authority, which

other Southern Democrats who had been backing the liberal public housing proviso in committee withdrew their support for it. As a result, the Banking and Currency Committee removed that section before reporting the bill to the full Senate.

Despite this setback, however, moderates of both parties combined on the Senate floor to restore to the bill a public housing provision conforming exactly to the President's January request. Presented by Majority Leader Knowland, the 140,000-unit authorization amendment passed easily (66–16), with Republican senators supporting it by 38–3; the only dissenting party members were liberals Ives, Langer, and Morse. The Senate then passed the omnibus housing bill by voice vote.

The sharp difference between the House and Senate versions with regard to public housing ensured a confrontation in conference.[18] On June 10, the House Rules Committee voted to recommend that House conferees be instructed not to compromise on the public housing section. Five days later, however, responding to pressures from the White House, Republican House leaders, and the American Federation of Labor, the committee reversed its action and changed the rule to permit the conferees a free hand. In committee, only Hugh Scott of the Republicans had opposed the ban on compromise from the outset, but in the reversal vote he was joined by fellow Republicans Leo Allen, Edgar Chenoweth, Harris Ellsworth, and Donald Nicholson. Clarence Brown and Carroll Reece voted against compromise on both occasions, and Henry Latham, the other Republican on the committee, voted against compromise the first time and was paired against it the second.[19] Opponents of public housing, de-

---

had been found guilty of segregation practices by the California District Court of Appeals.

[18] There were other notable differences, too, primarily in a number of "anti-scandal" provisions written into the bill by the Senate committee after a scandal in the Housing and Home Finance Administration was uncovered in April (after House action was completed). The Senate changes, which had the effect of rendering some of the federal guarantees to both builders and buyers less liberal, were generally accepted by House conferees with little objection.

[19] *New York Times*, June 11, June 16, 1954.

feated in the Rules Committee, determined to revive the no-compromise instruction during House consideration of the rule. Congressman Halleck rose quickly to the challenge, however, arguing against setting a precedent of tying "the hands of con-ferees" and emphasizing the importance of "orderly procedure." Chastened by their leader's urgings, Republicans then supported the rule without instruction, by a vote of 192–1 (the lone dissent-ing vote was Noah Mason).[20] The bill therefore went to confer-ence without stipulation.

The intensity of feeling in the House, so clearly apparent in the pre-conference maneuvers, was equally evident in the con-ference itself. Though the House conferees nominally compro-mised with the Senate version to the extent of providing authority for 35,000 *new* housing starts in fiscal 1955, they succeeded in adding the stipulation originally proposed by Representative Widnall during the April House debate: that such units could be built only in equal proportion to units of slum clearance. This limitation, according to public housing proponents, meant that not more than 10,000 new units were likely to be built, despite the allowance for a maximum of 35,000. The real tip-off came with the statement of Jesse Wolcott, who had opposed the Presi-dent's request throughout the battle. "With these limitations," said Wolcott, "we conferees believe we have done a masterful job on public housing . . . ." The settlement, lamented the Na-tional Housing Conference in its newsletter, was likely to "take the President off the hook, and kill public housing at the same time."[21] The House agreed to the conference report after turning back a recommittal motion, 156–234. Recommittal was opposed by Republicans, 50–155, in almost exact repetition of the party split on the four-year, 140,000-unit plan during the April debate. With less fanfare, the Senate accepted the conference compromise on a vote of 59–21, including a Republican vote of 38–4 (opposed

[20] *Ibid.*, June 18, 1954. The vote of the full House was 361–19.
[21] *Ibid.*, July 21, 1954; see National Housing Conference "Special Newsletter," Vol. 7, No. 16 (July 16, 1954), copy in Ives Papers.

were liberals Ives, Langer, and Saltonstall, and the strongly conservative John Williams).

On August 2, 1954, the President signed the housing bill into
law, pointing with pride to the many provisions implementing
his January recommendations. Almost as an aside at the conclusion of his statement, however, Eisenhower declared that the
job was "not all finished. . . . We shall need to continue our public
housing program until the needs can be met by private industry." [22] The Omnibus Housing Act, as a package, did come close
to meeting the President's request, but on its key social welfare
provision—public housing—Republican opposition, at least in
the House, had dealt him a sharp setback.

In another area of welfare policy Eisenhower had greater success. Although he had to wait until the second session, he obtained
from the Eighty-third Congress legislation which expanded and
revised the social security system. The President had pointed
toward this goal since early 1953, calling in his first State of the
Union message for greater "safeguards against the privations that
too often come with unemployment, old age, illness, and accident," and more specifically for extension of the social security
system "to cover millions of citizens who have been left out . . . ." [23]
The matter was given top priority, along with ten other administration proposals, as "must" legislation for 1953.

Social security revision, however, did not see the light of day
during the first session. Less than three weeks after the President's
request for expansion of the system, Daniel Reed, whose Ways
and Means Committee had jurisdiction over the legislation, declared that because "no patchwork job would suffice," he was
appointing a subcommittee to conduct a thorough study of the
problem. Since the administration was already embroiled with
Reed over the question of personal income tax cuts, the chairman's move was read by some observers as yet another challenge

[22] Statement upon signing the Housing Act of 1954, in *Public Papers . . . 1954*,
675.
[23] Message to Congress of Feb. 2, 1953, in *Public Papers . . . 1953*, 32.

to White House authority. Furthermore, Representative Carl T. Curtis of Nebraska, appointed by Reed to chair the subcommittee, had long favored changing social security from an actuarial to a "pay-as-you-go" system (which would ultimately have lowered benefits), a proposition which was opposed by the Eisenhower administration. But Curtis quickly announced that even though his subcommittee would not be made up of "yes-men," it expected "to work harmoniously with the Executive" during the course of its study. Reed, too, issued a statement designed to reassure his critics among administration and congressional Republicans, saying that he intended to help, rather than hinder, the President's efforts to revise social security.[24]

Congressional action on social security was all but nonexistent in 1953. The Curtis subcommittee moved very slowly, and the Ways and Means Committee proved more reluctant than Reed's earlier comments had suggested. Early in 1953, Representative Robert Kean introduced a bill (H.R. 3608) designed to extend coverage to six million additional workers and to raise the level of monthly earnings allowed to social security recipients. Kean denied having consulted with the administration, but the bill's provisions squared neatly with White House plans.[25] Nonetheless, Reed's committee did not act on the measure. Then, just two days before the 1953 session ended, the President transmitted to Congress a specific request for extension of the system to cover 10.5 million additional workers; at the same time, he promised that further recommendations for change would be forthcoming early in 1954. On the day Congress adjourned, Reed introduced "by request" a bill enbodying the President's request, although of course no action could be taken on it before the next year.

It is not clear whether Reed was adamantly opposed to the administration and blocked executive efforts to get a plan before Congress in the first session. When one newspaper reported that the President had tried to win Reed over "right up to the closing hours of Congress," Eisenhower's chief aide for congressional

24 *New York Times*, Feb. 21, Mar. 6, 1953.
25 *Ibid.*, Mar. 2, 1953.

liaison wrote Reed, obviously "for the record," characterizing the story as "a complete fabrication" and denying that the President had held up his social security message in an attempt to "placate" Reed.[26] The administration's relations with Reed, Curtis, and the subcommittee remained fairly cordial throughout the later months of 1953. At one point in late August, Curtis claimed that the Department of Health, Education, and Welfare was not giving him proper cooperation, but he did not complain about the conduct of the executive branch thereafter. Despite another disagreement between Eisenhower and the two Ways and Means members later in the fall over the wisdom of a scheduled January 1, 1954, increase (from 1.5 to 2 percent) in the social security tax, an open rift failed to develop.[27] Indeed, Reed's public statements on social security began to sound increasingly like the President's. On December 10, he came out for increased benefits and extended coverage, both of which were features of the administration's tentative program, and pledged to "maintain and strengthen the contributory principle of the program," a declaration which could be interpreted as assurance that no effort would be made to put the system on a pay-as-you-go basis.[28] Moreover, when Congressman Curtis in late December announced his own plan to change social security into a universal old-age pension system on the lines previously advocated by the U.S. Chamber of Commerce, there was no rallying of congressional Republicans to the measure, and Reed remained aloof.

The President presented his complete list of recommendations for social security revision in a special message on January 14, 1954. These proposed changes included extension of the program to cover 10.5 million more workers, increased monthly benefits, a liberalized retirement-earnings provision, and an increase in the annual taxable-earnings base from $3600 to $4200, as well as a number of other less sweeping alterations. Because of its long

---

26 Exact newspaper reference unknown; quotations from General Wilton B. Persons to Reed, Aug. 7, 1953, Box 35, Morgan Records, Eisenhower Papers.

27 *New York Times*, Aug. 26, Nov. 22, Dec. 13, 1953.

28 *Ibid.*, Dec. 11, 1953.

backlog of business, which included the tax revision and excise reduction bills, the Ways and Means Committee did not begin hearings on social security revision until April 1. It then took until May 28 to report its bill (H.R. 9366). The only serious disagreement among committee Republicans came over the provision for increasing the taxable-earnings base, but in the end the White House recommendation was adopted.[29] Conforming very closely to Eisenhower's January proposals, the bill glided through the lower house on June 1, passing by a vote of 356–8; the only two Republicans who voted against it were the strongly conservative Clare Hoffman of Michigan and Wint Smith of Kansas.

The social security bill continued to enjoy smooth progress to final enactment. The Senate Finance Committee took it up immediately after finishing work on the omnibus tax program, and after two weeks of hearings reported out a measure substantially like the House version. The Finance Committee's bill diverged most sharply from the House bill (and from the administration program) in failing to include some four million farmers and self-employed professionals under the expanded coverage. After limited debate which produced only minor amendments, the Senate passed the bill by voice vote. Conference action restored the provision extending coverage to farmers, and both houses then readily agreed to the measure. On signing the bill into law, the President, demonstrating a penchant for the building-block metaphor, spoke proudly of laying yet another "cornerstone."

If the social security revision bill represented a victory for the administration, another of its welfare-related programs, health reinsurance, represented the opposite. President Eisenhower had stressed the need for increased health coverage for the American people in the same 1953 message in which he first alluded to the need for extension of the social security system. Indeed, the situation was undeniably bad: although ninety-two million persons

---

[29] On the disagreement among GOP committee members, see *ibid.*, May 14, 1954. Noah Mason and James Utt refused to sign the committee report because of the taxable-earnings base increase.

were covered by voluntary health insurance programs, only one-fourth of all families with annual incomes below $2000 had any protection at all.[30]

Still, the White House proposed no health coverage legislation during the first session. In mid-autumn of 1953, Senator H. Alexander Smith, chairman of the Senate Committee on Labor and Public Welfare (and himself a liberal on welfare questions), wrote to HEW Secretary Oveta Culp Hobby to spur administration action. Smith's recommendations for "a comprehensive non-socialistic national health program" emphasized, in typical Republican fashion, local community organization and incentives for private, voluntary action. He also proposed, however, more direct assistance to individuals in the form of "offset" tax deductions for payment of health insurance premiums.[31] By January 1954 another New Jersey legislator, Representative Charles Wolverton, also began to lay plans for enacting a health security program, as he introduced legislation designed to encourage the expansion of the private health insurance system through a set of federal guarantees.

The administration's policy did not become known until January 18, when the President sent Congress his proposal for a limited health reinsurance system. Eisenhower's plan called for setting up a $25 million fund within the Treasury which the Secretary of Health, Education, and Welfare could use to guarantee to any approved private carrier of health insurance that the federal government would assume 75 percent of any "abnormal losses" incurred by that carrier as a result of offering health coverage to persons of high risk. The program was to become self-sustaining on the basis of carrier contributions within five years. Immediately, Smith and Wolverton introduced identical bills embodying the President's program. The House and Senate held hearings virtually simultaneously and reported the bills favorably within four days of each other in early July.

[30] See State of the Union message, Feb. 2, 1953, in *Public Papers . . . 1953*, 32; statistics from *New York Times*, July 18, 1954.
[31] Smith to Hobby, Oct. 28, 1953, Ives Papers.

133

The House, first to act, received the bill from Wolverton's committee on July 9. That evening Secretary Hobby, speaking from the White House, delivered a nationally televised address to rally support for the administration's plan. The reinsurance measure, she said, would enable sixty-three million Americans without coverage to enter into voluntary health plans and would broaden the coverage of those already protected.[32] But the administration propaganda effort, whatever its effect on the public, was not sufficient to counter the influence of strong lobbies at work on House members. One of the most effective was the American Medical Association, which viewed any health program as anathema. The AMA apparently persuaded at least some House Republicans to oppose the bill.[33] Among the most vocal Republican opponents of the reinsurance measure during debate in the House were Will Neal, himself a West Virginia physician, and James Dolliver, who spoke of the opposition of the medical profession in Iowa. Another important lobby was disclosed by Melvin Laird of Wisconsin, who condemned the bill as an unnecessary encroachment upon the private insurance sector.[34] Wolverton and Charles Halleck took the lead in defending the administration measure against such attacks, but with little luck. In an upset vote which evidently took the Republican leadership off guard, the House voted to recommit the bill by 238–134; Republicans split 75–120 on the recommittal vote.

The House decision provoked a flurry of reaction. Eisenhower, stung by the rebuff, issued an unusually harsh denunciation, charging that "the people who voted against this bill just don't understand what are the facts of American life."[35] Senator Smith, whose committee had favorably reported the reinsurance bill to the Senate the day before the House action, urged the upper chamber to press forward anyway. Senate debate, Smith argued, would help to place responsibility "where it belongs, on the peo-

[32] *New York Times,* July 10, 1954.

[33] See Charles Halleck to Mrs. A. Kiefer Mayer, July 16, 1954, Halleck Papers.

[34] *Congressional Record,* Vol. c, Part 8, 83d Cong., 2d Sess., 10397, 10406, 10409–10.

[35] Press conference remarks of July 14, 1954, in *Public Papers . . . 1954,* 633.

ple who would sabotage . . . the best program ever suggested."[36] Try as they might to revive the health reinsurance plan, however, neither Eisenhower nor his congressional lieutenants were able to bring it back from the dead.

The administration's reinsurance bill "got caught in a crossfire" between liberals and conservatives.[37] Certainly the bulk of Democratic opposition—though by no means all—came from advocates of a more extensive, centralized health program. Liberals had criticized the Eisenhower proposal from its inception for concentrating solely on supporting the businesses involved (the insurance carriers), while providing nothing in the way of direct guarantees to individual citizens. Even Senator Smith's suggestions to Secretary Hobby in October 1953 had included tax credits to help individuals afford health coverage. Among Republicans, however, opposition to the President's plan came primarily from conservatives, most of whom feared that it contained the seeds of socialized medicine. Of the seventy-five GOP House members who voted to kill the bill, twelve were freshmen and nine were either unscalable or uncommitted in welfare matters; forty-nine of the remaining fifty-four had conservative records in welfare policy. The President did convert many to his position; those forty-nine represented only 57 percent of House Republicans with conservative ratings in welfare policy. Still, however, his failure to win over enough of the Republican conservatives cost him dearly on the health reinsurance bill.

Analysis of the roll-call votes on welfare questions in 1953–1954 yields uneven information for the two houses of Congress. Because there were only four "welfare" roll calls in the Senate, two of which concerned housing and two unemployment insurance, a breakdown of Republican voting in that house tells little. Of those few roll calls, forty-one Republican senators supported the President every time they took a position, five took Eisenhower's side on all but one occasion (support scores of .67 or .75), one (Irving Ives of New York) scored .50 in administration sup-

---

[36] Smith's statement in *New York Times*, July 15, 1954.
[37] *Ibid.*, July 14, 1954; see also Donovan, *The Inside Story*, 229.

port, and two (North Dakota's William Langer, with .33, and Oregon's Wayne Morse, with .25) ranked as anti-Eisenhower.[38] Majority Leader William Knowland and the three committee chairmen most prominent in welfare matters—Homer Capehart (Banking and Currency), Eugene Millikin (Finance), and H. Alexander Smith (Labor and Public Welfare)—all had perfect support scores. It is impossible to generalize from so little information, but it is interesting that the two senators with "anti-Eisenhower" records on welfare ranked as strong liberals prior to 1953.

In contrast to the low number of welfare policy roll calls in the Senate, the lower house held a number of important recorded votes on such issues in 1953–1954 (see Appendix F). The twelve roll calls in the House included every major administration-backed program to come before the Eighty-third Congress, thus providing a sample large enough to allow generalization.

The vast majority of House Republicans supported the administration on matters of welfare policy. Of 217 who took positions on at least half of the welfare-related roll calls, forty-eight (22 percent) ranked as strong Eisenhower supporters, 141 (65 percent) as moderate supporters, twenty-five (11 percent) as "waverers," and only three and one as moderately and strongly opposed to the President, respectively (see Table 9). Those classified as opponents of the administration were all from the Midwest: Fred Busbey (Illinois), James Dolliver (Iowa), Noah Mason (Illinois), and Wint Smith (Kansas). Dolliver and Smith were conservatives and Busbey and Mason unscalable on welfare policy.

If the difference between "strong" (80 to 100 percent) and "moderate" (60 to 79 percent) support for Eisenhower is viewed as significant, then the voting of House Republicans in 1953–1954 provides some evidence that administration welfare programs appealed more to liberals than to conservatives within the party. Nineteen of thirty-four liberals on welfare policy (55.9

[38] Four (Hugh Butler, Dwight Griswold, Robert Taft, and Charles Tobey) failed to be recorded on at least two of the roll calls and so were not ranked.

## Table 9 "Eisenhower Support" by Republicans in the House of Representatives, Eighty-Third Congress, Welfare Policy*

| Category | Level of Support | | | | |
|---|---|---|---|---|---|
| | .80–1.00 | .60–.79 | .40–.59 | .20–.39 | .00–.19 |
| *Previous Scale Type* | | | | | |
| Strong liberal | 13 | 6 | 0 | 0 | 0 |
| Moderate liberal | 6 | 9 | 0 | 0 | 0 |
| Uncommitted, not scaled | 11 | 28 | 0 | 1 | 1 |
| Moderate conservative | 7 | 52 | 16 | 1 | 0 |
| Strong conservative | 0 | 11 | 3 | 1 | 0 |
| (Freshmen) | 11 | 35 | 5 | 0 | 0 |
| *Region* | | | | | |
| New England | 11 | 6 | 1 | 0 | 0 |
| Mid-Atlantic | 18 | 38 | 3 | 0 | 0 |
| Border | 2 | 9 | 3 | 0 | 0 |
| North Central | 11 | 44 | 10 | 1 | 1 |
| Plains | 0 | 16 | 3 | 2 | 0 |
| Far West | 6 | 28 | 4 | 0 | 0 |
| *Period of Entry* | | | | | |
| Pre-New Deal | 3 | 7 | 3 | 0 | 0 |
| New Deal | 3 | 22 | 6 | 0 | 1 |
| World War II | 13 | 26 | 3 | 2 | 0 |
| Postwar | 18 | 51 | 7 | 1 | 0 |
| Freshmen | 11 | 35 | 5 | 0 | 0 |
| *District Type‡* | | | | | |
| Metropolitan | 21 | 39 | 2 | 1 | 0 |
| Mid-urban | 12 | 38 | 8 | 0 | 1 |
| Small-town | 10 | 43 | 11 | 0 | 0 |
| Rural | 4 | 21 | 3 | 2 | 0 |
| TOTAL† | 48 | 141 | 24 | 3 | 1 |

* For roll calls used, see Appendix F; for individual scores, Appendix K.

†Excludes Reps. Clifford Case (N.J.) and Alvin Weichel (Ohio), who responded on fewer than half the roll calls on welfare policy in 1953–54, and Speaker Joseph Martin, who did not participate in House roll calls.

‡ Excludes Rep. George Bender (Ohio at-large), whose district was not classified.

percent) had strongly pro-Eisenhower records, compared with only seven of ninety-one conservatives (7.7 percent). But this tendency should not be overemphasized, for nearly all House Republicans, after all, had at least moderately pro-Eisenhower records. This fact, coupled with the President's frequent refusal to argue "principles" on welfare-related questions, would suggest that his ultimate stance on such measures usually represented acceptable Republican doctrine.

The records of the chairmen of the committees most significantly involved in welfare questions reveal that, as a group, they supported the President only moderately well: chairman Wolverton of Interstate and Foreign Commerce scored .92 in welfare matters, and both Rules chairman Leo Allen and Jesse Wolcott of the Banking and Currency Committee scored .73, but Daniel Reed (Ways and Means) and John Taber (Appropriations) each scored only .50. The seventeen-person Republican leadership organization included only four strong supporters of the President (Floor Leader Halleck, with a score of .92, among them), twelve who gave him moderate support, and one "waverer."

The support accorded by congressional Republicans to President Eisenhower's welfare proposals carried over into the distinct but related areas of agriculture and labor. In the former area this party support was sufficient to produce a notable policy triumph for the President, but in the latter he failed to accomplish anything in 1953–1954. Both reveal a good deal about the problems the administration faced and the tactics it used.

Eisenhower had spoken with almost systematic vagueness on farm policy during the 1952 campaign. Although groups on opposing sides of the farm price-support question interpreted his pre-election statements in various ways according to their own predilections, the President soon made clear his determination to reduce the prominent federal role in agriculture. After the customary nod to "economic stability and full parity of income for American farmers," Eisenhower went on in his 1953 State of the Union message to insist that "we must seek this goal in ways that minimize governmental interference in the farmer's affairs, that permit desirable shifts in production, and that encourage farmers themselves to use initiative in meeting changing economic conditions." [39] Such White House rhetoric, coupled with the appointment of the ardently conservative Ezra Taft Benson as Secretary of Agriculture, promised that there would be a serious reappraisal of the existing farm program, which called for rigid 90 percent price supports for the six basic storable commodities (corn, wheat, cotton, rice, peanuts, and tobacco).

The administration made no effort during 1953 to implement a farm policy, laboring instead to work out a program for 1954. The nature of Benson's influence within White House councils was plainly apparent. The Secretary thought agriculture to be "at a crossroad" where it would either "rush headlong down the road of socialistic controls and regimentation" or "turn gradually toward a kind of freedom and responsibility." Accordingly, he and two associates from the Agriculture Department presented a plan for a flexible system of price supports at a Cabinet meeting in late October 1953. Eisenhower, according to Benson, "for the first time . . . came out flatly in favor of" such a program. [40]

At least some in the administration felt it was high time for a decision. On the very day of Benson's Cabinet presentation, one farm policy adviser had written the White House that "the impression is around that there is no present [agriculture] program. . . . If there is a program, as I am sure there is, let us dramatize and emphasize it." [41] Eisenhower remarked indignantly in an October press conference that he "never said that there should be rigid price-support laws at 100 percent of parity, never." [42] But otherwise, the White House kept its plans to itself.

By December 1953, however, the farm program was taking shape. Just before the White House legislative planning confer-

[39] State of the Union Message, Feb. 2, 1953, in *Public Papers . . . 1953*, 27.

[40] Ezra Taft Benson, *Cross Fire: The Eight Years with Eisenhower* (Garden City, N.Y.: Doubleday, 1962), 73, 152–53.

[41] Memorandum from Victor A. Johnston to Wilton B. Persons, Gerald Morgan, and Jack Martin, Oct. 23, 1953, in Box 1, A67–19 Accessions, Morgan Records, Eisenhower Papers.

[42] Oct. 21, 1963, press conference remarks, in *Public Papers . . . 1953*, 710.

ence in mid-month, Secretary Benson had long talks with both George Aiken and Clifford Hope, chairmen respectively of the Senate and House committees on Agriculture. He proposed to them a sliding scale from 75 to 90 percent of parity on the basic storable commodities except tobacco. Representative Hope, a consistent proponent of rigid price supports, was particularly immune to administration pressures on behalf of flexible supports.[43] Nevertheless, President Eisenhower presented his sliding-scale program to Congress on January 11, 1954. Both houses opened hearings on the proposal during March, as "flexible" and "rigid" adherents prepared for battle.

Resisting all administration sales efforts, Congressman Hope's Agriculture Committee reported a bill, with only two dissenting votes (Pennsylvanians Paul Dague and Karl King), which included many of the administration's recommendations but retained rigid price supports at the level of 90 percent. During debate on the House farm bill (June 30 to July 2), Halleck took command of the pro-administration forces, since the nominal floor manager for the measure, Hope, was opposing the White House on its central feature. Halleck was given considerable latitude to use his own judgment in working for compromise. "Get as much of our program as you can," Benson claims to have instructed the floor leader on June 26. "You decide how much that is."[44]

Halleck decided to work for the principle of flexibility, rather than the 75 percent minimum, and got Representative Robert Harrison, a Republican from the heart of the farm belt, to sponsor an amendment to the committee bill substituting flexible supports, but on a scale extending only from 82.5 to 90 percent. The administration gave the Harrison amendment its full support and "used all possible pressures" on recalcitrant Republican House members, employing state political machines to put pressure on waverers and in some cases even threatening retalia-

---

[43] Benson, *Cross Fire*, 159; also Dean William I. Myers of Cornell Univ. to Eisenhower, Dec. 19, 1953, in OF 99-G-1, Eisenhower Papers.
[44] Benson, *Cross Fire*, 203.

tion at the polls if legislators voted wrong.[45] Speaker Martin, addressing the House from the floor, threatened that Eisenhower would veto any farm bill which included 90 percent supports and reminded his colleagues that such an eventuality would mean that, after the present law expired on December 31, 1954, a 1949 law providing flexible supports as low as 75 percent would go into effect anyway.[46] The political barrage paid off, as the Harrison amendment passed by 228–170, Republicans voting for it by 182–23.

The Senate, too, promised to make life difficult for the administration on its farm policy. In mid-June 1954, before the House had yet acted, Benson wrote despairingly to White House aide Gerald Morgan that Senator Aiken was working only for "the minimum legislation required for us to do an effective job."[47] The Secretary and his colleagues were further disturbed when the Senate Agriculture and Forestry Committee reported out a farm bill which differed in several respects from administration proposals. Most seriously, like the House committee draft, it called for the continuation of rigid 90 percent price supports for the basic commodities (though it did provide for 75 to 90 percent flexible supports by the end of 1955).

Senator Aiken decided that the best strategy was to go along with the majority of his committee, while reserving the right to fight on the floor any sections of the bill which conflicted with Eisenhower's requests. Consequently, after voting with the committee majority to report the bill, Aiken offered an amendment during the August 9 floor debate, substituting flexible supports of 80 to 90 percent. Aiken's proposal, further amended by Senator Andrew Schoeppel of Kansas to match the 82.5 to 90 percent span in the House-passed bill, squeaked through by a vote of 49–44. On the crucial roll call, thirty-seven of forty-eight Republicans voted for the flexible scale. In all, the Senate endured

[45] J. Roland Pennock, "Party and Constituency in Post-war Agricultural Price-Support Legislation," *Journal of Politics* 18, No. 2 (May 1956), 188.

[46] *Congressional Record*, Vol. c, Part 7, 83d Cong., 2d Sess., 9536.

[47] Memorandum dated June 17, 1954, in Box 1, A67–19 Accessions, Morgan Records, Eisenhower Papers.

fifteen roll calls on the 1954 farm bill (see Appendix G for a list); of the twelve on which the administration took a clear stand, half were settled in its favor. As the farm bill finally cleared both houses after conference action, the provision for the 82.5 to 90 percent flexible supports remained in, and the President signed it on August 28, 1954, with a genuine sense of accomplishment. Of the increase in the support floor from 75 to 82.5 percent the President was not the least bit critical. "It wasn't even a compromise," he told reporters. "I have [always] asked for a flexible system gradually applied."[48]

The Eisenhower administration had good reason to be proud of its achievement on the farm bill. It had converted congressional Republicans previously committed to rigid supports at an impressive rate.[49] In the House, forty-three of sixty-five (66 percent) such Republicans supported the President's position by voting for the Harrison amendment. Only among rigid-support representatives from the Plains states was the "conversion rate" lower than 70 percent. Among members of the House Agriculture Committee, the White House did less well, however: of ten Republican rigid-support adherents on the committee, only half voted for the Eisenhower position during House consideration of the 1954 bill. Chairman Clifford Hope remained adamantly opposed to the flexible program.

In the Senate there were no farm policy votes in the previous Congress against which Republican voting behavior in the Eighty-third Congress can be compared, but the large number of roll calls (sixteen) during 1954 permits some tentative conclusions about the kind of support the administration obtained from Republican senators on its farm program. Forty of forty-nine Republican senators taking stands on at least half the roll calls in 1954 strongly supported Eisenhower's program; two "wavered," two ranked as moderately anti-Eisenhower, and five

[48] Press conference remarks of July 7, 1954, in *Public Papers . . . 1954*, 623.
[49] "Previous commitment" to rigid price supports, in this context, means that the congressmen in question voted in 1952 *for* H.R. 8122, which extended supports on the basic commodities at the 90 percent level.

142

were strongly anti-administration. Regional differences were sharp. As in the House, the North Central and Plains states supplied the smallest percentages of Republicans with records of strong support (67 and 55 percent, respectively). By contrast, all Republican senators from New England and the Mid-Atlantic states strongly supported the President on the farm policy roll calls. Of the eight Republican members on the Agriculture and Forestry Committee, five—including chairman George Aiken—turned out to be strong administration loyalists on matters of farm policy; the other three all ranked as "antis." In the Senate, as in the House, the Eisenhower administration scored a major policy victory in its agriculture program, by largely unifying the Republican party behind an ideologically conservative policy.

In the realm of labor policy the White House did not fare as well. Although Eisenhower wrote later that when he came into office he "especially wanted prompt action in revising the Taft-Hartley Act," no administration labor program surfaced in 1953.[50] Taft, of course, as one of the authors of the original act, was slated to play a key role in any revision of it. He had apparently gained Eisenhower's agreement on a number of important points as preconditions to the Morningside Heights meeting of the previous September and was confident in the spring of 1953 that there would be no "weakening in the basic structure of the law."[51] Throughout the early months of the year, however, development of a coherent administration labor program was blocked by jurisdictional and ideological conflict between Secretary of Labor Martin Durkin and Secretary of Commerce Sinclair Weeks.

By late July, White House aides Bernard Shanley and Gerald Morgan, working with Republican congressional leaders, produced a nineteen-point proposal for amending the law.[52] Senator

---

[50] Eisenhower, *Mandate for Change*, 196.

[51] Robert A. Taft to Everett Dirksen, Aug. 6, 1952. Taft specifically outlined the congressmen in question voted in 1952 *for* H.R. 8122, which extended supports on Sept. 24, 1952. The quotation is from Taft's letter to Hon. Frank M. Dixon, Mar. 28, 1953. (All in Taft Papers.)

[52] Parmet, *Eisenhower and the American Crusades*, 327–28.

Taft's death on July 31 produced new difficulties, however. The next day, H. Alexander Smith, one of the participants in the ongoing discussions and chairman of the Senate Labor and Public Welfare Committee, counseled delay. It fell to Smith to forward to the White House a number of criticisms of the nineteen-point program which had been lodged by Thomas Shroyer, a man who had worked closely with Senator Taft in framing the 1947 law. In a covering memorandum to Shanley, Senator Smith urged a tactical retreat. "It would be very serious, as I see it," he wrote, "if this message [the nineteen-point proposal] came out in this form just as Senator Taft has passed away." Smith went on to concur with Shroyer's opposition to a provision approving certain secondary labor boycotts, and criticized three other points: one which would allow expulsion of union members by their leaders for "disclosure . . . of confidential information," another barring workers from holding "de-authorization elections" during an actual strike, and a third which recognized "the paramount authority of the Federal law" in the handling of labor disputes.[53]

Opposed from such prominent quarters, the President refrained from publicly announcing his program, pending further discussion and reworking of some of the specific points. One dramatic upshot of this decision was the resignation of Secretary of Labor Durkin, who later insisted in the face of official denials that the President had broken faith with him by withdrawing the nineteen-point program. Eisenhower, however, denied ever having made any such promises.[54] The administration continued to try to hammer out a workable labor program during the remaining months of 1953, working primarily with Senators Smith

[53] Memorandum, Smith to Shanley, dated Aug. 1, 1953, and enclosed memorandum from Shroyer to Smith, dated July 31, 1953, Smith Papers.

[54] See, for example, the President's press conference remarks on Sept. 30, 1953, in *Public Papers . . . 1953*, 624. Senators Smith and Saltonstall, both of whom were close to the situation, bore out the President's disclaimer in correspondence to one another (Smith to Saltonstall, Sept. 28, 1953, and Saltonstall to Smith, Oct. 6, 1953, Smith Papers).

and Irving Ives and Representative Samuel McConnell, who was chairman of the House Committee on Education and Labor. Ives, especially, played an important role, drafting an official statement on labor policy for the White House in late 1953.[55]

On January 11, 1954, President Eisenhower at last transmitted a fourteen-point message to Congress in which he set forth his labor program. The President urged many of the changes originally included in the ill-fated nineteen-point program but yielded several of the points to which Senator Smith and Thomas Shroyer had objected. As presented, Eisenhower's labor proposals of 1954 permitted secondary boycotts, but only on "struck" construction sites or against employers engaged in "farmed out work" for an employer whose workers were on strike; dropped the Communist-disclaimer oath requirement for union members; provided that striking workers could vote for their collective bargaining representatives; gave the right of "free speech" in labor disputes to management, as well as to labor; granted to states the right to take action in cases of labor disputes presenting danger to the public safety (even if such action conflicted with federal law); and ensured a secret ballot to workers voting on a proposed strike action. Noticeably absent was any recommendation for repeal of Section 14(b), the state "right-to-work law" provision, even though one of the nineteen points of mid-1953 had called for its deletion.

Hearings on the labor proposal were held in the appropriate committees of both houses during early 1954. Senator Smith's committee finished first. By a party-line vote of seven to six, the Labor and Public Welfare Committee reported a bill which followed closely the President's recommendations. Trouble loomed early, however, when a number of Republican senators, led by Barry Goldwater, insisted that the bill should include a stronger assertion of states' rights in handling labor disputes. This objection elicited such an uncertain response from the

---

[55] See Ives to Eisenhower, Oct. 16, 1953 (marked "Personal and Confidential"), with enclosure of draft statement to be issued by the President, Ives Papers.

White House that Senator Smith despaired at one point that Eisenhower did not "know quite what it [was] all about!"[56] Even though the states' rights issue remained unresolved, however, Senate Republicans supported the bill nearly unanimously in the single roll call held on it. Unfortunately for the administration, a Republican vote of 42–4 against a motion to recommit was canceled by a Democratic vote of 47–0 *for* it, and the bill was sent back to languish in committee. Voting with the Democrats were Republicans Langer, Malone, Morse, and Young. Three days after this Senate action, on May 10, Representative McConnell announced that the House committee would not pursue the matter further, and the administration's hopes were dashed.

Eisenhower's defeat in the area of labor policy cannot be ascribed to any failure on his part to respond to conservative Republicans in Congress, the states' rights controversy of early 1954 notwithstanding. On the contrary, the bill probably failed because at its center it so closely approximated traditional Republican hostility to organized labor. The measure did not even pick up the votes of any conservative Southern Democrats, and of the four Republicans opposing it, two were liberals on welfare policy (Langer and Morse), and one was unscalable (Malone).

President Eisenhower's labor, agriculture, and welfare policies met with mixed success in the Eighty-third Congress. The administration was able to secure flexible farm price supports and expansion of the social security system, both with strong Republican support. But in both cases the programs reflected ideological positions consistent with (or at least not at variance with) party tradition. Certainly, despite the carping of a few extremists, social security had moved beyond the field of partisan combat by the 1950s and was a program widely accepted and inevitably to be "conserved." It was a contributory system, which helped to quiet Republican consciences, and—what is probably more important —after nearly two decades of operation, social security was benefiting a considerable number of voters. Even on those issues where the President avowedly tried to steer a "middle way" and met

56 Smith Diary, Mar. 26, 1954, 132 (Smith Papers).

with less success (housing, health reinsurance, and labor), his programs adhered closely to orthodox Republicanism.

In contrast to his strong feelings on foreign policy matters, Dwight Eisenhower was not deeply committed to using federal means to meet the nation's welfare needs. The largely negative fate of many of his social welfare–related programs in 1953–1954 was the natural harvest of that apathy.

# CHAPTER SEVEN

# The Politics of Partnership

As presidential candidates will, Dwight D. Eisenhower talked a lot about the proper federal role in power and resource development during the 1952 campaign—especially in the West. He recommended a policy of "partnership," which he defined as pursuit of the "middle way" in power policy. In his first State of the Union message, the new President reiterated this viewpoint: "The best natural resources program for America," Eisenhower told Congress and the country in February 1953, "will not result from exclusive dependence on Federal bureaucracy. It will involve a partnership of the States and the local communities, private citizens, and the Federal Government, all working together."[1] This moderate, non-dogmatic approach to questions of power and resource development, the President promised, would characterize the Republican administration's policy. Almost a decade later, Eisenhower maintained that he had kept his promise, siding with neither public nor private power interests.[2]

Yet rather than carving out a new "middle way," President Eisenhower's "partnership" policy in power and resource development closely resembled the established Republican doctrine of minimal federal involvement. Particularly influential within

1 *Public Papers . . . 1953*, 26.
2 Eisenhower, *Mandate for Change*, 379.

the administration was Secretary of the Interior Douglas McKay, who resided "on the outermost edges of the conservative view" in the Cabinet.[3] This was a noteworthy position, considering the composition of that group. Since Eisenhower later emphasized "the harmony of . . . views" between himself and McKay,[4] it is not surprising that power and resource policies backed by the administration and enacted by the Eighty-third Congress strongly favored the private sector. Rhetoric aside, the years 1953–1954 witnessed the end of an era of active government involvement in the development of the country's natural resources.

Almost as soon as he took office, President Eisenhower set out to redeem one of his more specific campaign promises: to turn over to the individual states ownership of all submerged lands (including the mineral rights thereon) within "historic" state boundaries. Commonly, but erroneously, referred to as "tide-lands," these submerged lands contained vast quantities of pe-troleum already discovered and were estimated by some to represent mineral wealth of up to $300 billion.[5] Interest in the issue, therefore, ran rather high.

By 1953, the submerged lands debate had raged for nearly a decade. In 1945 President Truman upset long-standing assump-tions by laying federal claim to all "natural resources of the sub-soil and sea bed of the continental shelf," but a 1947 Supreme Court decision (*United States* v. *California*) left open the ques-tion of legal title to lands lying within the three-mile limit. Consequently, while the work of oil-leasing outfits proceeded normally after 1947, all royalties from such leases were im-pounded, pending legislative "demarcation" of state and federal rights, respectively, in the submerged lands. In 1952, the Eighty-second Congress tried to resolve the problem by enacting a bill quitting federal claims to all lands within three miles of the coast

---

[3] Hughes, *Ordeal of Power*, 67.

[4] Eisenhower, *Mandate for Change*, 87.

[5] "Tidelands" properly refers to those lands included within the area of normal tidal action, the ownership of which no one disputed. "Offshore" or "submerged" lands, on the other hand, are those which make up the ocean floor extending out from the low-tide line to the continental shelf.

(or three leagues, in the case of lands lying off the Florida and Texas coasts). But Truman vetoed the measure, branding it a "give-away" of national property.[6] As a parting shot, on January 16, 1953, the outgoing President proclaimed all offshore petroleum an official reserve of the United States Navy. Since President-elect Eisenhower was committed to the principle of state ownership of the submerged lands, Truman's move seemed designed to embarrass the new administration, as the *New York Times* said, by "invest[ing] the issue with moral and patriotic considerations . . . ."[7]

The Eisenhower administration moved quickly toward obtaining the legislation it desired. On February 9, Speaker Martin and Senator Taft declared that proper settlement of the submerged lands question ranked among the eleven pieces of "must" legislation for the first session of Congress. A week later both the House Judiciary and Senate Interior and Insular Affairs committees began hearings on the several bills already introduced. In their testimonies, administration officials agreed on the goal of state development of the offshore wealth but differed on the specific provisions the new legislation should include. Attorney General Brownell, who declared on February 16 that Truman's action of the previous month had not "in fact or in law, create[d] a naval petroleum reserve within the meaning of that statute [on naval reserves]," testified that the safest course would be to grant the states both mineral rights and leasing authority in the submerged lands, without giving them legal title.[8] Secretary of the Interior McKay differed with Brownell, urging that Congress quit all federal claims out to the "historic boundaries" of the states involved. His view was rejected in turn by the State Department, which warned that recognition of the "historic" boundaries of Florida and Texas (which extended three leagues, or 10½ miles seaward) could cause international complications. In the face of such con-

---

6 Ernest R. Bartley, *The Tidelands Oil Controversy: A Legal and Historical Analysis* (Austin: Univ. of Texas Press, 1953), 141–42, 161–62, 167, 170–73, 188, 227.
7 Jan. 17, 1953.
8 *Ibid.*, Feb. 17, Mar. 3, 1953.

flicting recommendations from the executive, the two committees proceeded on their own, but in the general direction favored by the President.

Bills were reported almost simultaneously in both chambers, but the lower house acted first. The House bill disregarded the advice of the State and Justice Departments by vesting in the states title to all submerged lands within their historic boundaries. The bill also contravened administration wishes by granting the states broad policy and taxing powers over the entire continental shelf. On the other hand, it fulfilled the President's request that Congress provide explicitly for federal ownership and development of mineral resources on the shelf seaward from the state limits. Eight members of the Judiciary Committee (including Republicans Usher Burdick, Kenneth Keating, and George Meader) dissented from the report, opposing the plan as a "windfall" to a handful of states. But sentiment in the House strongly favored the measure, and debate on the bill took only three days (March 30 through April 1). Although Keating secured an amendment to eliminate state taxing powers in the outer shelf, the fate of the bill was never in doubt. On April 1 it passed, as predicted, by a large margin; the vote was 286–108, with only 18 of 206 Republicans voting against it.

The Senate took much longer to come to the same conclusion. Beginning debate on the Interior and Insular Affairs Committee's bill (S.J. Res. 13) on April 1, the upper house did not reach a decision until May 5, because of a filibuster conducted by liberal Democrats and Independent Republican Wayne Morse. Although Guy Cordon of Oregon, as chairman of the subcommittee which had worked on the submerged lands bill, served as its floor manager, Senator Taft directed the larger administration strategy. In addition to ensuring the presence of Republican leaders on the Senate floor at all times and taking repeated actions designed to bring debate to a close,[9] Taft even persuaded the President to break his self-imposed rule of restraint in such cases and

9 *Ibid.*, Apr. 23, 1953; also Taft letter to eight Republican senators asking their assistance on the floor, dated Apr. 15, Taft Papers.

to intervene directly in the fray. With the majority leader's assistance, Eisenhower drafted and sent an uncharacteristic reply to a group of twenty-two Democratic and three Republican senators who had asked for his views regarding the outer shelf. "I hesitate to express an opinion on legislative procedure," he wrote on April 24, "but I am deeply concerned with the delay of the entire Administration program in the Senate."[10]

Finally a threat by the Republican leadership to keep the upper house in continuous session until the bill came up for a vote caused the anti-administration forces to capitulate. Morse expressed the sour mood of the vanquished when he cautioned that any further "raid on the public domain" would result in a "debate that will take them [the administration] into the fall."[11] On May 5, after voting down several amendments, the Senate passed S.J. Res. 13 by 56–35. Republicans voted for the bill, 35–10; only one Republican dissenter (Ferguson) had a conservative record on power and resource questions; four (Aiken, Langer, Morse, and Young) were liberals.

One important difference between the House and Senate bills remained to be settled. The House measure provided for federal development of resources submerged in the outer shelf as well as for state control closer to shore. Administration leaders had purposely kept such a provision out of the Senate bill, fearing that amendments would inevitably be offered to grant states all or part of the mineral wealth outside their historic boundaries, which might in turn disrupt the pro-administration coalition and thereby jeopardize passage of the whole bill.[12] The White House, which favored federal resource development outside the state boundaries, thus faced a dilemma: whether to insist that the conference include the House proviso or to accept the Senate bill and hope for another, later bill to establish federal rights in the outer shelf.

10 Eisenhower to Clinton Anderson, *Public Papers . . . 1953*, 219. See draft of that letter with Taft's handwritten revisions, which were incorporated into the final version, Taft Papers.

11 *New York Times*, May 2, 1953.

12 Bartley, *The Tidelands Oil Controversy*, 280.

Basing his recommendation on Speaker Martin's observation that "a conference report might be subject to additional [Senate] filibustering," General Persons pressed inside the administration for the course eventually adopted. "You might want to seek out Senators Taft and Cordon and get their views," Persons wrote Gerald Morgan after passage of the Senate bill. "For my money, if they would commit themselves to prompt action on a second bill, we might be better off to go [that] road."[13] The promise was obtained, and the House accepted the Senate bill. Two months later the second measure, calling for federal development of the shelf, also became law. The conference report was nearly rejected in the Senate when a number of Democrats objected to its failure to earmark royalties from the outer shelf for grants-in-aid to education. But in both houses the bill received overwhelming Republican support (193–12 in the House, 37–7 in the Senate), which ensured its success.

Since Republicans would most likely have supported the submerged lands legislation anyway, given the history of similar bills in the previous Congress, the Eisenhower administration had to exert no special pressures to obtain the necessary votes for passage. In neither chamber were there wholesale "conversions" of previous Republican opponents of the administration stand on the submerged lands question. In fact, Eisenhower's gains and losses among Republicans virtually canceled each other out. In the Senate, Arthur Watkins changed his 1952 position to support the President, but Francis Case did the reverse; in the House, four who had previously favored state ownership voted against the bill in 1953, while two previous opponents supported the bill. Prior liberalism or conservatism in the area of power and resource development does not seem to have been related to Republican opposition to, or support for, the submerged lands legislation in either house.

Having stressed states' rights in the "tidelands" controversy of 1953, the Eisenhower administration embraced another pillar

---

13 Wilton Persons to Gerald Morgan, May 6, 1953, in Box 9, A67–19 Accessions, Morgan Records, Eisenhower Papers.

of conservative orthodoxy, the private enterprise system, in its atomic energy proposals of 1954. The President's proposed atomic energy program also contained an "internationalist" emphasis, in urging the wider sharing of hitherto secret information to encourage cooperative development of the atom for peaceful uses, but the basic conflict over the 1954 bill came on its domestic provisions, and pitted private and public power advocates against each other. With the exception of fighting a move by some House Republicans to make the patent provisions in the act even more favorable to private industry, President Eisenhower fought doggedly for the cause of private enterprise. As in the case of the submerged lands controversy, the administration's conservative stance in the atomic energy debates of 1954 produced a high degree of Republican unity on roll calls held on the measure.

The Eisenhower atomic energy program took shape slowly, even though it was based largely on work begun by the Atomic Energy Commission under President Truman in 1952. In December 1952, the AEC, headed by Gordon Dean, published a report entitled *Atomic Power and Private Enterprise*, which declared that the time had come to plan for the use of atomic power in industry. By spring 1953, the commission reputedly was preparing a specific program which would permit the sharing of fissionable materials (whether by sale, lease, or loan) with private developers "under certain security and safety restrictions" and would authorize such private concerns "to design, construct and operate" nuclear reactors for the purpose of power production. Eisenhower, reportedly, was "enthusiastic about the new program." [14]

Although the Joint Congressional Committee on Atomic Energy (JCAE), under its new Republican chairman, Representative W. Sterling Cole of New York, prodded the AEC repeatedly, the latter failed to come up with a specific program. In May the commission sent the Joint Committee a policy statement and draft bill, but neither had been cleared by the Bureau of the Budget and so they lacked administration approval. Nevertheless, de-

[14] *New York Times*, Apr. 8, 1953.

spairing of any immediate White House initiative, chairman Cole began general JCAE hearings on the basis of this tentative draft in June 1953.[15] Cole, vice-chairman Senator Bourke Hickenlooper (Iowa), and other members of the Joint Committee hoped thus to be ready to push through major legislation during the second session.

Meanwhile, as the JCAE held its 1953 hearings, the AEC worked under its chairman, Lewis Strauss, on constructing a program fully acceptable to the White House. In September Strauss announced that the commission had reached a decision on whether to allow private atomic patents, but said that none of the group's recommendations would be made public until the President decided to make them so.[16] Within two months, however, press reports confirmed early rumors on the general nature of the forthcoming administration program. Reportedly the plan would permit private operation of nuclear reactors and otherwise encourage private initiative in the peacetime development of atomic energy. It would also give the AEC broader authority to share atomic information with friendly nations.

Shortly after this leak, Representative Cole announced that he would introduce legislation in 1954 designed to loosen restrictions on the use of atomic energy by the private sector, adding (as if in anticipation of criticism by public power advocates) that, of course, "there could be no atomic give-away . . . ."[17] The rumor that the President would recommend internationalizing American atomic secrets, however, elicited a different reaction from Cole. When the President's dramatic "Atoms for Peace" speech to the United Nations General Assembly on December 8, 1953, lent credence to reports that the administration would seek such authority, both Cole and Hickenlooper issued tart statements opposing the idea.[18]

[15] Harold P. Green and Alan Rosenthal, *Government of the Atom: The Integration of Powers* (New York: Atherton, 1963), 123.

[16] *New York Times*, Oct. 1, 1953.

[17] *Ibid.*, Nov. 5, Nov. 20, 1953.

[18] H. L. Nieburg, "The Eisenhower AEC and Congress: A Study in Executive-Legislative Relations," *Midwest Journal of Political Science* 6, No. 2 (May 1962), 128.

The President sent his atomic energy program to Congress on February 17, 1954. In nearly every detail the plan matched earlier predictions. Eisenhower asked for authority "to exchange with nations participating in defensive arrangements with the United States such tactical information as is essential to the development of defense plans and to the training of personnel for atomic warfare," as well as to provide to "friendly nations" certain kinds of "restricted data" and quantities of fissionable materials "for industrial and research use." No doubt partially in response to the earlier reactions from Cole and Hickenlooper, the President added that these recommendations were separate from, and more limited than, his proposal for an international pool of atomic information as outlined in the earlier "Atoms for Peace" address. In a section headed "Domestic Development of Atomic Energy," Eisenhower outlined his plan for bringing private enterprise into the atomic field. He asked Congress to permit private ownership or leasing of reactors and fissionable materials and to allow privately held patents in atomic energy; he also suggested that the holders of such patents be required "for a limited period . . . to license others to use an invention essential to the peacetime applications of atomic energy."[19] Finally, he asked also for a number of changes in security classification procedures in order to facilitate these arrangements. Shortly after submission of the presidential message, the AEC sent the JCAE two separate legislative drafts, one embodying the "international" (information-sharing) provisions and the proposed security changes, and the other covering the President's requests with respect to the role of private enterprise.

Until the atomic energy bill came up for debate in mid-summer 1954, the administration in effect relinquished control over its proposal to congressional leaders. Cole and Hickenlooper, both of whom believed that the AEC drafts gave the executive too much authority, produced their own bill. Introduced in both houses in mid-April, the Cole-Hickenlooper bill provided for congres-

[19] Message on Atomic Energy, Feb. 17, 1954, in *Public Papers . . . 1954*, 263–64, 268.

sional control over any international information sharing (through a careful definition of the sorts of "international agreements" into which the President might enter) and also ensured relatively close scrutiny by the JCAE of arrangements concluded between the government and any private atomic developers.[20]

Cole and Hickenlooper took it upon themselves to combine the information-sharing and private development provisions into one bill, ostensibly because the two problems were "interrelated," but in reality for tactical reasons. Whereas each of the two halves of the President's program had its own natural enemies (nationalists dedicated to extreme secrecy in all defense and security matters and public power advocates, respectively), combining them into a single bill might present those two groups with a dilemma as to whether the bill's advantages outweighed its specific disadvantages.[21] The administration eventually came to favor this strategy, and in fact the tactic seems to have worked, since the "nationalist" element of the Republican party, which was steeped in the virtues of the private enterprise system, ultimately gave the combination measure its strong support.

After hearings extending from May 3 to June 10, the Joint Committee on Atomic Energy reported identical bills to both houses, largely based on the Cole-Hickenlooper draft. Still, however, Representative Cole was disturbed at the committee's decision to call for compulsory licensing (i.e., sharing) of private atomic patents. Accordingly, he filed a minority report objecting to the provision as an example of "socialism run rampant" and promised a floor fight on the issue.[22]

It soon became apparent that the public versus private power rift would subsume all other controversies growing out of the atomic energy bill. The conflict was intensified by Eisenhower's directive of June 16, 1954, ordering the AEC to negotiate a contract with a specified private corporation for power to be deliv-

---

[20] Green and Rosenthal, *Government of the Atom*, 125–26; Nieburg, *Midwest Journal of Political Science* 6, No. 2, pp. 129–31.

[21] Green and Rosenthal, *Government of the Atom*, 125.

[22] Cole was joined in his dissent by Rep. James VanZandt (R.-Pa.); *ibid.*, 147.

ered to the commission's Paducah, Kentucky, installation. The ensuing controversy was dubbed "Dixon-Yates" after the surnames of the two men heading the private corporation. Events leading to the presidential directive had begun a year earlier, when Memphis city officials informed the administration that the city's power needs exceeded the amount TVA could supply. Even though faced with this request, however, the White House worked successfully to defeat a 1953 appropriations bill designed to permit TVA to construct an additional steam plant at Fulton, Tennessee (near Memphis). At the same time the President promised that a suitable alternative power source for Memphis would be found.

Budget Director Joseph Dodge formulated the plan ultimately adopted by the administration in the Dixon-Yates affair. At its core the strategy was simple: the AEC, which was using approximately 600,000 kilowatts of TVA power at the Paducah site, would find a private source to furnish its power needs, thereby freeing the 600,000 kilowatts for use in Memphis.[23] Casting about for private developers willing to supply the power needed at Paducah, the administration settled on Edgar Dixon and Eugene Yates, who agreed to build a $107 million steam generating plant at West Memphis, Arkansas, to produce the necessary amount. For reasons of "efficiency," however, the power would be injected into the TVA system near Memphis.[24] The Atomic Energy Commission would then pay Dixon and Yates, so that TVA would not be paying directly for privately supplied power. As added incentive to the two developers, the administration promised to pay all local, state, and federal taxes for the West Memphis plant —the argument being that since TVA paid no taxes, the government was losing nothing by making such an arrangement in lieu of permitting TVA to construct the new facility. Having determined his course, the President then issued his order to the AEC to negotiate the contract with Dixon and Yates. Reports that AEC chairman Strauss carried out Eisenhower's order over the objec-

---

23 Wildavsky, *Dixon-Yates*, 34–35.
24 *Ibid.*, 106–107.

tions of a majority on the commission provided additional ammunition to public power advocates already eager to attack the administration for its role in the episode.

The eruption of the Dixon-Yates controversy increased prospects of Democratic delay and opposition on the atomic energy bill. Nevertheless, the administration rejected pleas by Cole and Hickenlooper to drop the contract. With the atomic energy bill scheduled to be considered in the Senate first, White House officials passed the word to Majority Leader Knowland that the President would not back down.[25] Senate Democrats, again aided by Wayne Morse, took up the challenge, staging a filibuster which carried debate on the atomic energy bill from July 13 to July 27. In combination with the obstinacy of Senator Knowland (who refused to permit a recess so long as the filibuster continued), the filibuster produced several consecutive all-night sessions. During the course of these extended sessions, senators showed signs of exhaustion; at one point, for example, Knowland produced some smiles by referring to his colleague from Iowa as "the Senator from Hickenlooper."[26]

Predictably, nearly all debate—as well as Democratic-sponsored amendments to the bill—in the Senate centered on the role of private enterprise in atomic development, with the Dixon-Yates contract serving as a continuous frame of reference for both sides. Administration forces won an early victory through passage of an amendment offered by Homer Ferguson which permitted the AEC to make contracts for private power, but they had to yield ground on two other important points. First, although Republican senators tried for a time to defend the legitimacy of the tax relief planned for the Dixon-Yates corporation, they soon found their position untenable. The result was passage, by voice vote, of Senator Albert Gore's amendment banning any government contracts from providing direct repayment for taxes paid by a private contractor. On July 22 occurred a second, more sweeping

25 *Ibid.*, 118; Lewis Strauss, *Men and Decisions* (Garden City, N.Y.: Doubleday, 1962), 304–305.

26 *New York Times*, July 23, 1954.

159

"public power" triumph, as the Senate adopted, by a 45–41 vote, the amendment proposed by Colorado Democrat Edwin Johnson authorizing the AEC to produce electric power by nuclear fission and giving preference to cooperatives and public-owned agencies in the disposal of excess power from AEC plants. Hickenlooper later insisted that six Republican senators who voted with Morse and the Democrats in favor of the Johnson amendment "didn't know what they were voting for," but the six included three who eventually opposed the atomic energy bill itself (Cooper and Langer, who voted against, and Young, who was recorded as opposing it) and three others who came from "power-conscious" states (Case and Mundt from South Dakota and Dworshak from Idaho). Rather than demonstrating inattentiveness by a few Republican senators, the amendment likely served to unify those who most strongly favored public power.[27]

The wearying filibuster was finally broken on July 27, largely because Lyndon Johnson and other Democrats not prominently identified with the cause of public power threatened to break with their colleagues unless the latter agreed to limit debate.[28] The atomic energy bill then passed the upper house by a vote of 57–28. Only three of forty-seven Republican votes were cast against it (Cooper, Langer, and Morse), but some party members who remained loyal on the final roll call reportedly resented Knowland's "untraditional harshness" in keeping the Senate in continuous session. Moreover, a number of Republicans thought the administration had been unnecessarily inflexible on the Dixon-Yates matter, which by its nature could only be a temporary victory on the power issue. Especially unhappy were those Republicans who were standing for re-election in 1954 in states where the revival of the "power question" could be politically damaging.

The House took two days to do what had taken the Senate two weeks. Taking up the atomic energy bill on July 23, in the midst

27 Wildavsky, *Dixon-Yates*, 113.
28 *Ibid.*, 114–15.

of the Senate filibuster, the lower house acted on seventeen floor amendments and then passed the bill on July 26. Public power forces in the lower house were unable to duplicate the major victory of their Senate counterparts; an amendment designed to permit the AEC to produce electric power was beaten on a 72–146 standing vote. In other important floor actions, the House upheld the AEC's right to contract with Dixon and Yates and adopted Cole's amendment to allow "normal" (exclusive, seventeen-year) patents for nonmilitary atomic developments. Although the administration opposed Cole's proposal because it feared the development of private atomic monopolies, House Republicans voted for the patent amendment by the overwhelming margin of 190–6 (the total vote was 203–161). Even the normally loyal Halleck worked actively against the White House and on behalf of Cole's amendment, prodding a number of Republican JCAE members to back it.[29] Probably, the administration chose to let Cole save face and have his amendment, since the pending Senate bill contained a provision for five-year "compulsory licensing" of all private atomic patents, and the two versions would have to go to conference anyway. The House passed the atomic energy measure by 231–154, after writing into it seven other amendments. Republicans voted for it, 195–7; five of the opponents were liberals (Burdick, Hagen, Javits, O'Konski, Withrow), one (Bennett) was uncommitted on power questions, and one (Gross) was unscalable.

Since the House bill differed sharply from the Senate version on several controversial points, the fate of the 1954 atomic energy bill remained uncertain as the conferees met in early August. The resulting conference report provided for normal, exclusive patent rights to private developers of nonmilitary atomic power, adding only that the AEC would give preference in granting licenses to developers who promised to "share" their patent rights for five years. The report also limited AEC power production to "experimental" facilities and stipulated that any surplus power

29 Green and Rosenthal, *Government of the Atom*, 161.

produced by such experimentation would be sold preferentially to public and cooperative agencies only "insofar as practicable." The Senate, where passage of the initial bill had obviously depended on more liberal disposition of these questions, balked at the report; the original foes of the bill were able to muster enough additional votes to send it back to conference on August 13, rejecting it by 41–48. The eighteen senators who opposed the revised bill after favoring the Senate version on July 27 included Republicans Dworshak and Malone, both Westerners and liberals in power policy.

In their second try, the conferees came much closer to splitting the difference between the House and Senate versions: the phrase "insofar as practicable" was deleted from the section giving preference to public and cooperative agencies in the distribution of surplus AEC power, though the commission was still limited only to "experimental" power plants. In place of the "normal patent" provision, the second conference inserted a requirement for five-year "compulsory licensing" by all atomic patent holders (half of the period required by the Senate version). Thus adjusted, the atomic energy bill sailed through both houses by voice vote on August 16.

Eisenhower expressed general approval of the atomic energy act as he signed it into law on August 30, 1954. The program, he declared, would "advance both public and private development of atomic energy."[30] Within the administration, however, there was some consternation about the new law. Again the Budget Bureau report revealed the official reaction. Regarding the "international" (information-sharing) section of the bill, the BOB report observed that "the substance" of White House requests had been satisfied, but qualifications introduced by Congress could restrict the President's "freedom of action in foreign relations and give rise to awkward administration." Nor was the private development section entirely consistent with administration goals. Overall, the Bureau feared, the law could "result,

[30] *Public Papers . . . 1954,* 777.

over a period of time, in heavy commitments by and large costs to the Government . . . ."[31]

The administration won only a partial victory as a result of congressional action on the Cole-Hickenlooper bill in 1954. The Dixon-Yates contract, thoroughly and hotly criticized during the debate, discredited the administration and created much more intraparty strain than would otherwise have accompanied consideration of the bill.[32] There were repeated subterranean grumblings from Republicans about Knowland's tactics and White House "inflexibility." Although the administration succeeded in holding most House and Senate Republicans in line on the key roll calls, the private enterprise section of the bill had to be modified in a liberal direction during Senate consideration and, ultimately, by conference action. The survival of the "preference" principle for public and cooperative agencies, particularly, represented a victory for public power advocates.[33]

Yet together with the submerged lands legislation of 1953, the outcome of the Dixon-Yates and atomic energy controversies in Congress revealed a largely united Republican party. The eminently sound Republican doctrine which Eisenhower clothed in his new rhetoric of "partnership" produced a degree of party unity in the House and Senate matched only in the area of fiscal policy during 1953 and 1954. On the major "Eisenhower" roll

[31] Roger W. Jones, report to Eisenhower, Aug. 24, 1954, in Box 40, Reports on Pending Legislation, Eisenhower Papers.

[32] It also caused severe financial loss for Dixon and Yates. Although the contract was signed on Nov. 10, 1954, and approved three days later by the lame-duck GOP-controlled JCAE, the Democratic majority in the 84th Congress exerted great pressure against it. In July 1955, President Eisenhower canceled the Dixon-Yates contract in favor of a plan whereby the city of Memphis would build its own power plant. Hearings held during 1955 by the Senate Judiciary Subcommittee on Antitrust and Monopoly Legislation revealed the "questionable" role of Adolphe Wenzell during contract negotiations, causing a good deal of embarrassment for the administration. Dixon and Yates themselves fared worse, losing by virtue of a 1961 Supreme Court action the entire $1.87 million they had spent on the West Memphis project as of the time the contract was canceled.

[33] Wildavsky, *Dixon-Yates*, 117; Barrow Lyons, *Tomorrow's Birthright: A Political and Economic Interpretation of Our Natural Resources* (New York: Funk, 1955), 333.

calls in the Eighty-third Congress on power and resource development issues, 89 percent of House Republicans with near-complete records (193 of 217) ranked as strongly pro-Eisenhower; in the Senate, the figure was 78 percent (38 of 49). In neither chamber did a Republican member who had previously been a strong liberal on such matters support the President, while over 90 percent of the moderate and strong conservatives in both houses did so (see Table 10). Relatively few Republican senators from Plains states (56 percent) ranked as strongly pro-Eisenhower, but otherwise region did not affect Republican voting. Other than the small group of strong liberals, no subgroup in either house contained an exceptionally high percentage of opponents of administration policy. Judged by their roll-call behavior, Republican members of the Eighty-third Congress clearly approved of their President's power and resource policy.

Eisenhower's conservative approach to power and resource development questions also helped him secure congressional approval for construction of the St. Lawrence Seaway.[34] Ironically, the Seaway, a project which both of Eisenhower's "public power" predecessors had unsuccessfully urged on Congress, was finally enacted during the second session of the Eighty-third Congress. Unquestionably, the Republican Congress authorized United States participation in the venture largely because of the fiscal conservatism and anti-public power bias of the 1954 bill. Moreover, when Eisenhower argued for the project on grounds of national security, congressional Republicans took heed.

By 1953 the St. Lawrence Seaway represented the proverbial idea whose time had come. Canada had recently served notice to the United States that she would proceed to construct it alone, if necessary. The two governments had already concluded ar-

[34] In one respect the Seaway can be viewed also as a foreign policy question, since it involved international cooperation in a most obvious way. It is a measure of the uniqueness and complexity of the issue that the single Seaway roll call in the 82nd Congress could not be scaled on either the foreign policy or the power and resource development scale. Discussion of the 1954 Seaway bill seems most appropriate in the present chapter because much of its appeal to Republicans lay in the *absence* of provisions for public hydroelectric power production on the St. Lawrence River.

*Table 10*  "Eisenhower Support" by Republicans in the Eighty-Third Congress, Power and Resource Development*

| Previous Scale Type | Level of Support | | | | |
|---|---|---|---|---|---|
| | .80–1.00 | .60–.79 | .40–.59 | .20–.39 | .00–.19 |
| | SENATE | | | | |
| Strong liberal | 0 | 1 | 1 | 1 | 1 |
| Moderate liberal | 7 | 0 | 0 | 0 | 1 |
| Uncommitted, not scaled | 8 | 1 | 1 | 0 | 1 |
| Moderate conservative | 5 | 0 | 0 | 0 | 0 |
| Strong conservative | 10 | 1 | 0 | 0 | 0 |
| (Freshmen) | 8 | 1 | 0 | 1 | 0 |
| TOTAL† | 38 | 4 | 2 | 2 | 3 |
| | HOUSE | | | | |
| Strong liberal | 0 | 0 | 0 | 0 | 4 |
| Moderate liberal | 5 | 2 | 0 | 0 | 0 |
| Uncommitted, not scaled | 22 | 0 | 3 | 3 | 2 |
| Moderate conservative | 58 | 2 | 1 | 1 | 0 |
| Strong conservative | 61 | 0 | 2 | 1 | 0 |
| (Freshmen) | 47 | 1 | 2 | 0 | 0 |
| TOTAL‡ | 193 | 5 | 8 | 5 | 6 |

* For roll calls used, see Appendix H; for individual scores, Appendix K.

† Excludes Sens. Bowring and Reynolds (Neb.), Crippa (Wyo.), and Upton (N.H.), who responded on fewer than half the roll calls on power and resource development questions in 1953–1954.

‡ Excludes Reps. Angell (Ore.) and Lipscomb (Calif.), who responded on fewer than half the roll calls on power and resource development questions, and Speaker Martin, who did not participate in House roll calls.

rangements in 1952 for the province of Ontario and the state of New York to work out together final plans for a hydroelectric project in the International Rapids section of the St. Lawrence, an undertaking long connected with the Seaway idea. Finally, in the few years immediately prior to the Republican victory of 1952, large deposits of iron ore had been discovered in Labrador, an area which the proposed Seaway would make easily accessible to United States industrialists. Primarily because of the new-found ore deposits, American military strategists had also become increasingly interested in the Seaway.

Aware of these political and economic realities, and counting on the backing of a new President who had supported the Seaway idea as Army Chief of Staff in 1946,[35] proponents of American participation in the St. Lawrence project looked to the future with optimism in 1953. In January, Senator Alexander Wiley of Wisconsin and Representative George Dondero of Michigan introduced identical new versions of the Seaway proposal to the Eighty-third Congress. Unlike earlier Seaway bills, the Wiley-Dondero bills omitted provisions for federal construction of hydroelectric power facilities on the St. Lawrence, limited the proposed Seaway to waters east of Lake Erie, and provided for a self-liquidating agency, the St. Lawrence Seaway Development Corporation, to oversee actual construction. The new proposal called for expenditure of only about $100 million, compared with the $566 million price tag on earlier plans placed before the Congress. Some liberals were unhappy with its failure to provide for power development. Wayne Morse, for example, wrote Wiley that "unless you can give me some good reason for this change in your bill, I am not inclined to either support it or vote for it."[36] Republican sponsors of the toned-down 1953 measure, however, anticipated strong presidential support and prompt congressional action.

Initial White House reaction was puzzling and disappointing to supporters of the plan. Although "generally understood" to be pro-Seaway during the 1952 campaign,[37] the President failed to mention the project either in the 1953 State of the Union message or in his list of "must" legislation for the first session of the Eighty-third Congress. When questioned about his views on the Seaway in an early 1953 press conference, Eisenhower replied that, though he did not "mean to be evasive," he thought he

---

[35] Carlton Mabee, *The Seaway Story* (New York: Macmillan, 1961), 161.

[36] Morse to Wiley, Jan. 9, 1953, Alexander Wiley Papers, Wisconsin State Historical Society, Madison.

[37] Mabee, *The Seaway Story*, 161.

needed more time "to reach a real decision."[38] It was about this time that the President was first hearing the arguments of the railroad and mining lobbies so opposed to the project.

White House support came, but only gradually. Senator Taft announced on March 30, 1953, that Senate hearings on the Wiley bill would have to "go ahead without any recommendation from the White House," but wheels were already turning within the administration. In early April, the President told the Cabinet that he was sure he would eventually have to back the project, but he wanted to hear out the arguments of the opposition.[39] During the next few weeks Eisenhower did exactly that.[40] On April 23, the President took his first public stand on the Seaway since entering the White House. Pointing to a recommendation from the National Security Council that United States participation would be beneficial to national security, Eisenhower indicated in a letter to Wiley that he now approved of the Seaway bill. Yet in a press conference the same day the President refused to approve the Wiley-Dondero plan. All he would say at this point, he told newsmen, was that he "believed it desirable that we participate in some degree . . . ."[41] On the following day, however, he appointed a special subcommittee of the Cabinet to prepare recommendations regarding the Seaway. The subcommittee brought in a report favoring United States participation in construction of the Seaway in the International Rapids section; the Cabinet unanimously approved the recommendation on May 8. All things considered, concluded the *New York Times*, the Cabinet action "implied an endorsement" of the bill pending before Congress.[42]

Administration support was too limited to help Wiley and

---

38 Press conference remarks of Feb. 25, 1953, in *Public Papers . . . 1953*, 61.

39 Taft's remarks in *New York Times*, Mar. 31, 1953; see Donovan, *The Inside Story*, 76–77. Donovan also indicates that Sherman Adams, Attorney General Brownell, and Treasury Secretary Humphrey were strong advocates of the Seaway at Cabinet meetings. On Humphrey's role, see also Mabee, *The Seaway Story*, 162.

40 See Joseph Dodge to Oscar Webber, Apr. 21, 1953, Box 10, Joseph M. Dodge Records, Eisenhower Papers.

41 *Public Papers . . . 1953*, 207, 212; see *Mandate for Change*, 301.

42 *New York Times*, May 9, 1953.

Dondero in 1953. Senator Wiley hand-picked a Foreign Relations subcommittee "with an eye to assure a majority" for his bill, naming himself chairman; members favorable to the Seaway included Republicans Taft and Charles Tobey and Democrats Hubert Humphrey and Theodore Green, while two others (Knowland and Democrat John Sparkman) were neutral and Democrat Walter George opposed the project. Wiley then proceeded to conduct hearings much more forcefully than was his custom.[43] By early June these tactics produced favorable reports from both the subcommittee and the full Foreign Relations Committee (in the latter by a vote of 13–2, with all Republicans in favor), but the Senate leadership dropped plans to take the measure to the floor when Dondero's House Public Works Committee failed even to vote on whether to report the bill. Even in its new form, the bill still repelled representatives of coastal and port areas (especially in New England) and various railroad, coal, and ore-mining interests, all of whom regarded the Seaway as a federally subsidized economic rival. The Wiley-Dondero bill obviously needed much more of a push from above to make any real progress in the Eighty-third Congress.

Administration interest in the Seaway appeared to increase during late 1953. In November, President Eisenhower traveled to Ottawa to address the Canadian Parliament, where he spoke of the project as "a vital addition to our economic and national security."[44] The Seaway was thoroughly discussed at the White House legislative planning conference in mid-December, and ten days after the conference a "high Republican source" told the press that, in keeping with "White House wishes," the measure would receive top priority in the forthcoming session of Congress.[45] Because the Senate had long been the more receptive of the two houses to the project, administration strategists decided to try for early passage in that chamber in order then to be able to apply pressure on the House.

43 Harry R. Mahood, "The St. Lawrence Seaway Bill of 1954: A Case Study in Decision-Making in American Foreign Policy" (diss., Univ. of Illinois, 1960), 134.

44 *Public Papers . . . 1953*, 772.

45 *New York Times*, Dec. 29, 1953.

The increasingly favorable outlook for the Wiley-Dondero bill in the Senate during January 1954 reflected the intense White House activity in its behalf. Reporting the "conversion" of Colorado's Senator Millikin, whose influence would probably "swing at least three other votes from the Rocky Mountain area to the project," the *New York Times* declared on January 7 that President Eisenhower's newly aroused interest in the Seaway was responsible for increasing the "pressure on individual Senators to go along."[46] The administration's strategy included personal appeals by the President himself. On January 15, for example, Gerald Morgan suggested to Eisenhower that he make use of a scheduled conference with Senator Ralph Flanders of Vermont to "hit him on the St. Lawrence Seaway and try to get him committed to it."[47] Flanders was not persuaded, but within a week three other Republican senators dropped their opposition to the proposed waterway. Robert Hendrickson of New Jersey told the Senate that he was no longer opposed but was "uncommitted and still listening," while Senators H. Alexander Smith and Everett Dirksen switched to outright support for the Seaway, both citing Eisenhower's national security arguments as the cause.[48] Dirksen apparently was won over during a breakfast at the White House where Eisenhower "talked Seaway to him alone for two hours."[49] More dramatic, however, even if perhaps less directly owing to White House persuasion, was Senator John F. Kennedy's January 14 announcement during floor debate that he would vote for the bill (thereby becoming the first congressional representative from Massachusetts ever to do so) because he believed the importance of the Seaway transcended regional interest.

By the time Senate debate concluded on January 20, the verdict in that body was no longer in doubt. Flanders's motion to re-

[46] *Ibid.*, Jan. 7, 1954.

[47] Morgan to Eisenhower, Jan. 15, 1954, in Box 35, Morgan Records, Eisenhower Papers.

[48] *New York Times*, Jan. 19, Jan. 20, 1954. On Smith's reasons, see also Smith to Alexander Wiley, May 20, 1954, Smith Papers.

[49] Mabee, *The Seaway Story*, 165.

commit was beaten back handily (32–51), and immediately afterward the upper house approved the Seaway by a vote of 51–33. Senate Republicans gave strong support to the bill. Of forty-six who took a position, twenty-nine (63 percent) supported it. Regional proclivities clearly affected the division. While nearly all Republican senators from the North Central (six of eight), Plains (seven of eight), and Western states (nine of twelve) favored the bill, fewer than half from New England (four of nine) and the Mid-Atlantic states (two of eight) did so. The lone Border state Republican, Kentucky's John Sherman Cooper, supported the Seaway.

Administration influence—in addition to the intrinsically more conservative cast of the 1954 bill—accounted for a number of conversions within Republican ranks. Of twenty-one Republican senators who had voted to recommit the 1952 Seaway bill, nine supported the project in 1954. Among the conversions were one senator from New England (Margaret Chase Smith) and one from the North Central states (Dirksen), two each from the Plains (Frank Carlson and Andrew Schoeppel, both of Kansas) and the Mid-Atlantic states (H. Alexander Smith and Hendrickson), and three Westerners (Millikin, Wallace Bennett, and Arthur Watkins).[50] Eisenhower, with his reputation for expertise in national security, won some of these converts by arguing the security benefits of the Seaway. Those from Maine and the Western states, however, were most likely won over at least in part by effective log-rolling: the White House announced in January 1954 that it would back both a federal survey of the Passamaquoddy Bay area near Maine (to assess possibilities for hydroelectric development) and a development project on the upper Colorado River.[51] Indeed, the response of Republican

[50] Likewise, Wiley, in analyzing likely Republican voting on the Seaway in the 83rd Congress, had listed eight senators as opponents who eventually supported it in 1954 (Bennett, Carlson, Dirksen, Millikin, Payne, Schoeppel, and the two Smiths). Three others he listed as "unknown" (Barrett, Cooper, and Goldwater) also backed it. "Senate Analysis," Nov. 13, 1952, Wiley Papers.

[51] See *New York Times*, Jan. 21, 1954; William Willoughby, *The St. Lawrence Seaway: A Study in Politics and Diplomacy* (Madison: Univ. of Wisconsin Press, 1961), 259.

senators to the St. Lawrence Seaway bill of 1954 shows the Eisenhower administration at its politically most effective during the Eighty-third Congress. Literally, White House intervention seems to have brought about Senate passage of the Wiley-Dondero bill.

The administration strategy of concentrating on the Senate paid prompt dividends. Confronted with such impressive support for the Seaway in the upper house, several House Republicans who had previously opposed the project began at once to re-evaluate their positions. Included in this group were Floor Leader Charles Halleck, Armed Services Committee chairman Dewey Short (Missouri), and Representatives James Auchincloss (New Jersey) and Myron George (Kansas), both members of the crucially important Public Works Committee.[52] Within two weeks of the Senate action, the House committee voted by the lopsided margin of 23–6 to report the bill virtually intact. Only five of sixteen Republicans on Public Works (Charles Brownson, Alvin Bush, Will Neal, Frank Small, and Walter Stauffer) voted against the favorable report. Several long-time Republican foes of the Seaway, including Auchincloss, George, Harry McGregor (Ohio), and Hubert Scudder (California), voted with chairman Dondero and the committee majority. Of the dissenters, Bush and Stauffer, from Pennsylvania, and Neal, from West Virginia, could well have been responding to pressure from coal-mining and railroad interests. Charles Brownson (Indiana), who claimed to oppose the bill because the government was guaranteeing the bonds to be issued, was accused by Seaway supporters of yielding to pressure from the powerful railroad lobby. Small, from Maryland, undoubtedly opposed the Seaway as a competitive threat to the port of Baltimore. Since the Public Works Committee had refused even to vote on the bill a year earlier, its favorable action in February 1954 improved prospects for the St. Lawrence project.

The bill still had to clear one final and formidable hurdle before it could come before the House, where it was given at least

---

[52] *New York Times*, Jan. 22, 1954.

an even chance to pass. The Rules Committee, instead of promptly reporting a rule for debate on the measure, sat on it for more than two months. This delay reflected continuing opposition to the bill from several key Republican House leaders, including Speaker Martin, Representative Halleck, and Rules chairman Leo Allen. Dondero, complaining to Sherman Adams about "the failure of the House Leadership to get behind the announced policy of the Administration," urged that the President make a personal appearance in Congress on behalf of the Seaway bill. Such an appearance, Dondero argued, "would be precedent shattering—bold, courageous and challenging (would outdo FDR at his best)."[53] The White House obviously thought this sort of tactic unnecessary, but supplied sufficient pressure where it counted to induce the Rules Committee to act on April 29. By a vote of seven to five, the committee sent the Seaway bill to the House under a rule permitting only four hours' debate. Meanwhile, Vice President Nixon and Senator Knowland, responding to Senator Wiley's requests, had been hard at work attempting to win over Republicans in the California House delegation, as well as (in Nixon's case) a few selected New Englanders (Heselton, Nelson of Maine, and Patterson and Seely-Brown of Connecticut).[54]

As the House began consideration on May 5, the administration was optimistic. The strongest challenge to the Seaway proposal took the form of an amendment sponsored by Brownson which banned the government from guaranteeing the $105 million worth of bonds to be issued by the St. Lawrence Seaway Development Corporation. The amendment was obviously designed to appeal to conservative supporters of the project as well as to outright foes of the Seaway. By eliminating the federal guaran-

[53] Undated memorandum, Dondero to Sherman Adams, in Box 8, A67 Accessions, Morgan Records, Eisenhower Papers.

[54] See F. Hugh Burns, vice president of Great Lakes–St. Lawrence Association, to Sen. Wiley, Mar. 2 and Mar. 8, 1954, Wiley to Nixon, Mar. 3, and to Knowland, Mar. 9, all in Wiley Papers. Nixon and Knowland had good luck: in the California delegation, only two Republicans (Utt and Bramblett) opposed the Seaway; of the New Englanders wooed by Nixon, Heselton and Patterson voted for the bill, Nelson and Seely-Brown against.

tees, Brownson's proviso probably would have made it impossible to raise the $105 million and would thus have killed the Seaway. By this time, however, the White House believed it had the votes. On the eve of the House vote, White House aide Homer Gruenther confidently assured his colleagues that reports from the House whip organization and "spot checks with one leader in each state" showed the outlook to be "encouraging for the defeat of the Brownson Amendment and passage of the St. Lawrence Waterway."[55]

On the House floor, Halleck and Leo Allen both spoke on behalf of the bill and against Brownson's proposal, indicating that the White House had once again succeeded in converting the party leadership to its point of view. Generally, however, the administration avoided putting direct pressure on individual congressmen. As Gruenther explained to his colleagues, "we are making no individual and special appeals because it is believed that such is not presently necessary plus the fact that every time we make a special appeal to a Congressman to change his position, he eventually comes back with a request for a favor ranging in importance from one of the President's packages of matches to a judgeship or cabinet appointment for a 'worthy constituent.' "[56]

The confidence of Seaway backers was borne out by House action on May 6. On a standing vote of 79–173, the lower house rejected Brownson's amendment, turned back a recommittal motion by 157–242, and then approved the Seaway bill by 241–158. As in the Senate, regional differences were associated with the positions House Republicans took on the Seaway. Although 88 percent of the Republican congressmen who committed themselves on the final roll call on the Seaway took the administration position, the breakdown by region repeated the Senate pattern. North Central, Plains, and Western Republicans favored the measure by 91, 90, and 95 percent respectively. For Border state

---

[55] Memorandum, Gruenther to Wilton Persons, Gerald Morgan, and Jack Martin, dated May 5, 1954, Wiley Papers.

[56] *Ibid*. This would indicate that the *New York Times* was mistaken in its assertion that "strong Administration pressure was exerted for passage of the bill without change" (May 7, 1954).

representatives, on the other hand, the figure was 57 percent, and Mid-Atlantic and New England congressmen voted only 32 and 28 percent in favor of the Seaway.

It is likely that the bill's comfortable passage in the Senate, coupled with the conservative nature of the Wiley-Dondero proposal, changed the view of a number of Republican House members, though there is no previous House vote on the Seaway against which to measure the votes of Republicans in 1954. The rationale offered by Representative Vorys of Ohio for his vote in favor of the Seaway in 1954 probably held for a number of his colleagues. The Ohio congressman noted that his previous opposition to the St. Lawrence project had been based on a "feeling that my constituents should not be taxed for a project that would offer possible competition with the railroads of my district." In contrast, he explained, the 1954 bill proposed a "self-liquidating" corporation. The President had alluded to the importance of the Seaway for defense purposes, Vorys continued, and Canada intended to build it in any event.[57] Through such arguments was the administration able to convince the Republican-controlled Eighty-third Congress to approve the St. Lawrence project. Again on the Seaway issue a familiar pattern reappeared. Just as a conservative administration approach to fiscal matters, farm price supports, and power and resource questions helped to produce a high degree of Republican support in Congress, so too did the basically conservative Seaway proposal of 1953–1954.

There were no other major legislative actions which tested the administration's influence in power and resource questions in 1953–1954, but related issues did emerge which revealed the conservatism of Eisenhower's views. The President's aversion to public power was apparent in his half-hearted support of ongoing multi-purpose resource development projects such as the Tennessee Valley Authority (TVA), the Bonneville Power Administration (BPA), and the Southwestern Power Administration (SPA). His appointment of private power advocate Dr. William A. Pearl to head the BPA indicated that that agency's activities would, at

[57] Vorys form letter, dated May 7, 1954, Vorys Papers.

the very least, not be expanded.[58] Likewise, the administration reduced the size of the SPA staff and refused to honor certain of that organization's contracts with generation and transmission cooperatives in the region.[59] Eisenhower's budget requests for the major federal power administrations were also down sharply from Truman's requests for fiscal 1953: 80 percent less for the Southeastern Power Administration, 50 percent less for Southwestern, 25 percent less for Tennessee Valley, and 12 percent less for Bonneville.

President Eisenhower's lack of sympathy for TVA in particular received wide publicity. Referring to the authority in June 1953 as an example of "creeping socialism," the President failed to soften the impact by subsequent "clarification" for reporters. Explaining that he was "not out to destroy TVA," he characterized it as a "curious thing in . . . socialistic theory," and argued that it represented sectional favoritism. "It seems to me," he said, "that we have got to have some kind of reevaluation . . . ."[60]

Still, Eisenhower refrained from agreeing publicly with extreme conservatives that TVA should be sold to private interests. As he explained in late 1953, he did not "even know that it could be sold to private industry without doing something to wreck the whole system." He could not "comment on such a thing," the President concluded, "because that would be a pretty drastic step . . . ."[61] Basically, as Eisenhower explained, there were features of TVA that he found "alarming." He believed, moreover, that logic compelled equal treatment for other regions: ". . . if the Federal Government is committed to building power in the TVA and giving them [sic] 100 percent of all they will ever want," he asked rhetorically, "why don't I do it in the Mississippi Valley?"[62] Although he might accept the TVA as an accomplished

58 Joe Miller, "The Battle for Hell's Canyon," *The Reporter* 10, No. 10 (May 11, 1954), 24.

59 Lyons, *Tomorrow's Birthright*, 236.

60 Press conference remarks of June 17, 1953, *Public Papers . . . 1953*, 433–34.

61 Press conference remarks of Oct. 21, 1953, *ibid.*, 705.

62 Press conference remarks of Oct. 8, 1953, *ibid.*, 650; and of Nov. 10, 1954, *Public Papers . . . 1954*, 1038.

fact, the President was never comfortable with its provision of federally developed hydroelectric power.

The Hell's Canyon controversy also revealed the outlines of private power sentiment in the Eisenhower administration. At issue was the construction of hydroelectric power facilities on the Snake River between Idaho and Oregon. The Truman administration had favored construction of a high concrete dam and federally operated power generators and transmission facilities at Hell's Canyon. Consequently, Truman's Secretary of the Interior lodged formal objection in June 1952 against the Federal Power Commission's decision to grant a license to the privately owned Idaho Power Company for development of three low dams on the river. In early May 1953 Eisenhower's Interior Secretary, Douglas McKay, withdrew administration objections, thus clearing the way for private development at Hell's Canyon and ending hopes for a public power project in the area. Congressional Democrats and public power Republicans like Senators Morse and Langer were outraged, and introduced a bill (S. 2590) to transfer from the FPC to Congress the authority to grant licenses for power development in river basins where Congress had previously authorized comprehensive development.

Although S. 2590 did not reach the Senate floor during the Eighty-third Congress, the fight was acrimonious—"the most momentous power fight," according to one observer, "since ... Wendell Willkie took on the TVA."[63] Eisenhower's reactions to questions about the Hell's Canyon issue showed, if there had been any doubt, that McKay had not acted independently. Allowing that the "weight of the evidence" seemed to him "on the side of letting this thing be decided locally," the President went on to state that he believed the people of Idaho "definitely" favored a privately developed project.[64] The issue was not ultimately settled until 1957, in favor of the private power forces, but in 1953–1954 it was significant for what it revealed of Eisenhower's views. On the one hand, he declined to intervene force-

[63] Miller, *The Reporter* 10, No. 10, 23.
[64] Press conference remarks of May 14, 1953, *Public Papers ... 1953*, 286–87.

fully on the side of private interests, instead choosing to emphasize the values of local autonomy and grass-roots decision making. At the same time, however, as in the case of TVA, the President clearly demonstrated an aversion to expanding the role of the federal government in producing hydroelectric power.

On one final issue during 1953–1954–that of Niagara River power development–these same presidential tendencies surfaced. Like the Hell's Canyon dispute, the Niagara question enlisted the conflicting enthusiasms of private and public power advocates: in addition, a third alternative existed, that New York State might develop the needed facilities. Although the site for the proposed construction was wholly within the state of New York, a 1950 United States–Canadian treaty had provided that power development so near Niagara Falls required congressional approval.

At the outset of the Eighty-third Congress, advocates of the various possible means of development pressed their cases, in the form of legislative proposals: H.R. 4351 (Representative George Dondero), H.R. 2289 (Representative William E. Miller), and S. 689 (Senators Homer Capehart and Edward Martin) all provided for Niagara power development by private enterprise; H.R. 5066 (Representative Franklin D. Roosevelt, Jr.) and S. 1851 (Senator Herbert Lehman) stipulated federal development; and H.R. 5335 (Representative Frank Becker) and S. 1971 (Senator Irving Ives) called for state development. The administration did not enter actively into the matter, though it certainly opposed federal construction of the needed facilities. In deciding between the two remaining options, Eisenhower adhered to the principle of states' rights. When Secretary McKay, called to testify on the private development bill, asked the President what he should do, Eisenhower advised him to oppose the measure and to argue that the State of New York should be permitted to decide the issue.[65] Since Governor Dewey of New York was on record as

65 Arthur Minnich memorandum to Wilton B. Persons, July 6, 1953, Box 5, A67–19 Accessions, Morgan Records, Eisenhower Papers. See also Donovan, *The Inside Story*, 78–79.

favoring construction of the facilities by the New York State Power Authority, this was tantamount to supporting the state-development alternative.

Yet throughout the long conflict, Eisenhower tried to remain publicly aloof, answering questions about the issue only when pressed to do so. Although he had told reporters in May 1953 that he favored giving the authority to the State of New York "to then handle the thing as they saw best," by July he was hedging. Noting that "in the ordinary . . . case, the process would be referred to the Federal Power Commission," the President explained that he did not question Congress's right to make the decision itself, but felt he should take "no action nor even express a specific opinion . . . until the bill as drawn, and if passed" was presented to him.[66] In other words, Eisenhower had his preferences but was determined not to become directly involved in a struggle between states' rights and private enterprise.

Matters did not come to a head until early 1954. The House, following the report of its Public Works Committee, had approved H.R. 4351, a private development bill, in July 1953. The Senate was more reluctant to act, however. Fearing a filibuster if the bill went to the floor in the 1953 session, Senate leaders postponed hearings until early 1954. Meanwhile, the FPC granted a license to the New York State Power Authority to go ahead and build the facilities. Although the President at first approved the decision, by December 1953 the White House was urging the Court of Appeals to hear petitions from private firms which objected to the FPC ruling.[67] The messy situation demonstrated the wisdom of Eisenhower's earlier desire to avoid involvement. When the court upheld the FPC license, the administration decided once again to lower its profile. In early 1954, the White House backed a compromise bill introduced by Senator Case of South Dakota, but President Eisenhower steadfastly refused to involve himself directly. Instead, he continued merely to reiterate

---

[66] Press conference remarks of May 14, 1953, and July 8, 1953, in *Public Papers . . . 1953*, 286, 479.

[67] Willoughby, *The St. Lawrence Seaway*, 254; *New York Times*, Nov. 6, 1953.

his belief in local initiative, insisting that he would not "give a specific answer other than to state what my belief is." [68]

The Case bill (S. 2599) merely returned jurisdiction over the Niagara project to the FPC, but by the time it came before the Senate in August 1954, emotions were sufficiently heated that no floor action was possible. Eventually a similar bill passed the Eighty-fifth Congress (with sweeteners added to please advocates of both private and federal development alike), and New York State did undertake the Niagara project. But the issue was important in the Eighty-third Congress for the emotions it laid bare. Typical of the views of private power legislators was Senator Capehart's impassioned statement in March 1954 that if private industry were denied the right to undertake the development, then he was "ready to throw in the sponge . . . because I think we will eventually go a hundred percent socialistic as far as power is concerned . . . ." [69] On the other hand, such prominent Republicans as Governor Dewey and Senators Ives and Aiken reinforced the President's own preference for states' rights on the issue, and were nearly as adamant as Capehart in their opposition to granting development rights to private interests. Federal development was popular primarily among Democrats, as the other two alternatives divided Republicans.

The Niagara power controversy dramatized as well as any single issue the difficulties and ambiguities in Eisenhower's "partnership" power policy. From the time of the first 1952 campaign declarations on "partnership," critics claimed the concept was too vague. [70] The President and his defenders saw federal power development as acceptable for large multi-purpose projects for entire river basins (and in fact the administration pushed unsuccessfully in 1953–1954 for a federal water storage project on the upper Colorado), but in specific situations they almost always came down on the side of local initiative. When political exigen-

[68] See Lyons, *Tomorrow's Birthright*, 231–32; Eisenhower's press conference remarks of June 10, 1954, *Public Papers . . . 1954*, 553.

[69] U.S. Congress, Senate, Committee on Public Works. *Hearings . . . on H.R. 4351, S. 689, S. 1971, S. 2599, S. 2966*, 83d Cong., 2d Sess., 1954, p. 219.

[70] See Miller, *The Reporter* 10, No. 10, 24–25.

cies called for state development, as in the Niagara case, the President could support that alternative, but most often he sided with advocates of power development by private interests. Basically, Eisenhower favored a diminished role for the federal government in power and resource development. "As Federal power expands in a region," the President told a Western audience in 1954, "local enterprise becomes increasingly intimidated and discouraged .... Thus still more Federal intervention becomes necessary. ... The Administration ... and the present leadership in Congress—are unalterably opposed to such malignant growth of bureaucracy." [71]

To critics who charged that the "partnership" policy represented a sell-out to monopolistic private interests, the standard administration reply was that the real threat of monopoly came from federal power development, not private.[72] Essentially, for all his rhetoric about "partnership," Eisenhower supported the traditional Republican position on power policy: encouragement of local responsibility (especially local private interests) and limitation of any expansion of ongoing federal hydroelectric facilities. The overwhelming support which the President's power policies received from Republicans in both houses of the Eighty-third Congress bore witness to the impeccable partisan breeding of those policies.

[71] Address at dedication of McNary Dam, Walla Walla, Wash., Sept. 23, 1954, in *Public Papers ... 1954*, 859.

[72] *Ibid.*; see also Gabriel Hauge speech entitled "The Economics of Eisenhower Conservatism," delivered in San Francisco, Oct. 14, 1955, press release in OF 72–A–2, Eisenhower Papers; and statement by Assistant Secretary of the Interior Fred Aandahl before a Senate subcommittee in Dec. 1953 (U.S. Congress, Senate, Committee on Judiciary, Subcommittee on Antitrust and Monopoly, *Hearings on the New Power Policy and Marketing Criteria of the Department of the Interior*, 83d Cong., 1st Sess., 1953, p. 131).

# CHAPTER EIGHT

# Eisenhower and the Republican Congress

The common view of Dwight D. Eisenhower as President emphasizes his lack of control over both Congress as a whole and legislators of his own party in particular. As an essentially non-partisan chief executive, he is supposed to have neglected one of the most important roles of a President, that of party leader, and to have frequently surrendered the fate of his legislative proposals to the whims of a fickle Congress.[1]

Far from eschewing his role as party leader, however, Eisenhower deeply felt such a responsibility. He believed that each party should be united on policy and accountable to the American public, and he viewed "the responsibility of the President as party leader . . . as an inescapable duty, essential to democracy itself." Specifically, he thought the President should "devise a program that is in general conformity with the platform of his party, and do his best to get it enacted into law."[2] During the

---

[1] This stereotype is aptly described in Hughes, *Ordeal of Power*, 123. See also Campbell et al., *The Voter Decides*, 325; Adams, *Firsthand Report*, 19, 27; Bauer et al., *American Business and Public Policy*, 32; Laurin L. Henry, *Presidential Transitions* (Washington: Brookings Institution, 1960), 703; and Richard E. Neustadt, *Presidential Power: The Politics of Leadership*, rev. ed. (New York: Wiley, 1968), 159, 164–67.

[2] See Adams, *Firsthand Report*, 28; Eisenhower, *The White House Years: Waging Peace, 1956–1961* (Garden City, N.Y.: Doubleday, 1965), 640. Quotes are from Eisenhower's speech at Mount Rushmore National Monument, S.D., June 11, 1953, in *Public Papers . . . 1953*, 399, and press conference remarks of Feb. 10, 1954, *ibid.*, *1954*, 253.

years 1953–1954, given Republican majorities in both houses of Congress, Eisenhower did what he thought he should: he devised a program which in most respects reaffirmed the tenets of mainstream Republicanism, then worked to weld congressional Republicans to his cause.

The performance of Eisenhower's only Republican Congress shows that he was capable of leading his party and pushing his program to victory. By contemporary standards, President Eisenhower achieved a high degree of success in getting congressional approval for legislation he supported. Among more recent Presidents, only Lyndon B. Johnson met with greater success in his first two years, and Johnson had the advantage of much larger partisan majorities in both houses.[3] Of the roll calls examined in this study, Eisenhower won 81 percent of the time in the Senate (seventy of eighty-six roll calls) and 84 percent of the time in the House (forty-one of forty-nine roll calls). In a Congress which his party barely controlled, such support was impressive.

Republicans in both houses of the Eighty-third Congress responded well to their President's lead. In Senate and House combined, Eisenhower enjoyed the support of 90 percent or more of voting Republicans on over one-third of the "Eisenhower issue" roll calls; he was supported by at least 75 percent of them on more than two-thirds of such roll calls (see Table 11). In contrast, a majority of Republicans opposed the White House on only twenty-one of the 135 roll calls (15.6 percent). In general, House Republicans tended to give Eisenhower greater majorities than did their Senate counterparts, but in the upper chamber, too, the response was strikingly positive.

Because Republican majorities in the Eighty-third Congress were so thin, the President could not often win legislative vic-

---

[3] According to *Congressional Quarterly*, Eisenhower was supported by Congress on 89 percent of the roll calls on which he took a position in 1953 and on 83 percent in 1954. By comparison, congressional support for Kennedy in his first two years was 81 and 85 percent; for Johnson, 88 and 93 percent (under the extraordinary circumstances of his predecessor's assassination and the 1964 landslide which produced huge Democratic majorities in Congress); and for Nixon, 74 and 77 percent. See *Congressional Quarterly Almanac*, Vols. XXVI (1970), 1123, and XXVIII (1972), 42.

*Table 11* AGGREGATE REPUBLICAN SUPPORT FOR EISENHOWER IN THE EIGHTY-THIRD CONGRESS, BY ISSUE AREA

| Issue Area | Number of Roll Calls, 90% or more Republicans supporting President | Number of Roll Calls, 75–89% Republicans supporting President | Number of Roll Calls, 50–74% Republicans supporting President | Number of Roll Calls, fewer than 50% Republicans supporting President | Total Roll Calls |
|---|---|---|---|---|---|
| SENATE | | | | | |
| Foreign Policy | 3 | 6 | 10 | 4 | 23 |
| Fiscal-economic | 10 | 3 | 0 | 5 | 18 |
| Welfare | 4 | 0 | 0 | 0 | 4 |
| Power and resources | 8 | 9 | 0 | 1 | 18 |
| Other* | 3 | 14 | 3 | 3 | 23 |
| Total | 28 | 32 | 13 | 13 | 86 |
| HOUSE | | | | | |
| Foreign Policy | 2 | 3 | 7 | 3 | 15 |
| Fiscal-economic | 9 | 2 | 0 | 1 | 12 |
| Welfare | 7 | 1 | 1 | 3 | 12 |
| Power and resources | 6 | 0 | 0 | 1 | 7 |
| Other* | 0 | 1 | 2 | 0 | 3 |
| Total | 24 | 7 | 10 | 8 | 49 |
| BOTH HOUSES TOTAL | 52 | 39 | 23 | 21 | 135 |

* For the Senate, "other" roll calls include agriculture (16), executive control in foreign policy (4), labor (1), and St. Lawrence Seaway (2); for the House: agriculture (1), St. Lawrence Seaway (2).

tories with support from only his own party. Of his seventy triumphs on "Eisenhower issue" roll calls in the Senate, Republicans supplied enough votes for passage only eight times (11.4 percent); but on another twenty-four they supplied at least 90 percent of the necessary votes, and on twenty-three other administration victories, they provided 75 percent of the needed votes.

In the House, Republicans alone accounted for twelve of Eisenhower's forty-one victories (29.3 percent), gave at least 90 percent of the necessary votes on another fourteen, and provided at least 75 percent of the votes needed on five additional roll calls. In both houses, the administration needed far more Democratic votes for its foreign policy victories than for success in any other policy area. Table 12 demonstrates the extent of the Republicans' contributions to Eisenhower's success in the various issue areas.

If the small Republican majorities required that Eisenhower receive support from at least a minority of Democratic congressmen, such support was almost inevitably forthcoming. The internationalist views held by the President had been popular with most congressional Democrats since the end of World War II, while Eisenhower's conservatism in domestic affairs was bound to attract the bulk of conservative Southern and Border-state Democrats in both houses. Since there were twenty-nine Southern and Border-state Democrats in the Senate and 126 in the House, this source of support was valuable to a conservative President. Democrats from these two regions did prove to be Eisenhower's most zealous supporters in that party. In every domestic issue area, a far greater proportion of Southern and Border-state Democratic senators were Eisenhower supporters (with support scores of .60 or higher) than were Democrats from other regions (see Table 13). In the House, this held true on fiscal-economic and power and resource development questions, but not in welfare policy. On foreign policy questions, Democratic support for Eisenhower was more widely diffused throughout the regions.

Lists of leading Democratic supporters of Eisenhower's programs demonstrate greater Southern hospitality in the Senate than in the House. Senate Democrats giving the strongest overall support to Eisenhower included Spessard Holland of Florida (.83), Willis Robertson of Virginia (.74), Clyde Hoey of North Carolina (.65), George Smathers of Florida (.65), Price Daniel of Texas (.59), Lyndon Johnson of Texas (.58), and James Eastland of Mississippi (.56), all Southerners or Border-staters, and

### Table 12 EXTENT OF REPUBLICAN CONTRIBUTION TO EISENHOWER'S LEGISLATIVE VICTORIES, BY ISSUE AREA, EIGHTY-THIRD CONGRESS

| Issue Area | Number of Roll Call Victories for which Republicans supplied 100% of minimal majority | Number of Roll Call Victories for which Republicans supplied 90–99% of minimal majority | Number of Roll Call Victories for which Republicans supplied 75–89% of minimal majority | Number of Roll Call Victories for which Republicans supplied less than 75% of minimal majority | Total Roll-Call Victories |
|---|---|---|---|---|---|
| **SENATE** | | | | | |
| Foreign Policy | 1 | 4 | 3 | 11 | 19 |
| Fiscal-economic | 3 | 5 | 3 | 1 | 12 |
| Welfare | 1 | 3 | 0 | 0 | 4 |
| Power and resource development | 3 | 7 | 7 | 0 | 17 |
| Other* | 0 | 5 | 10 | 3 | 18 |
| Total | 8 | 24 | 23 | 15 | 70 |
| **HOUSE** | | | | | |
| Foreign Policy | 0 | 2 | 3 | 8 | 13 |
| Fiscal-economic | 7 | 3 | 1 | 0 | 11 |
| Welfare | 3 | 4 | 1 | 0 | 8 |
| Power and resource development | 2 | 4 | 0 | 0 | 6 |
| Other* | 0 | 1 | 0 | 2 | 3 |
| Total | 12 | 14 | 5 | 10 | 41 |
| **BOTH HOUSES** **TOTAL** | 20 | 38 | 28 | 25 | 111 |

\* For the Senate, "other" victories included agriculture (14), executive control of foreign policy (2), and St. Lawrence Seaway (2); for the House: agriculture (1), St. Lawrence Seaway (2).

Table 13  "Eisenhower Support" by Democrats in Eighty-Third Congress, Overall and in Specific Issue Areas, by Region *

| | Level of Support | | | | |
|---|---|---|---|---|---|
| Issue Area, Region | .80–1.00 | .60–.79 | .40–.59 | .20–.39 | .00–.19 |
| SENATE | | | | | |
| *Overall* | | | | | |
| South/Border states (29) | 1 | 3 | 20 | 5 | 0 |
| Others (19) | 0 | 2 | 13 | 4 | 0 |
| *Foreign Policy* | | | | | |
| South/Border states (29) | 6 | 11 | 6 | 4 | 2 |
| Others (17) | 7 | 5 | 0 | 5 | 0 |
| *Fiscal-Economic* | | | | | |
| South/Border states (29) | 0 | 7 | 12 | 10 | 0 |
| Others (19) | 0 | 1 | 8 | 8 | 2 |
| *Welfare* | | | | | |
| South/Border states (26) | 8 | 8 | 8 | 2 | 0 |
| Others (17) | 2 | 3 | 3 | 8 | 1 |
| *Power and Resources* | | | | | |
| South/Border states (28) | 10 | 8 | 0 | 1 | 9 |
| Others (18) | 2 | 1 | 0 | 4 | 11 |

only three from other regions: Carl Hayden of Arizona (.64) and the two senators from Rhode Island, John Pastore (.61) and Theodore Green (.57). In each of the separate domestic policy areas, too, Southern and Border-state Democrats headed the lists of administration supporters (see Appendix J). Conversely, except for power and resource development questions, Democrats from the two regions were underrepresented among the leading foes of Eisenhower's domestic programs (see Appendix J).

In the House, Democratic support for the administration program was regionally more diverse. Only four of the top ten Eisenhower backers among House Democrats were from the South

*Table 13* (CONTINUED)

| Issue Area, Region | Level of Support | | | | |
|---|---|---|---|---|---|
| | .80–1.00 | .60–.79 | .40–.59 | .20–.39 | .00–.19 |
| | | HOUSE | | | |
| *Overall* | | | | | |
| South/Border states (125) | 0 | 25 | 88 | 12 | 0 |
| Others (89) | 0 | 40 | 46 | 3 | 0 |
| *Foreign Policy* | | | | | |
| South/Border states (124) | 9 | 37 | 35 | 37 | 6 |
| Others (84) | 66 | 11 | 5 | 2 | 0 |
| *Fiscal-Economic* | | | | | |
| South/Border states (126) | 4 | 14 | 72 | 32 | 4 |
| Others (89) | 0 | 6 | 35 | 27 | 21 |
| *Welfare* | | | | | |
| South/Border states (124) | 9 | 57 | 47 | 11 | 0 |
| Others (89) | 15 | 59 | 15 | 0 | 0 |
| *Power and Resources* | | | | | |
| South/Border states (124) | 39 | 45 | 14 | 10 | 16 |
| Others (85) | 2 | 10 | 5 | 9 | 59 |

\* Figures in table represent the numbers of Democrats in each category. Figures in parentheses represent the number in each regional group for each issue area.

(Courtney Campbell of Florida, .75; Brooks Hays of Arkansas, .73; James Richards of South Carolina, .71; and Speaker Sam Rayburn of Texas, .70); the other six came from either the Northeast (Francis Walter of Pennsylvania, .72, and Harrison Williams of New Jersey, .72) or California (Cecil King, .75; Clyde Doyle, .72; Samuel Yorty, .71; and John Shelley, .70). Likewise, the Democrats who supported Eisenhower's position most strongly in each of the individual policy areas were not so preponderantly Southern as in the upper house (see Appendix J). Speaker Rayburn qualified as a moderate administration supporter (with a score of .70), but Democratic house whip John McCormack of Massachusetts (.56), like Senate Democratic leaders Lyndon

Johnson (.58) and Earle Clements (.54), ranked as neither "pro" nor "anti."

The strong backing which congressional Republicans gave to the President deflates the argument that Eisenhower presented a program more appealing to Democrats than to his own party. Indeed, the striking contrast between the degrees of support from the two parties clearly indicates that the administration program of 1953–1954 was solidly Republican. Only in foreign policy (where Eisenhower was admittedly tugging Republicans in a new direction) and welfare policy (where he attempted some "middle way" measures) did Democrats support the President nearly to the extent that Republicans did. Table 14 demonstrates the much more positive response of Republicans to Eisenhower's 1953–1954 policies.

Within Republican ranks, individual legislators usually did not support the President to the same degree across the spectrum of all policy areas. Consequently, the same individuals did not constitute the leading administration supporters from one type of issue to the next (see Appendix K, giving the scores of congressional Republicans in each of the four areas). On welfare questions in the Senate and fiscal-economic policy in the House, a number of Republicans registered perfect 1.00 support scores. But when those two cases are excluded, only two Republicans in the whole Congress ranked among the highest Eisenhower supporters in more than one issue area: Rep. William S. Mailliard of California scored 1.00 on both fiscal-economic and power and resource questions, and Senator John Sherman Cooper of Kentucky scored .87 on foreign policy and .94 on fiscal-economic questions. Otherwise, the leading administration supporters from area to area varied considerably (see Table 15).

Administration opponents within Republican ranks tended to be somewhat more consistent. In the Senate, Republicans Wayne Morse, William Langer, and Milton Young ranked among the leading opponents in three separate areas (the three domestic areas); no other Republican senator ranked among Eisenhower's strongest foes in more than one of the four areas. In the House,

*Table 14* "EISENHOWER SUPPORT" BY REPUBLICANS AND DEMOCRATS IN EIGHTY-THIRD CONGRESS, OVERALL AND BY ISSUE AREA*

| Issue Area, Party | Percent at Each Level of Support† | | | | |
|---|---|---|---|---|---|
| | .80–1.00 | .60–.79 | .40–.59 | .20–.39 | .00–.19 |
| SENATE | | | | | |
| *Overall* | | | | | |
| Republicans (46) | 50% | 39% | 4% | 7% | 0% |
| Democrats (48) | 2 | 10 | 69 | 19 | 0 |
| *Foreign Policy* | | | | | |
| Republicans (44) | 36 | 27 | 13 | 18 | 7 |
| Democrats (46) | 28 | 35 | 13 | 20 | 4 |
| *Fiscal-Economic* | | | | | |
| Republicans (47) | 21 | 70 | 4 | 2 | 2 |
| Democrats (48) | 0 | 17 | 42 | 38 | 4 |
| *Welfare* | | | | | |
| Republicans (49) | 84 | 10 | 2 | 4 | 0 |
| Democrats (43) | 23 | 26 | 26 | 23 | 2 |
| *Power and Resources* | | | | | |
| Republicans (49) | 78 | 8 | 4 | 4 | 6 |
| Democrats (46) | 26 | 20 | 0 | 11 | 43 |
| HOUSE | | | | | |
| *Overall* | | | | | |
| Republicans (219) | 43% | 50% | 6% | 1% | 0% |
| Democrats (214) | 0 | 30 | 63 | 7 | 0 |
| *Foreign Policy* | | | | | |
| Republicans (216) | 37 | 20 | 20 | 17 | 6 |
| Democrats (208) | 36 | 23 | 19 | 19 | 3 |
| *Fiscal-Economic* | | | | | |
| Republicans (219) | 95 | 3 | 1 | 0 | 0 |
| Democrats (215) | 2 | 9 | 50 | 27 | 12 |
| *Welfare* | | | | | |
| Republicans (217) | 22 | 65 | 11 | 1 | 0.5 |
| Democrats (213) | 11 | 54 | 29 | 5 | 0 |
| *Power and Resources* | | | | | |
| Republicans (217) | 89 | 2 | 4 | 3 | 2 |
| Democrats (209) | 20 | 26 | 9 | 9 | 36 |

* Figures represent percentages in each category. Numbers in parentheses represent total Republicans and Democrats, respectively, whose voting records were sufficiently complete to be classified in each area.

† Percentages are summed across rows.

189

Table 15 Leading Eisenhower Supporters among Republicans in Eighty-Third Congress, by Issue Area

SENATE

| Foreign Policy | | Fiscal-Economic | | Welfare | | Power and Resources | |
|---|---|---|---|---|---|---|---|
| Duff, Pa. | .94 | Bush, Conn. | .94 | 41 tied | 1.00 | Barrett, Wyo. | 1.00 |
| Ives, N.Y. | .94 | Cooper, Ky. | .94 | | | Bridges, N.H. | 1.00 |
| Payne, Maine | .91 | H. A. Smith, N.J. | .89 | | | Potter, Mich. | 1.00 |
| Wiley, Wis. | .91 | Flanders, Vt. | .88 | | | Purtell, Conn. | 1.00 |
| Cooper, Ky. | .87 | Upton, N.H. | .85 | | | Saltonstall, Mass. | 1.00 |
| Millikin, Colo. | .87 | 4 tied | .83 | | | Taft, Ohio | 1.00 |

HOUSE

| Foreign Policy | | Fiscal Economic | | Welfare | | Power and Resources | |
|---|---|---|---|---|---|---|---|
| Gubser, Calif. | 1.00 | 126 tied | 1.00 | Auchincloss, N.J. | 1.00 | Corbett, Pa. | 1.00 |
| Jackson, Calif. | 1.00 | | | Coudert, N.Y. | 1.00 | Mailliard, Calif. | 1.00 |
| Kearney, N.Y. | 1.00 | | | Kersten, Wis. | 1.00 | Morano, Conn. | 1.00 |
| Prouty, Vt. | 1.00 | | | Mailliard, Calif. | 1.00 | Rhodes, Ariz. | 1.00 |
| Scott, Pa. | 1.00 | | | Wigglesworth, Mass. | 1.00 | Saylor, Pa. | 1.00 |
| Wainwright, N.Y. | 1.00 | | | 17 tied | .92 | Springer, Ill. | 1.00 |

only Noah Mason of Illinois appeared among leading opponents of the administration in three areas (foreign, fiscal-economic, and welfare policies), while Usher Burdick of North Dakota, H. R. Gross of Iowa, Jacob Javits of New York, Alvin O'Konski of Wisconsin, and Wint Smith of Kansas each did so twice (see Table 16). These nine individuals, who could be said to represent the bedrock of Republican opposition to Eisenhower in 1953–1954, did not fit a single ideological pattern. All but Javits and Morse scaled as strong nationalists prior to 1953, but on domestic policy there was greater variation. Senator Young and Representatives Gross, Mason, and Smith were all strong conservatives on most or all domestic questions, while Senators Langer and Morse and Representatives Burdick, Javits, and O'Konski were domestic liberals. Since his leading party foes came from both extremes, it would seem that Eisenhower's approach fit somewhere within the Republican mainstream.

Neither were the general sources of Republican support for and opposition to the administration program the same from one issue area to another, although there were a few broad patterns. Except in fiscal and economic policy, regional differences exerted the most consistent influence. In both houses, Republicans from the East (New England, Mid-Atlantic, or both) supported the administration most readily, while those from the Midwest (Plains, North Central, or both) most often opposed its policies. Similarly, in the House, the type of district from which a Representative came seemed to be related to his support or nonsupport for Eisenhower's policies. Although district type did not account for significant differences in either fiscal or power and resources policy, in both foreign policy and welfare matters urban Republicans supported Eisenhower most frequently, while rural Republicans did so least frequently. In neither house did period of entry into Congress determine the degree of support a legislator gave to the President in any of the four policy domains.

Most significantly, in each of the four policy areas, the vast majority of congressional Republicans ranked as Eisenhower supporters (scoring at least .60). Forty-three percent of Republi-

*Table 16* LEADING EISENHOWER OPPONENTS AMONG REPUBLICANS IN EIGHTY-THIRD CONGRESS, BY ISSUE AREA

SENATE

| *Foreign Policy* | | *Fiscal-Economic* | | *Welfare* | | *Power and Resources* | |
|---|---|---|---|---|---|---|---|
| Malone, Nev. | .10 | Morse, Ore. | .11 | Morse, Ore. | .25 | Langer, N.Dak. | .00 |
| Bricker, Ohio | .11 | Langer, N.Dak. | .39 | Langer, N.Dak. | .33 | Tobey, N.H. | .00 |
| Welker, Idaho | .18 | Young, N.Dak. | .53 | Ives, N.Y. | .50 | Morse, Ore. | .06 |
| Capehart, Ind. | .20 | Williams, Del. | .56 | Young, N.Dak. | .67 | Young, N.Dak. | .31 |
| McCarthy, Wis. | .22 | 4 tied | .65 | 4 tied | .75 | Cooper, Ky. | .39 |
| Jenner, Ind. | .25 | | | | | Wiley, Wis. | .47 |

HOUSE

| *Foreign Policy* | | *Fiscal-Economic* | | *Welfare* | | *Power and Resources* | |
|---|---|---|---|---|---|---|---|
| C. Reed, Ill. | .11 | O'Konski, Wis. | .44 | Mason, Ill. | .17 | Case, N.J. | .00 |
| Bishop, Ill. | .13 | Burdick, N.Dak. | .55 | Busbey, Ill. | .33 | Gross, Iowa | .00 |
| W. C. Cole, Mo. | .13 | Javits, N.Y. | .58 | Dolliver, Iowa | .33 | O'Konski, Wis. | .00 |
| Gross, Iowa | .13 | Mason, Ill. | .64 | W. Smith, Kans. | .33 | Withrow, Wis. | .00 |
| Mason, Ill. | .13 | Fino, N.Y. | .67 | Shafer, Mich. | .40 | Burdick, N.Dak. | .14 |
| W. Smith, Kans. | .13 | Coudert, N.Y. | .73 | C. Hoffman, Mich. | .42 | Javits, N.Y. | .14 |

can House members (95 of 219) and 50 percent of those in the Senate (23 of 46) supported the administration viewpoint on at least 80 percent of the "Eisenhower issue" roll calls. Moreover, only three Republican senators (Langer, Morse, and Young) and two Republican House members (Mason and O'Konski) fell into the anti-Eisenhower category, overall (support scores below .40). Virtually all of the remainder (approximately half of the House Republicans and one-third of the Republican senators) ranked as moderately pro-Eisenhower, with support scores ranging from .60 to .79 (see Table 14, above). For domestic policy alone, of course, these figures would be skewed in a more "pro-Eisenhower" direction; in each of the three domestic areas, at least 80 percent of the Republicans in each house were administration supporters.

Republican party leaders in the two houses played a significant part in bringing about the President's success with the congressional wing of his party. Senator Robert Taft's role, of course, was crucially important at the outset of the Eisenhower administration. The Ohioan's decision to take the post of Senate majority leader showed that he was willing to work on behalf of the new President's program instead of opposing it, as some had feared he would. After losing what he knew to be his last chance at the Presidency in 1952, Taft seemed to dedicate himself completely to the task of making a success of the first Republican administration in two decades. This, he knew, required the cooperation of congressional Republicans—particularly the leadership—and the establishment of clear lines of communication between the White House and Capitol Hill. Aside from more generous motives, Taft also hoped to influence the new administration's policies. His decision to take the majority leader post, he explained to a supporter in late 1952, was motivated in part by a belief "that General Eisenhower's judgment will be better than it seems provided both points of view are presented to him."[4] Taft virtually transformed his public personality in early 1953, becoming less doctrinaire and more gregarious, as he

[4] Taft to Walter Hallanan, Dec. 27, 1952, Taft Papers.

worked unstintingly for the White House program among the congressional Republicans who held him in such high esteem.[5] In return, the senator enjoyed strong influence within the administration, where he was carefully and courteously treated and regularly consulted on policy formulation.[6]

Because Taft was far from conservative on many domestic issues,[7] highly influential in White House councils, and effective as a leader of the party controlling the Eighty-third Congress, his continued presence in the Senate might well have alleviated many of the administration's difficulties in 1953–1954. In particular the Ohioan's influence might have brought Eisenhower greater success in legislation affecting housing, health insurance, and labor policy, all of which proved to be disappointments to the White House in those years. On the other hand, Taft was less than enamored of the foreign aid program, so that the President might have encountered greater difficulty than he did in that major area in 1954. All things considered, however, the Eisenhower-Taft relationship of 1953 held great promise, and the Senator's death in the summer of that year undoubtedly worked a hardship on the new administration.

Taft's successor as Senate majority leader, William Knowland of California, was a man of very different stripe. Hand-picked for the succession by Taft, who viewed him as "safely Republican and adequately partisan in the traditional way," Knowland was generally more conservative than his predecessor on domestic questions and more closely identified with the so-called "Asia-firsters" on foreign policy issues.[8] According to a number of

[5] Richard H. Rovere, "Robert A. Taft, Majority Leader," first published Mar. 22, 1953, in *Affairs of State: The Eisenhower Years*, 110; also Jewell, *Senatorial Politics and Foreign Policy*, 59. According to his former colleague, John Bricker, Taft regarded his service as majority leader as the crowning achievement of his career (Bricker interview, Feb. 2, 1971, Columbus, Ohio). See also Patterson, *Mr. Republican*, 598.

[6] Jewell, *Senatorial Politics and Foreign Policy*, 60; Adams, *Firsthand Report*, 24; Patterson, *Mr. Republican*, 592–93.

[7] See Ch. 2, above; also Patterson, *Mr. Republican*, 329–34.

[8] White, *The Taft Story*. 253. See also Saltonstall Oral History Transcript, Eisenhower Project, Eisenhower Library, 13.

sources, Knowland was neither an effective spokesman for administration policy nor a strong party leader. "Bill Knowland didn't talk to anybody," one Republican senator reportedly said. "We never had any communication with Bill."[9] Knowland supported Eisenhower on 87 percent of the "Eisenhower issue" roll calls in the Eighty-third Congress, but he was not instrumental in the success of any single administration bill, with the possible exception of the atomic energy bill, where his power tactics brought success but also alienated numerous senators on both sides of the aisle. The administration often had to depend on Republicans other than Knowland for genuine advocacy and leadership in the Senate on important matters.

In the House, the most important Republican leaders were Speaker Martin, Floor Leader Halleck, and to a lesser extent Whip Leslie Arends. Martin, who as Speaker did not vote on issues before the House and usually took no part in floor maneuvers, generally supported the administration program. Along with Representatives Halleck and John Taber, he was regarded by Eisenhower as a loyal political ally.[10] On at least two occasions the Speaker even stepped down to deliver floor speeches in support of the administration (the 1953 foreign aid bill and 1954 farm bill), but he seems to have been motivated in general by a "lesser evil" attitude. Martin later wrote that he frequently stressed to party colleagues that support for Eisenhower's program represented "the best chance for the conservative cause" and that its defeat might well lead "the people [to] insist on moving to something more extreme."[11] While one outside observer has remarked on Martin's "great qualities of leadership" and reliability, Eisenhower's chief White House assistant sus-

---

9 Unnamed source, quoted in Randall B. Ripley, *Power in the Senate* (New York: St. Martin's Press, 1969), 96. See also William S. White, "The Fight for the Senate," *Harper's Magazine* 209, No. 1251 (Aug. 1954), 24; Adams, *Firsthand Report*, 25–26; James MacGregor Burns, *The Deadlock of Democracy: Four-Party Politics in America* (Englewood Cliffs, N.J.: Prentice-Hall, 1963), 192.

10 Eisenhower, *Mandate for Change*, 195.

11 Martin, *My First Fifty Years in Politics*, 232.

pected the Speaker's loyalties, labeling his approach "uninspired and lackadaisical."[12] Overall, Martin probably helped the administration more than he hindered it, but he could hardly be counted as the President's foremost House spokesman.

The most important Republican leader in the lower house was Charles Halleck, who came closer than anyone else to filling Taft's shoes after mid-1953. "Charlie Halleck explains to the President how members of both houses will react to a specific issue," remarked a White House aide at the time. "Before Mr. Eisenhower decides to push for a bill, he talks to Halleck about ways and means. Similarly, when Halleck says he can get a bill through, the President tells White House worriers: 'Charlie's guaranteed it.' "[13] The floor leader's credentials as an administration loyalist were nearly impeccable. He took a leading part in the floor fight on virtually every major piece of administration-sponsored legislation to come before the House in 1953–1954 and registered an overall support score of .92; in no issue area did he score below .86 in support of the President's position. Halleck's sterling record of support reflected his conception of the floor leader's role. "I do all my arguing in the huddles," he said in 1954, "but when the signals are called, the argument stops. My only idea then is to get the ball over the line. If I didn't feel that way about it, I shouldn't be leader."[14] Some House Republicans evidently resented Halleck's tendency to claim too much credit for administration victories. At one point in mid-1954, Eisenhower loyalist Hugh Scott specifically notified the White House that he and a number of other Republican representatives had supported Eisenhower's side on a particular roll call "because they wanted to show the country that they [were] in back of the President's program," and "not . . . because of Congress-

12 William H. Lawrence Oral History Transcript, Eisenhower Project, Eisenhower Library, 35; Adams, *Firsthand Report*, 26.

13 Unnamed source, in "These Are the Men Ike Listens To," *Newsweek* 43, No. 24 (June 14, 1954), 27.

14 Scheele, *Charlie Halleck*, 154; also Halleck Oral History Transcript, Eisenhower Project, Eisenhower Library, 22.

man Halleck." [15] On the whole, however, the floor leader's work in the Eighty-third Congress merited the kind of praise which Eisenhower frequently accorded to him.[16]

In addition to the Republican party hierarchy in the two houses, the administration could usually count on receiving help from the committee chairmen most directly involved in the various major pieces of legislation. On occasion the chairman presented some problem to the White House, as in the case of Daniel Reed of the House Ways and Means Committee on 1953 tax legislation, Clifford Hope (House Agriculture) on the 1954 farm bill, Jesse Wolcott (House Banking and Currency) on public housing, and Representative Sterling Cole and Senator Bourke Hickenlooper (Joint Committee on Atomic Energy) on the 1954 atomic energy bill. But on the whole, Republican committee heads cooperated with the White House. Because they achieved their positions as a result of seniority, these men often possessed considerable prestige outside their own committees and were therefore valuable allies.

The support scores of chairmen in both houses were strikingly high. Among major committee chairmen in the two houses, only Daniel Reed fell below the minimum "pro-Eisenhower" score of .60, with a score of .58. In the Senate, nearly all chairmen of important committees scored over .80: Policy chairman Homer Ferguson had a score of .83, Eugene Millikin (Finance) .87, Styles Bridges (Appropriations) .84, H. Alexander Smith (Labor and Welfare) .92, and George Aiken (Agriculture) .80. Only chairmen Alexander Wiley of Foreign Relations (.68) and Homer Capehart of Banking and Currency (.65) fell below the .80 cutoff, thereby ranking as only moderately pro-Eisenhower. In the House, fewer committee chairmen could be counted on with such regularity, though all but Reed ranked as pro-Eisenhower. Those

15 Memorandum, Charles F. Willis to Sherman Adams, July 29, 1954, in OF 99, Eisenhower Papers.

16 See, for example, Eisenhower's foreword in Scheele, *Charlie Halleck*, 1, and Eisenhower to Halleck, Aug. 8, 1953, OF 99, Eisenhower Papers.

who scored at least .80 in support of the President were Leo Allen (Rules) .88, Robert Chiperfield (Foreign Affairs) .80, Clifford Hope (Agriculture) .87, Samuel McConnell ( Education and Labor) .82, and Charles Wolverton (Interstate and Foreign Commerce) .88. Moderately pro-Eisenhower chairmen included George Dondero (Public Works) .69, John Taber (Appropriations) .75, and Jesse Wolcott (Banking and Currency) .77.

In part, of course, the strong loyalty of influential party members in the two houses reflected the President's willingness to compromise and the leaders' own particular sense of responsibility for getting favorable congressional action on the administration program. But probably just as important was President Eisenhower's oft-remarked propensity to work through "regular" party channels in Congress.[17] Because of his chain-of-command approach, the President worked especially closely with the older, more senior Republicans in the two houses. Some observers have concluded that this tendency led to White House neglect, and eventually alienation, of younger, rank-and-file Republican representatives and senators who would otherwise have been strong Eisenhower supporters.[18] Indeed, some did feel neglected. "If there is any liaison between the White House and the rank and file of the Members of the House," Representative T. Millet Hand of New Jersey wrote to Sherman Adams in early 1954, "I am not aware of it." Hand went on to say that the White House should try to reach "not only . . . the leadership of the Congress, but . . . all of the Republican members . . . ."[19]

Yet this feeling of neglect did not affect the voting of junior

[17] See Hughes, *Ordeal of Power*, 126; Joyner, *The Republican Dilemma*, 82; and Randall B. Ripley, *Majority Party Leadership in Congress* (Boston: Little, Brown, 1969), 122.

[18] See Joyner, *The Republican Dilemma*, 82; and Campbell et al., *The Voter Decides*, 324.

[19] Hand to Adams, Jan. 20, 1954, OF 99, Eisenhower Papers; see also similar criticisms by Rep. John Heselton, in a letter to Adams dated July 16, 1953, in OF 99, Eisenhower Papers, and by Rep. Clarence Brown, as noted in I. Jack Martin's memorandum of a Nov. 1953 meeting between Brown and the President (memorandum in possession of Mrs. I. Jack Martin, Kensington, Md.).

congressional Republicans. The freshman and postwar groups, which together included relatively few with leadership positions and so can be equated with "rank and file," were composed of strong administration supporters in roughly the same proportion as all Republican legislators collectively: 44 percent of these groups in the Senate and 48 percent in the House had scores of .80 or higher. In both houses, however, freshmen scored higher than those from the postwar period: 70 percent of the Senate freshmen and 59 percent of the House freshmen were strongly pro-Eisenhower. Notwithstanding the President's methods and preferences, then, Republican support for his programs in the Eighty-third Congress was not linked closely with seniority (see Table 17).

The Eisenhower administration has also been criticized for virtually cutting adrift liberal Republicans, many of whom had been among the President's earliest boosters for the nomination in 1952.[20] Some "Eisenhower men" and party liberals did experience frustration. For example, Senator Irving Ives, who helped advise Eisenhower on labor policy during the 1952 campaign, wrote in December 1953 that Republican liberals had "received little or no encouragement from the White House . . . . Thus far, perhaps unfortunately, there has been too great a tendency to appease and placate the reactionaries and isolationists in our party."[21] Jacob Javits, one of the twenty Republican congressmen who wrote to Eisenhower urging his candidacy in early 1952, later echoed Ives's complaint, though the passage of time evidently caused him to accept the situation more philosophically. According to Javits, liberal Republicans "were pretty much headed off by Sherman Adams at the door. But then . . . he headed off most everybody." Javits added that he did not "think that the liberals had any right to have any illusions about their reception at the White House. The President had given them no particular

20 See Childs, *Eisenhower: Captive Hero*, 227; White, *The Taft Story*, 226.
21 Ives to Mrs. G. B. Williams of the Geneva *Daily Times*, Dec. 11, 1953, Ives Papers.

*Table 17* "Eisenhower Support" by Republicans in the Eighty-Third Congress, all Issue Areas, by Period of Entry*

| | Percent at Each Level of Support† | | | | |
|---|---|---|---|---|---|
| Period of Entry | .80–1.00 | .60–.79 | .40–.59 | .20–.39 | .00–.19 |
| | SENATE | | | | |
| New Deal (7) | [43%] | [57%] | [0%] | [0%] | [0%] |
| World War II (12) | 67 | 17 | 0 | 17 | 0 |
| Postwar (17) | 29 | 53 | 12 | 6 | 0 |
| Freshmen (10) | 70 | 30 | 0 | 0 | 0 |
| TOTAL (46)‡ | 50 | 39 | 4 | 7 | 0 |
| | HOUSE | | | | |
| Pre–New Deal (13) | [38%] | [46%] | [15%] | [0%] | [0%] |
| New Deal (32) | 38 | 47 | 13 | 3 | 0 |
| World War II (46) | 35 | 54 | 9 | 2 | 0 |
| Postwar (77) | 42 | 56 | 3 | 0 | 0 |
| Freshmen (51) | 59 | 39 | 2 | 0 | 0 |
| TOTAL (219)** | 43 | 50 | 6 | 1 | 0 |

*Figures given are percentages of the total Republican membership in each category, exclusive of those with incomplete records. In parentheses are the numbers included in each period-group.

† Percentages are summed across rows.

‡ Does not include Sens. Bowring, Hugh Butler, Crippa, Griswold, Reynolds, Taft, and Tobey, whose records were incomplete (fewer than 41 responses in all areas combined).

** Does not include Speaker Martin.

reason for thinking that he would be particularly congenial to them."[22]

As in the case of rank-and-file Republicans, original "Eisenhower men" did not avenge the President's lack of special attention to them by turning against his program. Aside from a few glaring exceptions, they gave Eisenhower strong support. Of the fourteen returning Republican House members who had signed

[22] Javits Oral History Transcript, Eisenhower Project, Eisenhower Library, 8. See also Rep. Winston Prouty's advice to Adams to give "a little encouragement and recognition" to "the 'before Chicago' [pre-nomination] Eisenhower members in the House" (Prouty to Adams, Jan. 19, 1954, in CF 3–A, Eisenhower Papers).

the February 1952 letter urging Eisenhower's candidacy, only one had a support score in the Eighty-third Congress below .79 (Javits, with .65); ten scored .90 or higher. Of seven senators in the Eighty-third Congress who had favored Eisenhower before the 1952 convention,[23] four (Carlson, Duff, Flanders, and Saltonstall) scored .80 or higher in support of the President's 1953–1954 program, two (Cooper and Thye) scored between .60 and .79, and only one (Morse, who became disillusioned with Eisenhower during the course of the 1952 campaign) ranked as moderately anti-Eisenhower, with a score of .31.

Those on the Republican liberal wing (disregarding the matter of early support for Eisenhower's candidacy) were not quite so enthusiastic. Of fifteen Republican House members who scaled as liberal on at least one of the three domestic issue areas during the Eighty-second Congress and had no conservative ratings, only five (33 percent) scored as strongly pro-Eisenhower, seven (47 percent) as moderately pro-Eisenhower, and three (20 percent) as "waverers." These figures compare unfavorably with those for all House Republicans: 43, 50, and 6 percent, respectively.[24] In the Senate, the sample was smaller and the findings less conclusive. Of the four Republican senators qualifying as "liberals" on the basis of the criteria listed above, two ranked as administration supporters (Duff with .91 and Aiken with .80) and two as opponents (Langer and Morse) in the Eighty-third Congress.[25] As Ives and Javits pointed out, moreover, liberal Republicans did not enjoy especially open access to the Eisenhower White House. From a compilation of lists submitted by various White House and departmental officials in late 1953,

---

[23] See David et al., *Presidential Nominating Politics in 1952* (5 vols.), *passim.*

[24] If another criterion for "liberalism" is used, the results are only slightly different, though somewhat more favorable to the President. Eleven House members scaled as "strong liberals" in at least two of the three domestic issue areas. Of that total, five (45 percent) ranked as strongly pro-Eisenhower, four (36 percent) as moderately pro-Eisenhower, one (9 percent) as a waverer, and one (9 percent) as moderately anti-Eisenhower.

[25] Using the criterion described in the preceding note, three GOP senators could be called liberals—Aiken, Ives, and Morse. Ives (.83) and Aiken (.80) ranked as pro-Eisenhower, while Morse, at .31, was an "anti."

naming Republican congressmen and senators well known to them, it is possible to measure roughly the degree of contact (or at least the potential for it) between individual Republicans and the administration. On the basis of these lists, only six of the liberal Republicans in the House (Gordon Canfield, Robert Corbett, Hal Holmes, Javits, Leroy Johnson, and John Saylor) had more than the average number of "contacts" in the executive branch; of the liberal Republican senators, only Duff exceeded the average.[26]

On the basis of the roll-call behavior of the original "Eisenhower Republicans" and Republican liberals in Congress, two conclusions emerge. First, the President's failure to give special treatment to those in the party who had been for him "before Chicago" (that is, before the 1952 nomination) did not necessarily cause them to turn against his program in 1953–1954. On the other hand, Republican members of the Eighty-third Congress with the most liberal records prior to 1953 were somewhat less likely to be strong backers of the administration program than Republican legislators generally. This suggests that, despite Eisenhower's having been labeled a "liberal" Republican in 1952, his domestic policies in 1953–1954 were not especially liberal.

Republican party support for the Eisenhower program in the Eighty-third Congress reveals a few interesting patterns which uphold the conventional wisdom regarding "Eisenhower Republicanism." The so-called "Eastern establishment," for example, did form a nucleus of strong support for the President within the party. In the House, forty-four of the ninety-five Republicans (46 percent) who scored at least .80 on the "Eisenhower" roll calls came from the New England or Mid-Atlantic

[26] In the House, the average number of contacts with individuals in the executive branch was 2.4, while the Senate average was 4.0. Lists were submitted in response to a request from the President's congressional liaison staff. Those from White House aides Harlow, Jack Martin, Robert Cutler, Gabriel Hauge, Bernard Shanley, Murray Snyder, and Charles Willis, the Foreign Operations Administration, and the Departments of State, Treasury, Interior, and Health, Education and Welfare may be found in Box 1, A67–19 Accessions, Morgan Records, and Box 4, Homer Gruenther Records, Eisenhower Papers.

states, even though representatives from those two regions accounted for only 36 percent of the total Republican House membership. In the upper house, thirteen of twenty-three (57 percent) strongly pro-Eisenhower Republican senators came from the Northeast, though only seventeen of the forty-six (37 percent) who were scored for the Eighty-third Congress represented that section. In both houses, conversely, Republicans from the Midwest (North Central and Plains) were the least likely to support the Eisenhower program.

Furthermore, the "Eisenhower wing" of the party possessed a strongly urban and suburban flavor. In the House, degree of urbanization in the districts of Republican members related directly to the strength of their support for the Eisenhower programs. Sixty-three percent of Republican congressmen from metropolitan districts (forty of sixty-four) ranked as strong administration supporters. Corresponding figures for Republicans from the other types of districts were: mid-urban, 47 percent (twenty-eight of sixty); small-town, 33 percent (twenty-one of sixy-four); and rural, 17 percent (five of thirty). It is, of course, difficult to establish a causal connection between constituency type and a congressman's roll-call behavior, but the strength of the relationship indicates that Republican representatives with urban or suburban backgrounds tended to feel personally, or at least to perceive among their constituents, an identification with the President's programs.

Quantitative analysis of the response of the Republican Eighty-third Congress shows that President Eisenhower commanded a good deal of support in his party. It also demonstrates that while the same individuals did not lend the strongest support from one issue area to the next, nevertheless there were identifiable "types" upon whom the President could rely with particular confidence. Among these types were party leaders, Easterners, and freshmen in both chambers, and House members representing urban districts. These relationships existed only in an aggregate sense; both the truth of the generalizations and the exceptions to them are readily apparent in Table 18, which gives the overall support

*Table 18* "Eisenhower Support" Scores of Individual Republicans in the Eighty-Third Congress, all Issue Areas Combined

| | SENATE | | |
|---|---|---|---|
| Member* | Overall Support Score† | Region | Period of Entry |
| H. A. Smith, N.J. | .92 | Mid-Atlantic | WW II |
| Upton, N.H. | .92 | New England | Freshman |
| Duff, Pa. | .91 | Mid-Atlantic | Postwar |
| Bush, Conn. | .90 | New England | Freshman |
| Payne, Maine | .90 | New England | Freshman |
| Flanders, Vt. | .88 | New England | Postwar |
| Carlson, Kans. | .87 | Plains | New Deal |
| Knowland, Calif. | .87 | West | WW II |
| Millikin, Colo. | .87 | West | WW II |
| Saltonstall, Mass. | .87 | New England | WW II |
| Hendrickson, N.J. | .86 | Mid-Atlantic | Postwar |
| Kuchel, Calif. | .86 | West | Freshman |
| Purtell, Conn. | .86 | New England | Freshman |
| Beall, Md. | .85 | Mid-Atlantic | Freshman |
| Cordon, Ore. | .85 | West | WW II |
| Bridges, N.H. | .84 | New England | New Deal |
| Bennett, Utah | .83 | West | Postwar |
| Ferguson, Mich. | .83 | North Central | WW II |
| Ives, N.Y. | .83 | Mid-Atlantic | Postwar |
| Dirksen, Ill. | .82 | North Central | New Deal |
| Aiken, Vt. | .80 | New England | WW II |
| Hickenlooper, Iowa | .80 | Plains | WW II |
| Potter, Mich. | .80 | North Central | Freshman |
| Barrett, Wyo. | .79 | West | Freshman |
| M. Smith, Maine | .79 | New England | WW II |
| Watkins, Utah | .77 | West | Postwar |
| J. Butler, Md. | .76 | Mid-Atlantic | Postwar |
| Martin, Pa. | .75 | Mid-Atlantic | Postwar |
| Schoeppel, Kans. | .74 | Plains | Postwar |
| Cooper, Ky. | .73 | Border | Freshman |
| Thye, Minn. | .73 | North Central | Postwar |
| Goldwater, Ariz. | .71 | West | Freshman |
| Jenner, Ind. | .69 | North Central | Postwar |
| Wiley, Wis. | .68 | North Central | New Deal |
| Case, S.Dak. | .66 | Plains | New Deal |
| Capehart, Ind. | .65 | North Central | WW II |
| Bricker, Ohio | .64 | North Central | Postwar |
| Dworshak, Idaho | .64 | West | New Deal |
| Welker, Idaho | .64 | West | Postwar |

*Table 18* (CONTINUED)

SENATE (*Cont.*)

| Member | Overall Support Score | Region | Period of Entry |
|---|---|---|---|
| Williams, Del. | .63 | Mid-Atlantic | Postwar |
| Mundt, S.Dak. | .61 | Plains | New Deal |
| Malone, Nev. | .53 | West | Postwar |
| McCarthy, Wis. | .52 | North Central | Postwar |
| Young, N.Dak. | .35 | Plains | WW II |
| Morse, Ore. | .31 | West | Postwar |
| Langer, N.Dak. | .23 | Plains | WW II |

HOUSE

| Member | Overall Support Score | Region | Period of Entry | District Type |
|---|---|---|---|---|
| Mailliard, Calif. | .98 | West | Freshman | Metro. |
| Kersten, Wis. | .95 | No. Cen. | Postwar | Metro. |
| Ayres, Ohio | .94 | No. Cen. | Postwar | Metro. |
| Holmes, Wash. | .94 | West | WW II | Small-town |
| Wainwright, N.Y. | .94 | Mid-Atl. | Freshman | Rural |
| F. Bolton, Ohio | .92 | No. Cen. | WW II | Metro. |
| Frelinghuysen, N.J. | .92 | Mid-Atl. | Freshman | Metro. |
| Halleck, Ind. | .92 | No. Cen. | New Deal | Small-town |
| Judd, Minn. | .92 | No. Cen. | WW II | Metro. |
| Tollefson, Wash. | .92 | West | Postwar | Mid-urban |
| Widnall, N.J. | .92 | Mid-Atl. | Postwar | Small-town |
| Merrow, N.H. | .91 | New Eng. | WW II | Mid-urban |
| Patterson, Conn. | .91 | New Eng. | Postwar | Mid-urban |
| J. Allen, Calif. | .90 | West | Postwar | Metro. |
| Auchincloss, N.J. | .90 | Mid-Atl. | WW II | Small-town |
| Holt, Calif. | .90 | West | Freshman | Metro. |
| Oakman, Mich. | .90 | No. Cen. | Freshman | Metro. |
| Springer, Ill. | .90 | No. Cen. | Postwar | Mid-urban |
| Bender, Ohio | .89 | No. Cen. | New Deal | — |
| Gubser, Calif. | .89 | West | Freshman | Mid-urban |
| Jackson, Calif. | .89 | West | Postwar | Metro. |
| Johnson, Calif. | .89 | West | WW II | Mid-urban |
| Scott, Pa. | .89 | Mid-Atl. | WW II | Metro. |
| L. Allen, Ill. | .88 | No. Cen. | New Deal | Mid-urban |
| Arends, Ill. | .88 | No. Cen. | New Deal | Small-town |
| O. Bolton, Ohio | .88 | No. Cen. | Freshman | Small-town |
| L. Curtis, Mass. | .88 | New Eng. | Freshman | Metro. |

*Table 18* (CONTINUED)

| | | HOUSE (*Cont.*) | | |
|---|---|---|---|---|
| Member | Overall Support Score | Region | Period of Entry | District Type |
| Ford, Mich. | .88 | No. Cen. | Postwar | Mid-urban |
| Harden, Ind. | .88 | No. Cen. | Postwar | Small-town |
| Kean, N.J. | .88 | Mid-Atl. | New Deal | Metro. |
| Merrill, Ind. | .88 | No. Cen. | Freshman | Mid-urban |
| Rogers, Mass. | .88 | New Eng. | Pre-N.D. | Mid-urban |
| Sadlak, Conn. | .88 | New Eng. | Postwar | Mid-urban |
| Seely-Brown, Conn. | .88 | New Eng. | Postwar | Small-town |
| Wigglesworth, Mass. | .88 | New Eng. | Pre-N.D. | Metro. |
| Wolverton, N.J. | .88 | Mid-Atl. | Pre-N.D. | Metro. |
| Cretella, Conn. | .87 | New Eng. | Freshman | Mid-urban |
| Hope, Kans. | .87 | Plains | Pre-N.D. | Small-town |
| Morano, Conn. | .87 | New Eng. | Postwar | Mid-urban |
| Riehlman, N.Y. | .87 | Mid-Atl. | Postwar | Metro. |
| Warburton, Del. | .87 | Mid-Atl. | Freshman | Mid-urban |
| Westland, Wash. | .87 | West | Freshman | Mid-urban |
| Gamble, N.Y. | .86 | Mid-Atl. | New Deal | Metro. |
| Goodwin, Mass. | .86 | New Eng. | WW II | Metro. |
| Hillings, Calif. | .86 | West | Postwar | Metro. |
| Hinshaw, Calif. | .86 | West | New Deal | Metro. |
| Hosmer, Calif. | .86 | West | Freshman | Metro. |
| Ostertag, N.Y. | .86 | Mid-Atl. | Postwar | Metro. |
| St. George, N.Y. | .86 | Mid-Atl. | Postwar | Small-town |
| Vorys, Ohio | .86 | No. Cen. | New Deal | Metro. |
| R. Wilson, Calif. | .86 | West | Freshman | Metro. |
| Younger, Calif. | .86 | West | Freshman | Metro. |
| Pelly, Wash. | .85 | West | Freshman | Metro. |
| Broyhill, Va. | .84 | Border | Freshman | Metro. |
| Derounian, N.Y. | .84 | Mid-Atl. | Freshman | Metro. |
| LeCompte, Iowa | .84 | Plains | New Deal | Small-town |
| Lipscomb, Calif. | .84 | West | Freshman | Metro. |
| Ray, N.Y. | .84 | Mid-Atl. | Freshman | Metro. |
| Rhodes, Ariz. | .84 | West | Freshman | Mid-urban |
| Scudder, Calif. | .84 | West | Postwar | Rural |
| Young, Nev. | .84 | West | Freshman | Small-town |
| Carrigg, Pa. | .83 | Mid-Atl. | Postwar | Mid-urban |
| Cunningham, Iowa | .83 | Plains | WW II | Mid-urban |
| Hill, Colo. | .83 | West | WW II | Rural |
| Horan, Wash. | .83 | West | WW II | Mid-urban |
| Hyde, Md. | .83 | Mid-Atl. | Freshman | Small-town |
| Kearney, N.Y. | .83 | Mid-Atl. | WW II | Mid-urban |
| Osmers, N.J. | .83 | Mid-Atl. | New Deal | Metro. |

*Table 18* (CONTINUED)

| | | HOUSE (*Cont.*) | | |
|---|---|---|---|---|
| Member | Overall Support Score | Region | Period of Entry | District Type |
| Prouty, Vt. | .83 | New Eng. | Postwar | Rural |
| Robsion, Ky. | .83 | Border | Freshman | Metro. |
| Bates, Mass. | .82 | New Eng. | Postwar | Mid-urban |
| Becker, N.Y. | .82 | Mid-Atl. | Freshman | Metro. |
| Brownson, Ind. | .82 | No. Cen. | Postwar | Metro. |
| T. Curtis, Mo. | .82 | Border | Postwar | Metro. |
| Devereux, Md. | .82 | Mid-Atl. | Postwar | Small-town |
| Dorn, N.Y. | .82 | Mid-Atl. | Freshman | Metro. |
| Heselton, Mass. | .82 | New Eng. | WW II | Mid-urban |
| McConnell, Pa. | .82 | Mid-Atl. | WW II | Small-town |
| W. Miller, N.Y. | .82 | Mid-Atl. | Postwar | Metro. |
| Radwan, N.Y. | .82 | Mid-Atl. | Postwar | Metro. |
| Saylor, Pa. | .82 | Mid-Atl. | Postwar | Small-town |
| Kearns, Pa. | .81 | Mid-Atl. | Postwar | Mid-urban |
| McDonough, Calif. | .81 | West | WW II | Metro. |
| Stringfellow, Utah | .81 | West | Freshman | Small-town |
| Baker, Tenn. | .80 | Border | Postwar | Small-town |
| Bonin, Pa. | .80 | Mid-Atl. | Freshman | Mid-urban |
| Chiperfield, Ill. | .80 | No. Cen. | New Deal | Small-town |
| Dague, Pa. | .80 | Mid-Atl. | Postwar | Small-town |
| Hale, Maine | .80 | New Eng. | WW II | Mid-urban |
| Hess, Ohio | .80 | No. Cen. | Pre-N.D. | Metro. |
| C. Jonas, N.C. | .80 | Border | Freshman | Mid-urban |
| Meader, Mich. | .80 | No. Cen. | Postwar | Mid-urban |
| Norblad, Ore. | .80 | West | Postwar | Small-town |
| R. Simpson, Pa. | .80 | Mid-Atl. | New Deal | Rural |
| Stauffer, Pa. | .80 | Mid-Atl. | Freshman | Mid-urban |
| Case, N.J. | .79 | Mid-Atl. | WW II | Metro. |
| W. S. Cole, N.Y. | .79 | Mid-Atl. | New Deal | Mid-urban |
| Cotton, N.H. | .79 | New Eng. | Postwar | Small-town |
| Vursell, Ill. | .79 | No. Cen. | WW II | Rural |
| Angell, Ore. | .78 | West | New Deal | Metro. |
| Bramblett, Calif. | .78 | West | Postwar | Small-town |
| Canfield, N.J. | .78 | Mid-Atl. | WW II | Metro. |
| Chenoweth, Colo. | .78 | West | WW II | Mid-urban |
| Corbett, Pa. | .78 | Mid-Atl. | New Deal | Metro. |
| Dawson, Utah | .78 | West | Freshman | Mid-urban |
| Fenton, Pa. | .78 | Mid-Atl. | New Deal | Small-town |
| Fulton, Pa. | .78 | Mid-Atl. | WW II | Metro. |
| Hiestand, Calif. | .78 | West | Freshman | Metro. |
| Keating, N.Y. | .78 | Mid-Atl. | Postwar | Metro. |

*Table 18* (CONTINUED)

| | Overall Support Score | Region | Period of Entry | District Type |
|---|---|---|---|---|
| HOUSE (*Cont.*) | | | | |
| Member | | | | |
| Schenck, Ohio | .78 | No. Cen. | Postwar | Metro. |
| Bosch, N.Y. | .77 | Mid-Atl. | Freshman | Metro. |
| Coudert, N.Y. | .77 | Mid-Atl. | Postwar | Metro. |
| Ellsworth, Ore. | .77 | West | WW II | Small-town |
| Graham, Pa. | .77 | Mid-Atl. | New Deal | Small-town |
| James, Pa. | .77 | Mid-Atl. | Postwar | Metro. |
| Latham, N.Y. | .77 | Mid-Atl. | WW II | Metro. |
| Mumma, Pa. | .77 | Mid-Atl. | Postwar | Mid-urban |
| Small, Md. | .77 | Mid-Atl. | Freshman | Small-town |
| Williams, N.Y. | .77 | Mid-Atl. | Postwar | Mid-urban |
| Wolcott, Mich. | .77 | No. Cen. | Pre-N.D. | Small-town |
| Byrnes, Wis. | .76 | No. Cen. | WW II | Mid-urban |
| Crumpacker, Ind. | .76 | No. Cen. | Postwar | Mid-urban |
| George, Kans. | .76 | Plains | Postwar | Small-town |
| Hillelson, Mo. | .76 | Border | Freshman | Mid-urban |
| Hruska, Neb. | .76 | Plains | Freshman | Metro. |
| Kilburn, N.Y. | .76 | Mid-Atl. | WW II | Small-town |
| Taylor, N.Y. | .76 | Mid-Atl. | WW II | Small-town |
| Wampler, Va. | .76 | Border | Freshman | Rural |
| Gwinn, N.Y. | .75 | Mid-Atl. | WW II | Metro. |
| Hunter, Calif. | .75 | West | Postwar | Mid-urban |
| Taber, N.Y. | .75 | Mid-Atl. | Pre-N.D. | Small-town |
| E. Wilson, Ind. | .75 | No. Cen. | WW II | Rural |
| Bentley, Mich. | .74 | No. Cen. | Freshman | Small-town |
| Harvey, Ind. | .74 | No. Cen. | Postwar | Mid-urban |
| Pillion, N.Y. | .74 | Mid-Atl. | Freshman | Metro. |
| Reece, Tenn. | .74 | Border | Pre-N.D. | Rural |
| D'Ewart, Mont. | .73 | West | WW II | Small-town |
| R. Hoffman, Ill. | .73 | No. Cen. | Postwar | Metro. |
| E. Jonas, Ill. | .73 | No. Cen. | Postwar | Metro. |
| Knox, Mich. | .73 | No. Cen. | Freshman | Rural |
| Mack, Wash. | .73 | West | Postwar | Small-town |
| T. Martin, Iowa | .73 | Plains | New Deal | Mid-urban |
| A. L. Miller, Neb. | .73 | Plains | WW II | Rural |
| Scherer, Ohio | .73 | No. Cen. | Freshman | Metro. |
| Belcher, Okla. | .72 | Border | Postwar | Mid-urban |
| R. Harrison, Neb. | .72 | Plains | Postwar | Rural |
| Sheehan, Ill. | .72 | No. Cen. | Postwar | Metro. |
| Weichel, Ohio | .72 | No. Cen. | WW II | Mid-urban |
| Betts, Ohio | .71 | No. Cen. | Postwar | Small-town |
| Cederberg, Mich. | .71 | No. Cen. | Freshman | Small-town |

*Table 18* (CONTINUED)

| | | HOUSE (*Cont.*) | | |
|---|---|---|---|---|
| *Member* | *Overall Support Score* | *Region* | *Period of Entry* | *District Type* |
| C. Curtis, Neb. | .71 | Plains | New Deal | Metro. |
| Fino, N.Y. | .71 | Mid-Atl. | Freshman | Metro. |
| Krueger, N.D. | .71 | Plains | Freshman | Rural |
| E. T. Miller, Md. | .71 | Mid-Atl. | Postwar | Rural |
| Poff, Va. | .71 | Border | Freshman | Mid-urban |
| Talle, Iowa | .71 | Plains | New Deal | Small-town |
| Van Zandt, Pa. | .71 | Mid-Atl. | New Deal | Mid-urban |
| Bush, Pa. | .70 | Mid-Atl. | Postwar | Small-town |
| Jenkins, Ohio | .70 | No. Cen. | Pre-N.D. | Rural |
| Jensen, Iowa | .70 | Plains | New Deal | Small-town |
| Laird, Wis. | .70 | No. Cen. | Freshman | Small-town |
| Beamer, Ind. | .69 | No. Cen. | Postwar | Small-town |
| Davis, Wis. | .69 | No. Cen. | Postwar | Mid-urban |
| Dondero, Mich. | .69 | No. Cen. | New Deal | Mid-urban |
| Golden, Ky. | .69 | Border | Postwar | Rural |
| McCulloch, Ohio | .69 | No. Cen. | Postwar | Small-town |
| Wharton, N.Y. | .69 | Mid-Atl. | Postwar | Small-town |
| Bray, Ind. | .68 | No. Cen. | Postwar | Small-town |
| Coon, Ore. | .68 | West | Freshman | Rural |
| Lovre, S. Dak. | .68 | Plains | Postwar | Rural |
| McVey, Ill. | .68 | No. Cen. | Postwar | Metro. |
| O'Hara, Minn. | .68 | No. Cen. | WW II | Rural |
| Thompson, Mich. | .68 | No. Cen. | Postwar | Small-town |
| Velde, Ill. | .68 | No. Cen. | Postwar | Mid-urban |
| Adair, Ind. | .67 | No. Cen. | Postwar | Mid-urban |
| Church, Ill. | .67 | No. Cen. | Postwar | Mid-urban |
| Hand, N.J. | .67 | Mid-Atl. | WW II | Mid-urban |
| Nicholson, Mass. | .67 | New Eng. | Postwar | Mid-urban |
| Rees, Kans. | .67 | Plains | New Deal | Mid-urban |
| Scrivner, Kans. | .67 | Plains | WW II | Mid-urban |
| Van Pelt, Wis. | .67 | No. Cen. | Postwar | Small-town |
| Hoeven, Iowa | .66 | Plains | WW II | Small-town |
| C. Reed, Ill. | .66 | No. Cen. | New Deal | Mid-urban |
| Andresen, Minn. | .65 | No. Cen. | Pre-N.D. | Small-town |
| Bow, Ohio | .65 | No. Cen. | Postwar | Mid-urban |
| C. Brown, Ohio | .65 | No. Cen. | New Deal | Small-town |
| Budge, Idaho | .65 | West | Postwar | Small-town |
| Dolliver, Iowa | .65 | Plains | WW II | Rural |
| Javits, N.Y. | .65 | Mid-Atl. | Postwar | Metro. |
| King, Pa. | .65 | Mid-Atl. | Postwar | Mid-urban |
| McGregor, Ohio | .65 | No. Cen. | WW II | Small-town |

*Table 18* (CONTINUED)

|  | HOUSE (*Cont.*) | | | |
| Member | Overall Support Score | Region | Period of Entry | District Type |
| --- | --- | --- | --- | --- |
| Phillips, Calif. | .65 | West | WW II | Small-town |
| S. Simpson, Ill. | .65 | No. Cen. | WW II | Small-town |
| Berry, S. Dak. | .64 | Plains | Postwar | Small-town |
| Clevenger, Ohio | .64 | No. Cen. | New Deal | Rural |
| W. C. Cole, Mo. | .63 | Border | Freshman | Small-town |
| Gavin, Pa. | .63 | Mid-Atl. | WW II | Rural |
| Hagen, Minn. | .63 | No. Cen. | WW II | Rural |
| Neal, W.Va. | .63 | Border | Freshman | Small-town |
| W. H. Harrison, Wyo. | .62 | West | Postwar | Rural |
| McIntire, Maine | .61 | New Eng. | Postwar | Small-town |
| Nelson, Maine | .61 | New Eng. | Postwar | Small-town |
| Short, Mo. | .61 | Border | Pre-N.D. | Small-town |
| Utt, Calif. | .61 | West | Freshman | Mid-urban |
| D. Reed, N.Y. | .58 | Mid-Atl. | Pre-N.D. | Small-town |
| Withrow, Wis. | .58 | No. Cen. | Pre-N.D. | Small-town |
| L. Smith, Wis. | .57 | No. Cen. | WW II | Mid-urban |
| Clardy, Mich. | .56 | No. Cen. | Freshman | Mid-urban |
| Shafer, Mich. | .55 | No. Cen. | New Deal | Mid-urban |
| Bennett, Mich. | .54 | No. Cen. | WW II | Rural |
| Busbey, Ill. | .53 | No. Cen. | WW II | Metro. |
| Bishop, Ill. | .52 | No. Cen. | WW II | Rural |
| Burdick, N.Dak. | .52 | Plains | New Deal | Rural |
| Andersen, Minn. | .51 | No. Cen. | New Deal | Rural |
| C. Hoffman, Mich. | .51 | No. Cen. | New Deal | Rural |
| W. Smith, Kans. | .44 | Plains | Postwar | Rural |
| Gross, Iowa | .43 | Plains | Postwar | Small-town |
| Mason, Ill. | .39 | No. Cen. | New Deal | Mid-urban |
| O'Konski, Wis. | .33 | No. Cen. | WW II | Small-town |

* The seven Republican senators who responded on fewer than half (43) of the total roll calls, and their support scores were: Bowring (Neb.) .95; Crippa (Wyo.) .91; Taft (Ohio) .78; Reynolds, (Neb.) .77; H. Butler (Neb.) .70; Griswold, (Neb.) .65; and Tobey (N.H.) .29.

† Includes responses on the Bricker amendment, Bohlen nomination, St. Lawrence Seaway, agriculture, and labor, where applicable (in addition to four major issue areas).

scores as well as relevant descriptive information for each Republican member of Congress in 1953–1954 (except those with an insufficient number of responses on the "Eisenhower issue" roll calls).

Roll-call analysis does not by itself verify or disprove hypotheses regarding the ideological nature of Eisenhower's 1953–1954 program or of "Eisenhower Republicans" in the Eighty-third Congress. It is not really possible to divide congressional Republicans of the period into "liberal" or "conservative" camps, since Guttman scale scores are in no sense additive (that is, scores from separate issue areas cannot be added together to produce a single meaningful score). Moreover, the rather subjective method of distinguishing "liberals" attempted above leads to a tentative conclusion that individually they did not respond to the Eisenhower program in the same way. Examination of the nature and extent of party support for the President's policies in particular areas, however, can provide some useful clues about the ideological thrust of the administration program.

On some questions, previous ideological differences among Republicans did affect their relative enthusiasm for administration policies in 1953–1954. In foreign policy, for example, Eisenhower received far greater support from internationalists than from nationalists: well over three-fourths of the internationalist Republicans in the Eighty-third Congress ranked as strong Eisenhower supporters on foreign policy, while hardly any of the nationalists did so (see Table 19). In domestic areas, the results were less clear-cut, although conservatives on power and resource questions were substantially more attracted to the President's policies in that area than were liberals. On fiscal-economic policy, on the other hand, there was virtually no difference between the responses of liberals and conservatives, since nearly all Republicans were strongly pro-Eisenhower on such matters. On welfare questions, an ambiguous picture appeared: in the Senate, conservatives supported Eisenhower in far greater proportions than liberals, while in the House the reverse was true. This ambiguity is but one more indication that adminis-

*Table 19*  IDEOLOGICAL CLASSIFICATIONS OF "STRONGLY PRO-EISENHOWER" REPUBLICANS IN EIGHTY-THIRD CONGRESS, BY ISSUE AREA

| Ideological Position, Eighty-second Congress | Percent of Group Scoring as "Strongly" Pro-Eisenhower, 1953–1954 | |
|---|---|---|
| SENATE | | |
| *Foreign Policy* | | |
| Internationalists | [89%] | (N=9) |
| Nationalists | [ 0%] | (N=20) |
| *Fiscal-Economic* | | |
| Liberals | [11%] | (N=9) |
| Conservatives | [10%] | (N=21) |
| *Welfare* | | |
| Liberals | [38%] | (N=8) |
| Conservatives | [87%] | (N=23) |
| *Power and Resources* | | |
| Liberals | [58%] | (N=12) |
| Conservatives | [94%] | (N=16) |
| HOUSE | | |
| *Foreign Policy* | | |
| Internationalists | [76%] | (N=38) |
| Nationalists | [ 7%] | (N=81) |
| *Fiscal-Economic* | | |
| Liberals | [92%] | (N=38) |
| Conservatives | [95%] | (N=98) |
| *Welfare* | | |
| Liberals | [56%] | (N=34) |
| Conservatives | [ 8%] | (N=91) |
| *Power and Resources* | | |
| Liberals | [45%] | (N=11) |
| Conservatives | [94%] | (N=126) |

tration welfare policies were somewhat hybrid in their specific details and sometimes produced unusual voting coalitions, despite their adherence to basic Republican traditions.

Obviously, Eisenhower's programs cannot be ideologically typed solely on the basis of the way Republicans of various persuasions responded to them. Such analysis, however, clearly reveals the internationalism underlying the administration's foreign policy positions, as well as the conservatism of its power and resource development policies. Moreover, even though results are mixed from area to area, for all three domestic areas combined, conservative Republicans were more likely to be strong Eisenhower supporters (scoring .80 or higher) than liberal Republicans: the average percentage of conservatives who ranked as strongly pro-Eisenhower for each of the domestic policy areas was 64.7, compared with an average of 50 percent of the liberals. Conclusions can only be tentative, but the figures seem to support the thesis that Eisenhower's program appealed greatly to conservative Republicans in the Eighty-third Congress.

## *The End of the Eighty-third: the Elections of 1954*

President Eisenhower did not want to see his Republican Congress go. Far from surreptitiously preferring a Democratic triumph in 1954, as some observers speculated, the President not only appreciated that Republicans had given him good support in 1953–1954, but also believed that governmental accountability to the public could be maintained only if the same party controlled Congress and White House alike.[27] Consequently, the White House played a major role in the 1954 campaign. By his own later reckoning, Eisenhower delivered over forty partisan speeches during September and October, requiring him to travel over 10,000 miles.[28] In late October, the President capped his efforts by delivering a campaign speech over a network of 123 television and 471 radio stations, followed the next day by a

[27] Eisenhower, *Mandate for Change,* 431–33, 436.
[28] *Ibid.,* 436.

1,500-mile whirlwind speaking tour of four states.[29] In addition to Eisenhower's efforts, Vice President Nixon stumped actively for Republican congressional candidates throughout the campaign, and the Congressional Committee of the Citizens for Eisenhower group (first established in 1952) was reactivated to help the party's congressional candidates across the country.[30]

Administration hopes and efforts were not enough, however. On election day, the voters returned Democratic majorities to both houses of Congress. Although Democratic gains were not overwhelming, they were sufficient. The party controlled the new House by 232–203 and the Senate by 48–47 (with Wayne Morse counted an Independent, until he formally switched to the Democratic party in February 1955). Included among Republican losers were three incumbent senators (John Sherman Cooper, Guy Cordon, and Homer Ferguson), three sitting House members trying for Senate seats (Wesley D'Ewart in Montana, William Henry Harrison in Wyoming, and Herbert Warburton in Delaware), and nineteen incumbent representatives: Homer Angell (Oregon Third), C. W. Bishop (Illinois Twenty-fifth), Edward Bonin (Pennsylvania Eleventh), Fred Busbey (Illinois Third), Kit Clardy (Michigan Sixth), William C. Cole (Missouri Sixth), Angier Goodwin (Massachusetts Eighth), Louis Graham (Pennsylvania Twenty-fifth), Harold Hagen (Minnesota Ninth), Jeffrey Hillelson (Missouri Fourth), Allan Oakley Hunter (California Twelfth), Edgar Jones (Illinois Twelfth), Charles Kersten (Wisconsin Fifth), D. Bailey Merrill (Indiana Eighth), Will Neal (West Virginia Fourth), Charles Oakman (Michigan Seventeenth,) Frank Small, Jr. (Maryland Fifth), S. Walter Stauffer (Pennsylvania Nineteenth), and William Wampler (Virginia

29 On the Oct. 28 speech arrangements, see James L. Murphy to Stanley M. Rumbough, Jr., Oct. 25, 1954, OF 138–A–4 (4), Eisenhower Papers; on the speaking tour, see Eisenhower, *Mandate for Change*, 434–37, and Parmet, *Eisenhower and the American Crusades*, 381–82.

30 See Eisenhower's letter of gratitude to Nixon, Oct. 27, 1954, *Public Papers . . . 1954*, 975–76. On the Citizens for Eisenhower activities, see James L. Murphy to Charles F. Willis, Dec. 30, 1953, and Willis to Sherman Adams, Feb. 10, 1954, Box 51, Robert E. Hampton Records, Eisenhower Papers.

Ninth).[31] Republican newcomers did win five House seats and two Senate seats held by Democrats, but of nineteen Republican-held seats which the party singled out for "top priority" attention during the campaign, eight were lost. Republican incumbents also lost in three of the four "top priority" Senate races.[32]

As in most American elections, the reasons for the 1954 results are difficult to assess. A number of observers blamed high unemployment, but this was probably a serious factor only in the particularly hard-hit industrial pockets in Illinois, Michigan, and Pennsylvania (where Republicans lost a total of one Senate and eight House seats); in other industrial areas, such as in Ohio and Indiana, unemployment levels were lower and the Republicans did not lose ground.[33] Also frequently mentioned was the "farm problem," and particularly farm discontent resulting from the Eisenhower-Benson flexible price-support program. Again, however, the problem was regional. Where farm prices were relatively stable—as in Iowa and Kansas—Republicans held their own (even picking up a Senate seat in the former and a House seat in the latter). The Republican share of the vote did decline in dairy- and poultry-farming areas (such as Minnesota, upstate New York, parts of Pennsylvania, and Wisconsin), but agricultural discontent probably contributed to only four Republican losses, at most: Cole and Hillelson (Missouri), Bishop (Illinois), and Stauffer (Pennsylvania).[34] Even more specifically regional in its impact was the power policy question. Senators Cooper of Kentucky and Cordon of Oregon both suffered somewhat in power-

31 Angell lost in the Republican primary, and his conqueror then lost to Democrat Edith Green in November.

32 See National Citizens for Eisenhower Congressional Committee interoffice memorandum, J. Allen Overton to James L. Murphy, Aug. 9, 1954, OF 138-A-4, Eisenhower Papers.

33 *U.S. News & World Report* 37 (Nov. 12, 1954), 29-31; Richard Lewis, "The Issues that Counted: Illinois," *Nation* 179, No. 20 (Nov. 13, 1954), 419; *Business Week*, Nos. 1314 (Nov. 6, 1954), 29, and 1315 (Nov. 13, 1954), 29.

34 *Ibid.*, 29; *U.S. News & World Report* 37 (Nov. 12, 1954), 29; Samson Halleck, "The Issues that Counted: Iowa," *Nation* 179, No. 20, 417; *New Republic* 131, No. 20 (Nov. 15, 1954), 3; V. O. Key, Jr., "The 'Moral Victory' of the Republicans," *ibid.*, No. 23 (Dec. 6, 1954), 11.

conscious areas for their identification, either directly or indirectly, with Eisenhower's partnership policy;[35] but the power issue was only one of several in both states.

The elections as a whole did not represent sharp repudiation of the Eisenhower program. Commentators pointed out repeatedly that Republican losses were not especially large when measured against usual mid-term losses by the party in power. Moreover, the results of House races involving Republican incumbents demonstrated that administration supporters were apt to do better than Republican mavericks: nearly one-fifth of all pro-Eisenhower House Republicans who ran for re-election in 1954 (thirty-seven of 191) bettered their 1952 vote, while none of the fifteen anti-Eisenhower Republicans did so. Of the thirty-seven House incumbents who received a greater share of the vote in 1954 than they had in 1952, seventeen had strongly supported Eisenhower in 1953–1954 (scored .80 or higher), and twenty had been moderate administration supporters (.60 or higher). According to Sherman Adams, the feeling inside the administration was that the election had given "a green light for continuing the . . . middle-of-the-road program." To Nixon, the outcome seemed "a virtual stand-off."[36]

Eisenhower's personal status emerged intact, if not enhanced. His intervention had seemed to help Republicans wherever he had gone during the campaign. Speaker Martin, otherwise disappointed with the results, captured the essence of the situation, writing that the President's "efforts were wonderful and prevented what might have been a great disaster."[37]

Some even thought the outcome would help the President within his own party, and there was some basis for such a view.[38]

---

[35] *U.S. News & World Report* 37 (Nov. 12, 1954), 72, 84; Joe Miller, "Oregon: Can the Issues be Ignored?", *The Reporter* 11, No. 11 (Nov. 4, 1954), 33–34; Wildavsky, *Dixon-Yates*, 133.

[36] Adams, *Firsthand Report*, 168; Nixon statement in *U.S. News & World Report* 37 (Nov. 12, 1954), 46; see also *Business Week*, No. 1314 (Nov. 6, 1954), 25.

[37] Rep. Joseph Martin to Eisenhower, Nov. 5, 1954, OF 138–A–4 (1), Eisenhower Papers; see also Richard Rovere, "Letter from Washington," *New Yorker* 30, No. 39 (Nov. 13, 1954), 115.

[38] William G. Carleton, "Triumph of the Moderates," *Harper's Magazine* 210,

Among Republican House incumbents, only six of the ninety-five (6 percent) who had strongly pro-Eisenhower records were defeated, while three of the fifteen (20 percent) with anti-Eisenhower records lost their seats. Of the Republican senators who lost, two (Cordon and Ferguson) were strongly pro-Eisenhower and the other (Cooper) was moderately pro-Eisenhower, but these losses were countered by the election to the Senate of six Republican House members, all of whom were administration supporters: George Bender of Ohio (who had a support score of .89 in 1953–1954), Clifford Case of New Jersey (.79), Norris Cotton of New Hampshire (.79), Carl Curtis of Nebraska (.71), Roman Hruska of Nebraska (.76), and Thomas Martin of Iowa (.73).

The all-important fact was, however, that the President's party had lost control of Congress. Eisenhower could not have known it, of course, but he had lost permanently his chance to head a "responsible" party government. For the next six years he would have to deal with an opposition-led legislative branch, resembling more and more the President "above party" which many had predicted he would be from the outset. In his first two years, however, working with a Congress which his own party controlled, Dwight D. Eisenhower had led—and in the tradition of "political" Presidents. If that leadership did not significantly change the Republican party, it was not for lack of force, but rather because Eisenhower's views did not differ much from the views of most Republicans.

---

No. 1259 (Apr. 1955), 31–32, 37; also Rovere, *New Yorker* 30, No. 39, 116; *Business Week*, No. 1314 (Nov. 6, 1954), 26.

# The Eisenhower Leadership: Style and Substance

President Eisenhower's party leadership achievements have gone largely unrecognized. This has happened not only because he was stereotyped early as "nonpolitical," but also because his use of glib terms like "modern Republicanism" and "dynamic conservatism" led many to think he aimed at bringing about a transition in Republicanism that in fact failed to occur in the 1950s. By his own words and behavior, Eisenhower helped perpetuate these public assumptions. Indeed, some have even viewed his ability to foster such images as politically astute in itself.[1] The story of Eisenhower and the Eighty-third Congress, however, shows the common assumptions to be wrong. The President was committed to the idea that he should lead his party, and he did so. Accordingly the output of that Republican Congress bore an obvious Eisenhower stamp. An important factor in the White House achievement was the President's well-developed method of working with (and on) Republican members of Congress.

## Methods: The Eisenhower Style

The Eisenhower administration's methods of liaison with Congress show the President's strong concern for leading Congress.

---

[1] See Sidney Hyman, "Eisenhower's Presidency—the Known and the Foreseeable," *The Reporter* 14, No. 6 (Mar. 22, 1956), 16; also Parmet, *Eisenhower and the American Crusades*, 175, 577.

White House contact with Capitol Hill was steady, frequent, and extensive during the years 1953–1954, often involving Eisenhower himself. Much of the President's personal diplomacy, according to one White House aide, was "off the record," so that press and public alike were unaware of it.[2] The Eisenhower technique included good listening: the President claimed that he spent hours listening to the arguments of various Republican leaders, "sometimes a little hopelessly," in an effort "to get them to understand, to give."[3] His tact and considerable reservoir of charm often produced important political results, the most striking being his successful courtship of Daniel Reed following the tax fights of early 1953. Representative Richard Simpson, a protectionist who became a valuable administration ally in the reciprocal trade battles of both sessions of the Eighty-third Congress, also responded to direct presidential appeals, and Senator Taft's indispensable cooperation on nearly every important issue until his death in July 1953 obviously reflected the warm and courteous treatment he received at the White House.

Complementing the President's informal personal diplomacy was the more formalized device of the legislative leadership meeting, described by Eisenhower as "by far the most effective" of all administration liaison efforts.[4] Held almost weekly at the White House, these conferences provided an opportunity for "joint consideration of important public problems" and specific planning for the Republican legislative program.[5] Regular participants in the leadership meetings included the President; Vice President Nixon; leading White House aides; Senators Taft, Knowland, Millikin, Saltonstall, and (in 1954), Ferguson; Speaker Martin; and Representatives Halleck and Arends. Other powerful congressional Republicans were also invited as topics within their areas of particular influence or expertise came up.

---

[2] See statement of Bryce Harlow, in Abraham Holtzman, *Legislative Liaison: Executive Leadership in Congress* (Chicago: Rand McNally, 1970), 246.

[3] Hughes, *Ordeal of Power*, 125.

[4] Eisenhower, *Mandate for Change*, 194, 300.

[5] From the President-elect's press release of Dec. 17, 1952, announcing the first such meeting, in OF 99, Eisenhower Papers.

Congressmen Daniel Reed and Leo Allen often attended on this *ad hoc* basis. White House personnel who attended with some degree of regularity were Adams, Earle Chesney, Robert Cutler, Homer Gruenther, Bryce Harlow, James Hagerty, Jack Martin, Gerald Morgan, Arthur Minnich, Wilton Persons, Maxwell Rabb, Bernard Shanley, and Murray Snyder.[6] These weekly meetings evidently offered a chance for free and open exchange. As one regular participant said, they "were always open. You always had an opportunity to say your part if you wanted to." Yet the President, according to another observer, "more than [held] his own in the sessions."[7]

A more dramatic example of Eisenhower's technique of consultation with party leaders was a three-day conclave held at the White House in December 1953 to which he invited virtually every Republican leader in Congress (including the chairmen of nearly all standing committees), ostensibly to plan the 1954 legislative program. In fact, however, the conference amounted to a briefing where the legislative leaders mostly "looked and listened, with much to absorb, nothing to ratify, and little time for argument." Typically at the conference, a Cabinet official or appropriate staff member would present the proposed 1954 program in a particular area to the congressional leaders most directly concerned with it. Administration spokesmen tactfully informed the legislators that actual language "remained in a preliminary stage, pending these consultations," and the President invited the leaders' reactions but did not ask for their concurrence to the proposals.[8] In view of some of the problems which had to be worked out with the various committee chairmen during 1954 on such measures as housing, atomic energy, social security, and health insurance, the December leadership conference

6 Taken from the President's Appointment Books, 1953 and 1954, Eisenhower Papers.

7 First quotation from Saltonstall Oral History Transcript, Eisenhower Project, Eisenhower Library, 114: the second is from a column by Bob Considine in New York *Journal American*, June 8, 1954, clipping in Box 1, Charles Masterson Records, Eisenhower Papers.

8 Richard Neustadt, "Presidency and Legislation: Planning the President's Program," *American Political Science Review* 49, No. 4 (Dec. 1955), 991.

obviously failed to produce complete party unity on the 1954 legislative program. Nevertheless, it gave Republican congressional leaders considerable publicity and a sense of participation, both of which undoubtedly helped the administration in a general way. Furthermore, at the three-day conference Eisenhower reportedly "spoke with the new and firmer tone of one taking a more resolute view of his role as a leader"—a tone which could not have been lost on so politically sensitive a group.[9]

In addition to regular meetings with the party's legislative leaders, the administration employed the Senate Republican Policy Committee as a channel for communication with Republicans in the upper house. The Policy Committee, chaired during most of the Eighty-third Congress by Homer Ferguson, performed a largely educative role. Eisenhower invited Ferguson to all the weekly leadership meetings during 1954 and sent Cabinet members and lesser administration officials to speak directly to the committee on behalf of White House plans. Throughout 1953–1954 Ferguson worked hard to bring about a sense of unity within his committee and among Senate Republicans generally, and the Policy Committee was an effective tool in building intraparty harmony.[10]

The problem of executive-legislative liaison received a great deal of attention from the White House. In the first weeks of the new administration, Sherman Adams decreed that "certain members of the Staff" would "review" any requests by members of Congress to see the President. A year later, again on Adams's instructions, a memo was circulated within the White House announcing that henceforth a member of the liaison staff would sit in on all meetings held between the President and a member of Congress which had been called at the congressman's request.[11]

9 Donovan, *The Inside Story*, 224, 226; see also Neustadt, *American Political Science Review* 49, No. 4, 995.

10 Bone, *Party Committees and National Politics*, 180, 345, 350–51; also Jewell, *Senatorial Politics and Foreign Policy*, 91.

11 "Excerpts from Minutes of Staff Meeting of January 29, 1953," in OF 72–A (1), and Staff Memorandum from Murray Snyder, dated Jan. 9, 1954, in Box 6, A67–19 Accessions, Morgan Records, Eisenhower Papers.

Eisenhower also set up in the White House for the first time a publicly acknowledged congressional liaison unit with a staff of its own.[12] The five-man liaison team during the Eighty-third Congress included General Wilton Persons, Homer Gruenther, Bryce Harlow, Gerald Morgan, and (after the first session) I. Jack Martin. All had prior experience in working with Congress, and Harlow, Martin, and Morgan each had ties with important congressional Republicans.[13]

Apparently the Eisenhower "team approach" worked very effectively in legislative liaison. General Persons, a diplomatic and skillful conciliator himself, ran a thorough and well-organized operation.[14] Gruenther and Harlow customarily worked with House members while Martin and Morgan dealt mostly with the Senate, but occasionally the whole staff focused its attention on one house or the other. Frequently an individual liaison officer was given primary responsibility for a particular piece of legislation; Gerald Morgan and Jack Martin seem to have received a large share of such topical assignments in 1953 and 1954.[15] Specialization within the staff never reached the point of assigning particular Republican legislators to one or another of the staff members on a permanent basis, but in times of need such formal individual assignments were made temporarily.[16] On those occasions, Persons also called on other members of the White House staff to "cover" the congressmen and senators whom they knew especially well. General Persons also made an attempt to system-

[12] Holtzman, *Legislative Liaison*, 16.

[13] *Ibid.*, 236–38; Neustadt, *American Political Science Review* 49, No. 4, 984n. See also a letter from Christian Herter to Herbert Brownell endorsing Morgan for a liaison appointment, Nov. 21, 1952, in OF 72–A–2, Eisenhower Papers.

[14] Neustadt, *American Political Science Review* 49, No. 4, 1016n; Stephen Horn, *Unused Power: The Work of the Senate Committee on Appropriations* (Washington: Brookings Institution, 1970), 196. On Persons's strengths, see Hughes, *Ordeal of Power*, 66; Saltonstall Oral History Transcript, 135; and Halleck Oral History Transcript, 24, both in Eisenhower Project, Eisenhower Library.

[15] See progress report on legislation from desk of Homer Gruenther, dated May 18, 1954 (in possession of Mrs. I. Jack Martin, Kensington, Md.).

[16] See undated, unsigned memorandum, listing all legislators along with individual White House "contacts," in folder on "Secret Pacts and Executive Agreements," OF 116–H–4, Eisenhower Papers.

atize the work of the liaison teams of the various executive departments, calling regular Saturday morning meetings at which agents from each department would discuss with the White House liaison staff their forthcoming problems and needs. On the basis of these discussions, Persons then prepared the agenda for the President's weekly meeting with the Republican congressional leaders.[17]

Complaints and suggestions inevitably arose regarding the White House liaison effort. Within the staff, some objected to General Persons's desire to oversee personally the work of his entire staff. Harlow, for example, wrote Persons in early 1953 that such centralization kept the rest of the liaison officers in the dark concerning overall strategy and that the situation seemed "to place too high a premium on your memory."[18] Another member of the administration believed that the liaison staff was too small, and suggested to Sherman Adams that several more members be added. Adams replied abruptly that the "suggestion is logical enough; in fact, you can easily extend it to having the staff increased so that every ten taxpayers could have a liaison in the White House. This might require a building which would be ten stories high in Lafayette Park."[19] Nothing was done to enlarge the staff.

Members of Congress also offered ideas for improving executive-legislative liaison. Among the suggestions set forth by congressional Republicans during 1953 were White House use of former congressmen as liaison men, regular meetings between the President and all congressional committee heads as a group, and provision for Republican legislators to accompany members of the executive branch into their districts whenever the latter visited.[20]

17 Holtzman, *Legislative Liaison*, 259.

18 Memorandum dated Mar. 21, 1953, Box 4, A67–19 Accessions, Morgan Records, Eisenhower Papers.

19 Charles F. Willis to Adams, Aug. 20, 1953, and Adams's reply, Sept. 14, 1953, in OF 72–A(3), Eisenhower Papers.

20 Rep. John Heselton to Adams, July 27, 1953, Rep. George Bender to Eisenhower, June 5, 1953, both in OF 99, and Rep. John Allen to Bryce Harlow, May 12, 1953, in GF 3–A, Eisenhower Papers.

Although none of these specific suggestions was adopted, the administration did work hard between the two sessions of the Eighty-third Congress to improve its system, directing the various executive departments to upgrade the quality and coordination of their dealings with Congress and drawing together a comprehensive list of those Republican members of Congress "well known" to individual presidential aides and high departmental officials.[21] On the basis of the administration's improved record on legislation during the second session and the decline in direct congressional criticism, it seems that the liaison staff established itself as an effective arm of the White House by 1954.

The institutionalization of executive-legislative liaison created some problems for the administration in its dealings with members of Congress. The size of the staff itself was partly responsible. In November 1953 one aide reported to Persons that many legislators showed "a lack of knowledge and a curiosity regarding the organization of the White House staff and the personalities involved."[22] In addition, numerous Republican senators and representatives apparently resented the tiers of aides and assistants which they had to penetrate to reach the President. For this state of affairs Sherman Adams correctly drew most of the congressional criticism.[23]

Conflict also arose between congressional Republicans and the White House over the continued appearance before House and Senate committees of career officials held over from previous Democratic administrations. As Representative Taber wrote a colleague in early 1953, many Republicans felt the administration was leaning "too much on the Lame Ducks who have been

[21] See aide-memoire of Cabinet meeting of Oct. 30, 1953, in Box 2, A67–19 Accessions, Morgan Records, and memorandum from Homer Gruenther to numerous Eisenhower aides, dated Nov. 9, 1953, Box 4, Gruenther Records, Eisenhower Papers.

[22] Stanley Rumbough, Jr., to Wilton B. Persons, Nov. 5, 1953, in OF 72–A(3), Eisenhower Papers.

[23] See, for example, Associated Press wire release of Rep. Joseph Carrigg (R.-Pa.) in which he denounces Adams, dated Nov. 11, 1954, in OF 72–A–2(2), Eisenhower Papers; statement in the *Arizona Republic* (Phoenix), June 27, 1954, and Hughes, *Ordeal of Power*, 64.

trying to make trouble for it and for us."[24] The White House soon acted to overcome this problem, however. Citing four examples which had "caused considerable irritation at the Capitol," Gerald Morgan suggested to Vice President Nixon in April 1953 that "no policy-making holdover official from the previous Administration be permitted to appear before a Congressional Committee...."[25]

The Eisenhower administration also caused itself problems by failing to coordinate its testimony in committee hearings. In view of the conflicting and ambiguous statements by Cabinet members Brownell, Dulles, and Weeks on the submerged lands question, and by Dulles and Weeks on reciprocal trade, Gabriel Hauge's statement of concern in August 1953 was a model of understatement: "Looking back on our first Congressional session," Hauge wrote to Sherman Adams, "I wonder how well we are organized with respect to the coordination of testimony in support of a particular piece of legislation on the Hill."[26] After Hauge's memo was called to his attention, Budget Bureau official Roger Jones assured the White House that "we are in pretty good shape, but we have to designate lead horses on some of the major matters. The problems last session came chiefly from inexperience and failure to let [the] White House or Budget know in several cases that the issue was up...."[27] Departmental officials testifying before Congress during the second session generally avoided the kinds of contradictions which marked 1953.

President Eisenhower's conduct of liaison with congressional Republicans challenges the view that he was an inept political leader. Although he may have been naïve in the ways of partisan politics when he took office in January 1953, the new President was no stranger to politics insofar as it involved the arts of negotiation, compromise, and patient prodding. He had built his

24 Taber to Rep. Charles G. Oakman of Michigan, Mar. 23, 1953, Taber Papers.

25 Memorandum dated Apr. 24, 1953, in OF 99–E(1), Eisenhower Papers.

26 Memorandum dated Aug. 7, 1953, in Box 5, A67–19 Accessions, Morgan Records, Eisenhower Papers.

27 Roger W. Jones to Gerald Morgan, Nov. 16, 1953, Morgan Records, Eisenhower Papers.

reputation before 1952 largely on his ability to bring about effective reconciliation of divergent viewpoints, welding the sometimes stubborn powers of Western Europe into a relatively harmonious team in times of both war and peace. There was no reason to think he would suddenly find himself bereft of such skills once in the White House.

Eisenhower quickly learned what he needed to know to become a party leader. This included using patronage to achieve political goals, as demonstrated by his handling of Representative Reece of Tennessee in the excess profits tax struggle of 1953. In March 1953, the President issued an executive order (No. 10440) which in effect made possible the removal of large numbers of bureaucrats who had been protected under the civil service. Finally, he used the threat of selective campaigning for Republicans in the 1954 elections.[28] Since his immense personal popularity was undiminished after nearly two years in office, this no doubt remained a potent weapon in dealing with Republicans whose seats were relatively insecure. Eisenhower also understood some of the finer points of party politicking, such as the value of publicity to a member of Congress. In deciding which Republican legislators might have their pictures taken with him, for example, the President admitted that he took "a little bit of a check . . . to see whether on the important things in which I believe he has generally been along."[29]

Eisenhower also employed profitably the tactic of compromise. Repeatedly during the two sessions of the Eighty-third Congress, he built up strong Republican support and won passage for particular programs by trimming his requests. The most obvious examples were the reductions in administration requests for public housing starts in both 1953 and 1954, but the upward adjustment of the floor for flexible farm price supports, the successive one-year "as is" extensions of the reciprocal trade program, and the accommodations reached on excises and dividend credit pro-

---

[28] Parmet, *Eisenhower and the American Crusades*, 215–16; Eisenhower, *Waging Peace*, 642; Donovan, *The Inside Story*, 229.

[29] Press conference remarks of July 28, 1954, in *Public Papers . . . 1954*, 663.

visions in 1954 tax legislation all represented tactical compromises by the President which ensured victory for his policies. Through a combination of conciliation, persuasion, and political maneuver, Eisenhower slowly but effectively established White House influence among Republicans on Capitol Hill.

### Eisenhower Republicanism

Eisenhower's efforts as a party leader largely succeeded. At a time when the Republican party, long out of power, faced a potential watershed in its ideological orientation,[30] its members in Congress consistently supported the new President's program. As a result, administration policy generally became public policy. Thus the story of Republican rule in 1953–1954 not only illuminates the nature of Eisenhower's influence within his party, but affords an opportunity to analyze the phenomenon known as "Eisenhower Republicanism."

Without question, President Eisenhower exercised strong influence on the Republican party in matters of foreign policy. By the time the Eighty-third Congress adjourned, the party's congressional wing had accepted in broad outline the level of activity abroad which had characterized the foreign policy of Truman and Acheson. A large majority of Republican members in both houses voted in favor of the Eisenhower mutual security program in both 1953 and 1954, even if at levels somewhat lower than the President initially requested. Moreover, Republican legislators continued to support such programs in each of the three succeeding Congresses during the Eisenhower presidency.

While the party's nationalist element made life temporarily difficult for the President over the Bricker amendment, that effort to circumscribe executive authority in foreign affairs was defeated in early 1954, and only one year later (during the Eighty-

---

30 See Washington *Post*, Oct. 15, 1952, p. 15; Roland N. Stromberg, *Republicanism Reappraised* (Washington: Public Affairs Press, 1952), 90; Richard Rovere, "The Republican Prospects," *Harper's Magazine* 206, No. 1237 (June 1953), 36, 39; Graebner, *The New Isolationism*, 119; and Lubell, *The Future of American Politics*, 224.

fourth Congress) Republicans voted 43–1 in the Senate and 185–2 in the House to grant President Eisenhower discretionary powers of unprecedented breadth to deal with the Formosa crisis. Never again during his years in the White House was the executive branch's control of foreign policy making challenged by a bloc of any size within the Republican party.

Finally, although the administration had to reduce the scope of its reciprocal trade program in both 1953 and 1954, a substantial majority of Republicans in both houses supported the measure in both sessions. In later fights over extension of this internationalist program, moreover, the party remained loyal to the President. In both 1955 and 1958, approximately 60 percent of House Republicans and 80 percent of Republican senators sided with the White House in support of reciprocal trade. In virtually all major facets of foreign policy, then, Eisenhower's internationalist influence prevailed in the congressional wing of his party.

But American political parties are not customarily defined by their foreign policies, and on the domestic side the story differed somewhat. Arthur Larson, in a 1956 book entitled *A Republican Looks at His Party*, propounded the thesis that a "New Republicanism" emerged in the early Eisenhower years. Others have since echoed Larson's view.[31] After noting several accomplishments of the Eisenhower administration and the Republican-controlled Congress in 1953–1954, Larson summarized: "All this does not slip comfortably into some well-worn niche like 'liberal' or 'New Deal' or 'pro-labor' or 'pro-business' or 'left' or 'right.' This is because the New Republicanism is a set of ideas keyed explicitly to contemporary mid-century facts, while the familiar categories, drawn from earlier decades, are now largely obsolete."[32]

[31] Larson, *A Republican Looks at His Party* (New York: Harper, 1956), *passim.* For reiteration of this idea, see Burns, *The Deadlock of Democracy*, 194; Henry, *Presidential Transitions*, 543; Joyner, *The Republican Dilemma*, vi; Pusey, *Eisenhower the President*, Preface.

[32] *A Republican Looks at His Party*, 2. Larson later wrote that his 1956 book was largely completed by March 1954, making its judgments particularly relevant

This "New Republicanism" has had several definitions. Eisenhower himself, who labeled his Republican creed variously as "the middle way," "progressive moderation," and "dynamic conservatism," often cited as his guiding inspiration Abraham Lincoln's belief that the government should perform for the people only those services which they were incapable of performing for themselves. The Lincoln precept was also cited by members of Congress who viewed themselves as "modern Republicans."[33] Sherman Adams described the domestic goals of the modernized party somewhat more specifically, as "moderate government, with a sound fiscal policy, but with more willingness than the Republican administrations of the past to serve the needs of the people in common welfare . . . ." Larson's definition, the most extensive, ranges from "acknowledging reverently the existence of a God of order, justice and love" to a defense of local government, private enterprise, and free, untrammeled negotiations between labor and management.[34]

The "New Republicanism," however, was more rhetoric than reality. The transformation in foreign policy was not matched in domestic policy. At least since the days of Warren G. Harding, the Republican party had been the conservative force in American politics, as its adherents glorified individualism and the rights of property while rejecting egalitarianism and tendencies to centralized government.[35] These values dominated the domestic policy positions of most congressional Republicans when Eisenhower came to the White House, and the new President did little to change the situation. But Eisenhower did not want to effect any transformation of his party on such matters. Nearly

---

to this study (*The President Nobody Knew*, 45). See also William S. White, "Has Eisenhower Changed the G.O.P.?", *New York Times Magazine* (Mar. 18, 1956), 70.

33 See, e.g., the statements of Jacob Javits and Leverett Saltonstall in "What's a Modern Republican?", *U.S. News & World Report* 18 (May 3, 1957), 132–33.

34 Adams, *Firsthand Report*, 299; Larson, *A Republican Looks at His Party*, 198–203.

35 See James P. Young, *The Politics of Affluence: Ideology in the United States Since World War II* (Scranton, Pa.: Chandler Publishing, 1968), 123–24; also Ellsworth Barnard, *Wendell Willkie: Fighter for Freedom* (Marquette: Northern Michigan Univ. Press, 1966), 167.

all the administration's 1953–1954 programs reflected long-standing conservative Republican goals such as balanced budgets, lower taxes, encouragement of private enterprise, and reduction in the scope of federal activity. Indeed, Larson, while attempting to stress the novelty of his party's stance in the 1950s, offers an almost classic description of orthodox twentieth-century Republicanism: "The New Republicanism believes that the way to have the country prosper is to stop inflation, check government spending, balance the budget, encourage business venturing and confidence, maintain and increase consumer purchasing power, reduce government competition and interference to a minimum and . . . maintain just the right amount of government scrutiny to avoid excesses that damage the public interest . . . ." Such goals appeared in every Republican party platform from 1936 forward.[36] President Eisenhower revealed his orthodoxy quite clearly in a speech to a convention of Young Republicans in 1953. "We have instituted what amounts almost to a revolution in Federal Government . . . ," he told his listeners. "We have been finding things it can stop doing rather than new things for it to do."[37]

Opposition to "big government" was the most obvious carry-over of traditional Republican attitudes during the Eisenhower administration. One of the early actions of the new President was the establishment of a Commission on Intergovernmental Relations. Although the commission was formally charged with designating new areas and programs into which federal efforts might be directed, its real purpose was clear from the President's language in asking Congress to set up the body. "In many cases, especially within the past twenty years," Eisenhower stated, "the Federal government has entered fields which, under our Constitution, are the primary responsibilities of state and local governments. . . . [This] has led to duplication and waste. It is time

[36] Larson, *A Republican Looks at His Party*, 45; see platforms for 1936–48 in Porter and Johnson, comp., *National Party Platforms*, 365–70, 389–94, 407–13, and 450–54.

[37] Speech of June 11, 1953, at Mount Rushmore National Monument, S.Dak., in *Public Papers . . . 1953*, 403.

to relieve the people of the need to pay taxes on taxes." Ultimately the commission returned a report basically sympathetic to the President's point of view.[38]

President Eisenhower's desire to reduce the activities of the federal government showed up frequently in 1953–1954. This anti-centralist tendency characterized such measures as the submerged lands act of 1953 and the atomic energy and omnibus farm acts of 1954, all of which aimed at a reduction of the role of the federal government relative to state and private activity. Even the Eisenhower programs on social security (where the system was extended and defended largely on the grounds that it would ultimately decrease the need for direct government aid to the aged and unemployed) and health reinsurance (which aimed at propping up the private health insurance carriers rather than directly involving the federal government in health activities) were essentially anti–"big government" in spirit.

To say that Eisenhower adhered to traditional Republican conservatism is not, however, to impute that he overtly favored business. The administration's fiscal-economic policies in 1953–1954 demonstrated the President's aversion to government intervention on behalf of any single interest or bloc in American society. Eisenhower's dedication to a more liberal trade program, for example, showed that he was not particularly interested in becoming the protector of American businessmen. And if the omnibus tax bill of 1954 showed favoritism to business and stockholding interests, the President's simultaneous request for continuation of the existing corporate tax rate certainly did not. In fact, although Eisenhower had a number of businessmen in his Cabinet and in other important advisory positions, he was in some respects less a "government interventionist" than Republicans like Coolidge and Hoover, who talked of "rugged individualism" while employing the strength of the federal government to advance the interests of American business.

---

[38] Special Message to Congress, Mar. 20, 1953, in *Public Papers . . . 1953*, 140. The commission report, issued on June 28, 1955, called in effect for the minimization of central governmental authority.

Others of Eisenhower's early programs revealed that this "hands off" approach applied to domestic matters in general. In his attempt to revise the Taft-Hartley law, the President was trying to remove the federal government as much as possible from all labor disputes—on either side. Also, when Eisenhower decided in early 1953 to end all price, wage, and rent controls, but failed to support the idea of stand-by controls, he displayed a willingness to yield influence over wages (and the demands of labor) as well as over the prices charged by producers. Underlying these decisions were orthodox Republican attitudes of respect for property and the individual, and dislike for strong central government.

President Eisenhower's repeatedly expressed devotion to the private enterprise system grew more from his strong belief in the dignity and legitimate rights of the individual than from an identification with any particular interest group. In some ways, he viewed the individual and the government as adversaries, as he revealed in describing the years of his Presidency as a period of "Republican efforts to preserve the importance of the individual as against the state . . . ."[39] By supporting tax reductions, opposing rigid farm price supports, ending wage and price controls, and proposing his health reinsurance package of 1954, the President tried to fulfill his party's commitment. This faith in the dignity and worth of the individual explains why a President with such strongly conservative fiscal and economic beliefs would propose programs such as extended social security coverage, health reinsurance (no matter how "business-oriented"), and government-built public housing.

If Eisenhower embodied the anti-centralist and individualist emphases associated with Republicanism in the twentieth century, so too did he represent the moralistic strain inherent in American conservatism.[40] For him, religion, morality, and spiritualism were inseparable from the American system of govern-

[39] Eisenhower, *Waging Peace*, 654.
[40] See, for example, Russell Kirk, *The Conservative Mind: from Burke to Santayana* (Chicago: Henry Regnery, 1953), esp. 414.

ment. "The real source of our strength is moral and spiritual," he told one audience during the 1952 campaign. "As a nation we are what we are because of what we believe." And the relationship was reciprocal: "Our American ideals," he remarked at another point in the same campaign, "are . . . the well-spring of our own spiritual and moral strength . . . ."[41] Throughout his years in the White House, Eisenhower reiterated this theme, which, while it did not shape any specific program, revealed much about his basic political outlook. In linking morality inextricably with the dignity and freedom of individuals, Eisenhower was actually carrying forward a strong neo-Puritan thread present in twentieth-century American conservatism, and hence in the modern Republican party.[42]

Both his words and his performance after taking office in 1953 show that Dwight D. Eisenhower was far from a Republican New Dealer. It is no accident that Republican senators and representatives with the most liberal records in domestic policy before 1953 were not the leading "Eisenhower men" in the Eighty-third Congress. Eisenhower later wrote that in early 1953 he "wanted to make it clear that we would not be simply a continuation of the New Deal and Fair Deal, either in purpose or execution." This goal was thoroughly consistent for a man who, on his own admission, had decided to try for the Republican nomination in 1952 because he thought that "a long-term continuation of the domestic policies then supported by the Democratic administration would be ruinous to the nation."[43] Eisenhower's inadvertent public reference to TVA as "creeping socialism"—a slip for which he was privately chastised by one of his chief advisers[44]—revealed his true political convictions much more accurately than his 1952

41 Speeches at Buffalo, Oct. 23, and Newark, N.J., Oct. 17, in *New York Times*, Oct. 24, Oct. 18, 1952.

42 On Eisenhower's spiritualistic and moralistic tendencies, see Hughes, *Ordeal of Power*, 53–54, and William L. Miller, *Piety Along the Potomac: Notes on Politics and Morals in the Fifties* (Boston: Houghton, 1964), 23–24.

43 Eisenhower, *Mandate for Change*, 120, 113.

44 The reference occurred in an off-the-cuff speech at Custer State Park, S.D., on June 11, 1953 (*New York Times*, June 12, p. 13); see memorandum, Gabriel Hauge to Eisenhower, June 22, 1953, Hauge Records, Eisenhower Papers.

campaign utterances about the need for a "floor of security."

Certainly the legislative program which the administration presented to the Eighty-third Congress did not represent a continuation of liberal Democratic policies, either in spirit or in content. The Eisenhower programs closest to the New Deal–Fair Deal philosophy, the 1954 housing act and extension of the social security system, were both essentially conservative in spirit. The housing act, even though it continued the public housing program, set construction levels far lower than those of the Truman years and otherwise minimized the role of the federal government in the housing industry. Administration arguments for extension of the social security program relied heavily on the potential of the system to make all other federal relief unnecessary. The only other quasi-liberal measure presented by President Eisenhower during 1953–1954 was the health reinsurance program, which was killed by the House in 1954. In the context of the long-standing public debate over national medical needs, however, Eisenhower's proposal to provide guarantees to the private insurance sector was much closer to the conservative Republican position (which feared any federal involvement in health programs as "socialized medicine") than to Truman's liberal proposal for compulsory national health insurance. In the areas of fiscal policy and power and resource development, the Eisenhower administration's programs were almost unerringly conservative.

Eisenhower's retention of such programs as public housing and social security, as well as his oft-expressed (if infrequently implemented) commitment to marshaling the full strength of the federal government against the threat of economic depression, did in a general way represent the official entry of the Republican party into the New Deal "political orbit."[45] But conservatism in the United States has never been static; just as it rests on certain intellectual presuppositions, it has also consisted of response and reaction to ongoing changes in American

45 Reference is to Samuel Lubell's "sun-and-moon" theory of American politics (see *Future of American Politics*, 190–96).

234

society. Given the political and economic realities of the mid-twentieth century, conservative acquiescence to some of the features of the New Deal was therefore inevitable. Even Herbert Hoover agreed. "To go back is impossible," Hoover told Eisenhower in early 1953, "but many will not believe this . . . . All you can do is to try to turn away gradually from the path leading to paternalism . . . ."[46] Many of the most conservative members of the Republican party agreed with Hoover and were ready to accept the irreversibility of government programs like social security and labor-management relations laws. In making his own peace with such programs, Eisenhower was doing nothing daring, nor was he moving his party to a new, liberal position.

Where, then, does Eisenhower fit into the modern Republican party? Those who believe the 1950s witnessed the birth of a "New Republicanism" tend to see his nomination, election, and administration as a final victory for the party's liberal "presidential wing" over its "Old Guard" congressional wing.[47] Eisenhower is portrayed as the ideological heir of the party's presidential nominees in the preceding decade, Wendell Willkie and Thomas E. Dewey. Since Eisenhower, like Willkie and Dewey, was the candidate of the "Eastern establishment," according to this view the power shift within the party was regional as well as ideological. Yet Eisenhower's support for the 1952 nomination was not entirely regional. It came from Kansas, California, and states in between, in addition to New York and the East. Moreover, while Easterners among Republican congressmen often stood in the front ranks of Eisenhower supporters during the Eighty-third Congress, party members from all sections supported their President on nearly all important issues. Finally, except in foreign policy, Eisenhower's programs did not deviate much from what most congressional Republicans were already willing to accept as public policy, no matter what their region.

46 Eisenhower, *Mandate for Change*, 430–31.
47 See White, *New York Times Magazine* (Mar. 18, 1956), 69, 70; and Malcolm Moos, *The Republicans: A History of Their Party* (New York: Random House, 1956), 519–25.

Eisenhower's place in his party has been misunderstood, in part because commentators have tended to exaggerate the schism in Republicanism in the post–New Deal era. It is true that Wendell Willkie, as the party's presidential candidate in 1940, was much more willing than most Republicans then or later to see the federal government take strong steps to guarantee the civil rights and social and economic welfare of American citizens.[48] Despite his biographers' claims,[49] however, Willkie's influence on the party was not very great. Even the eventual acceptance by Republicans of an internationalist foreign policy owed much more to the necessities of post-1945 world politics and to Eisenhower's presidency than it owed to Willkie's leadership in the early 1940s. As a converted Democrat, the Indianan was viewed by Republican party professionals as an outsider, and he was suspected more than emulated. He never truly spoke for a "wing" within the party proper.

Dewey, on the other hand, was on balance no more liberal than Eisenhower. Indeed, in 1944 numerous party conservatives supported Dewey to block Willkie's possible renomination, because they believed the New Yorker was a "safe" party man.[50] Even Robert Taft felt Dewey's domestic views were acceptable; he disliked Dewey's arrogant and cold manner more than his ideological position. In fact, Taft thought Dewey's nomination in 1948 was due in part to the perception by some conservatives that he, Taft, was more liberal than the New York governor.[51] In the 1944 campaign, when for tactical reasons Dewey was more outspoken than in 1948, the governor blasted the New Deal for producing "a controlled and regulated society under a Government which destroys incentive" and warned of the coming of a "cor-

[48] See summaries of Willkie's beliefs in Barnard, *Willkie*, especially 429 and 472–75; and Donald B. Johnson, *The Republican Party and Wendell Willkie*, Vol. XLVI of Illinois Studies in the Social Sciences (Urbana: Univ. of Illinois Press, 1960), especially 313.

[49] See Bernard, *Willkie, passim*, and Johnson, *Republican Party and Wendell Willkie*, 308–309.

[50] Barnard, *Willkie*, 466; Leon Friedman, "The Election of 1944," in Schlesinger and Israel, eds., *History of Presidential Elections*, IV, 3020.

[51] Patterson, *Mr. Republican*, 270–72, 378, 417, 424.

porate state."[52] Like other Republican standard-bearers before him, Dewey emphasized orthodox Republican doctrines of economy, thrift, and private initiative. Eisenhower did acquire many of Dewey's old supporters and believed in many of the things Dewey believed in, but that did not place the General outside the Republican mainstream in 1952.

During Eisenhower's first two years in office, rhetoric and the very real shift of the Republican party toward internationalism combined to create an aura of change and revitalization about the GOP. But aside from foreign policy, there was no "Eisenhower revolution" for the Republican party.[53] This fact became increasingly apparent as the years passed; those who have written about the politics of the 1950s agree that President Eisenhower shifted noticeably to the right during his second term.[54] In 1957, Eisenhower himself observed that he had probably "grown more conservative" in his years in the White House, and lashed out against "the New Deal–Fair Deal toboggan of loose spending, centralization, punishment of business and fiscal irresponsibility."[55] Language so similar to that of orthodox Republicanism prior to 1952 hardly supports the idea that a "New Republicanism" emerged under Eisenhower's direction. In the end, the thirty-fourth President proved to be too regular a Republican to effect any basic transformation in his party.[56] Instead of ushering in a new political era, the years 1953–1954 signaled the return and reaffirmation of traditional Republicanism.

[52] Dewey speeches in Friedman, *History of Presidential Elections*, IV, 3033, 3075–76, 3086.

[53] See Milton Viorst, *Fall From Grace*, 184.

[54] Hughes, *Ordeal of Power*, 333; Larson, *The President Nobody Knew*, 142–43; James L. Sundquist, *Politics and Policy: The Eisenhower, Kennedy, and Johnson Years* (Washington: Brookings Institution, 1968), 420, 426, 428.

[55] Press conference remarks of May 15, 1957, and speech to Republican National Conference, June 7, 1957, in *Public Papers . . . 1957*, 354, 458.

[56] Halleck Oral History Transcript, Dulles Project, Princeton Univ., 7. Also Bricker interview, Feb. 2, 1971, Columbus, Ohio.

APPENDIXES

| Scale Type Defined* | Roll Call | Positive Response | P+† |
|---|---|---|---|
| | FOREIGN POLICY | | |

*Senate*

| | | | |
|---|---|---|---|
| 0 | H.R. 5113 (1951 MSA Authorization): Amendment restoring full $8.5 billion request | yes | .05 |
| 1 | S. 2594 (Defense Production Act Amendments of 1952): Fulbright amendment authorizing President to appoint representatives to International Materials Conference. | yes | .17 |
| 2 | S. 2550 (Immigration and Nationality Act): Lehman amendment repealing discriminatory quotas. | yes | .21 |
| 3 | H.R. 5113: Conference Report. Motion to recommit. | no | .21 |
| | S. 3086 (1952 MSA Authorization): Long amendment reducing by $200 million. | no | .22 |
| | S. 2550: Passage over veto. | no | .22 |
| 4 | H.R. 5113: Dirksen amendment to cut $250 million from European economic aid. | no | .24 |
| 5 | S. 3086: Welker amendment reducing by $500 million. | no | .26 |
| 6 | S. 2550: Humphrey motion to recommit. | yes | .27 |
| 7 | H.R. 5113: Dirksen amendment to cut $500 million from European economic aid. | no | .30 |
| 8 | S. 3086: Welker amendment to cut by $1 billion. | no | .33 |
| 9 | Japanese Peace Treaty—Jenner, M. Smith reservation that nothing therein limits U.S. control over its foreign policy, military establishment, etc., or Japanese sovereignty. | no | .44 |
| 10 | ———: Jenner, M. Smith reservation that nothing abrogates U.S. claim for direct military cost of the occupation. | no | .49 |

\* Scale score assigned to legislators responding positively to given roll call and all those following (allowing for permissible scale "errors").

† Proportion of total Republican legislators with recorded responses taking the positive position on given roll call.

| Scale Type Defined | Roll Call | Positive Response | P+ |
|---|---|---|---|
| 11 | H.R. 5113: Long amendment to cut $350 million from European economic aid. | no | .50 |
| 12 | ———: Adoption of conference report. | yes | .51 |
| 13 | H.R. 5684 (1951 MSA Appropriation): Passage. | yes | .66 |
| 14 | H.R. 7005 (1952 MSA Authorization): Adoption of conference report. | yes | .70 |
| 15 | S. 3086: Passage. | yes | .71 |
| 16 | H.R. 5113: Passage. | yes | .81 |
| 17 | (No positive responses) | | |

*Ideological Classifications:* Strong internationalist, types 0–2; moderate internationalist, 3–6; uncommitted, 7–10; moderate nationalist, 11–14; strong nationalist, 15–17.

*House*

| | | | |
|---|---|---|---|
| 0 | H.R. 1612 (Trade Agreements Extension Act of 1951): R. Simpson "peril points" amendment. | no | .03 |
| 1 | H.R. 7289 (State-Justice-Commerce Appropriations for 1953): Taber motion to recommit with insistence on barring funds for International Materials Conference. | no | .04 |
| 2 | H.R. 7005 (1952 MSA Authorization): Vorys amendment to cut European economic aid by $615 million. | no | .05 |
| 3 | H.R. 5678 (Immigration and Nationality Act): Passage over veto | no | .11 |
| 4 | H.R. 8370 (Supplemental Appropriations for 1953): Crawford amendment to cut European military aid by $145 million. | no | .12 |
| 5 | H.R. 7005: Vorys amendment to cut Asian economic and military aid by $111 million. | no | .19 |
| 6 | H.R. 4740 (State-Justice-Commerce-Judiciary Appropriations for 1952): Conference report. Rooney motion to agree to Senate amendment limiting U.S. contributions to international organizations to one-third of the latter's budgets (rather than lower figure). | yes | .21 |

| Scale Type Defined | Roll Call | Positive Response | P+ |
|---|---|---|---|
| 7 | ————: Clevenger motion to recommit with instructions to cut Voice of America funds by $15 million. | no | .26 |
| 8 | H.R. 7005: Adoption of conference report | yes | .44 |
| 9 | H.R. 5684 (1951 MSA Appropriation): Passage. | yes | .46 |
| 10 | H.R. 7005: Passage. | yes | .47 |
| 11 | H.R. 5113 (1951 MSA Authorization): Passage. | yes | .49 |
| 12 | S. Con. Res. 36 (European Consultative Assembly): Passage. | yes | .60 |
| 13 | H.R. 3791 (India Emergency Assistance Act): Passage. | yes | .67 |
| 14 | H. Res. 539 (Katyn Forest Massacre): Agreement to allow U.S. investigating commission to sit outside U.S. | yes | .75 |
| 15 | H.R. 3576 (Displaced Persons Act Amendment of 1951): Passage. | yes | .88 |
| 16 | (No positive responses) | | |

*Ideological Classifications:* Strong internationalist, 0–3; moderate internationalist, 4–7; uncommitted, 8–10; moderate nationalist, 11–13; strong nationalist, 14–16.

FISCAL AND ECONOMIC POLICY

*Senate*

| | | | |
|---|---|---|---|
| 0 | H.R. 4473 (Revenue Act of 1951): Committee amendment to restore provision that corporations pay tax on "excess" profits over 85 percent of those during base period (rather than 75 percent). | no | .05 |
| 1 | S. 1717 (Defense Production Act of 1951): Douglas amendment to delete limitation on rollbacks. | yes | .16 |
| 2 | S. 719 (Amend Robinson-Patman Act): Passage. | no | .19 |
| 3 | S. 2594 (Defense Production Act Amendments of 1952): Cain amendment to give city councils power | | |

| Scale Type Defined | Roll Call | Positive Response | P+ |
|---|---|---|---|
| | to veto a federal decision to restore rent controls in an area. | no | .21 |
| 4 | S. 1717: Morse amendment to eliminate exemption of agricultural commodities from price rollbacks. | yes | .24 |
| 5 | S. 2594: Dirksen amendment suspending all price and wage controls by Sept. 1, 1952, unless President determines that shortages exist. | no | .26 |
| 6 | ———: Dirksen amendment deleting sections extending price and wage controls. | no | .41 |
| 7 | S. 2170 (Price Control Revision): Passage. | yes | .41 |
| 8 | S. 1717: Wherry amendment banning price rollbacks. | no | .42 |
| 9 | ———: Case amendment exempting certain small business from price regulation. | no | .50 |
| 10 | ———: Dirksen amendment ending rent controls except in "critical defense" areas. | no | .58 |
| 11 | ———: Passage. | yes | .76 |
| 12 | ———: Williams amendment suspending agricultural price supports. | no | .91 |
| 13 | (No positive responses) | | |

*Ideological Classifications:* Strong liberal, 0–2; moderate liberal, 3–5; uncommitted, 6–8; moderate conservative, 9–11; strong conservative, 12–13.

*House*

| | | | |
|---|---|---|---|
| 0 | H.R. 4473 (Revenue Act of 1951): Reed motion to recommit. | no | .07 |
| 1 | H.R. 8210 (Defense Production Act Amendments of 1952): Wheeler amendment to end rent controls by Sept. 30, 1952, except in "critical defense" areas. | no | .14 |
| 2 | ———: Cole amendment to guarantee customary markups to wholesalers and retailers. | no | .16 |
| 3 | H.R. 3871 (Defense Production Act of 1951): Hope amendment prohibiting quotas or limitations on |  |  |

| Scale Type Defined | Roll Call | Positive Response | P+ |
|---|---|---|---|
| | amount of livestock handled or slaughtered by any processor. | no | .20 |
| 4 | H.R. 8210: Talle amendment suspending ceiling for any material which has sold below ceiling price for three months, etc. | no | .20 |
| 5 | H.R. 3871: Committee amendment to delete authority to control commodity speculation. | no | .22 |
| 6 | H.J. Res. 278 (Temporary Controls Extension): Cooley amendment banning rollbacks or imposition of ceilings during temporary extension. | no | .28 |
| 7 | H.R. 4431 (District of Columbia Emergency Rent Act): Passage. | yes | .32 |
| 8 | H.R. 3871: Cole amendment prohibiting ceilings on any livestock that do not allow all processors reasonable profit. | no | .35 |
| 9 | ———: Committee amendment to prohibit ceiling on any agricultural commodity lower than 90 percent of price received by producers as of May 19, 1951. | no | .37 |
| 10 | S. 2594 (Defense Production Act Amendments of 1952): Adoption of conference report. | yes | .39 |
| 11 | H.R. 8210: Barden amendment to end price and wage controls by July 31, 1952. | no | .41 |
| 12 | H.J. Res. 278: Adoption of rule providing for consideration. | yes | .54 |
| 13 | H.R. 3871: Cole motion to recommit. | no | .56 |
| 14 | ———: Passage. | yes | .61 |
| 15 | ———: Adoption of conference report. | yes | .65 |
| 16 | (No positive responses) | | |

*Ideological Classifications:* Strong liberal, 0–2; moderate liberal, 3–6; uncommitted, 7–10; moderate conservative, 11–13, strong conservative, 14–16.

| Scale Type Defined | Roll Call | Positive Response | P+ |
|---|---|---|---|

**WELFARE POLICY**

*Senate*

0    H.R. 3709 (Labor-FSA Appropriations for 1952): Ferguson amendment to increase cut in funds for personnel services from 5 to 10 percent.    no    .05

1    ————: Neely amendment to restore funds to Public Health Service, Office of Vocational Rehabilitation, and Children's Bureau.    yes    .14

2    ————: Lehman amendment to exempt Public Health Service from 5 percent cut.    yes    .19

3    S. 445 (Public Health Assistance to States): Passage.    yes    .29

4    H.R. 7072 (Independent Offices Appropriations for 1953): Committee amendment authorizing 45,000 (rather than 5,000) public housing starts.    yes    .32

5    H.R. 3709: Malone amendment to increase overall committee cut from 5 to 10 percent.    no    .33

6    H.R. 3880 (Independent Offices Appropriations for 1952): Dirksen amendment reducing public housing authorization from 50,000 to 5,000 new starts.    no    .53

7    H.R. 3709: Douglas amendment reducing funds for grants to states for maternal and child welfare by $3 million.    no    .63

8    (No positive responses)

*Ideological Classifications:* Strong liberal, 0–1; moderate liberal, 2–3; uncommitted, 4–5; moderate conservative, 6–7; strong conservative, 8.

*House*

0    H.R. 3880 (Independent Offices Appropriations for 1952): Gossett amendment cutting public housing authorization from 50,000 to 5,000 starts.    no    .12

1    ————: Phillips motion to recommit conference report and insist on public housing and other fund reductions.    no    .16

2    H.R. 7072 (Independent Offices Appropriations for 1953): Phillips motion to recommit conference re-

| Scale Type Defined | Roll Call | Positive Response | P+ |
|---|---|---|---|
|  | port and insist on public housing authorization reduction. | no | .16 |
| 3 | ————: Fisher amendment cutting public housing authorization from 25,000 to 5,000 starts. | no | .23 |
| 4 | H.R. 3880: Phillips motion to recommit second conference report and insist on public housing authorization reduction. | no | .28 |
| 5 | H.R. 7072: Fisher motion to recommit second conference report and insist on public housing authorization reduction. | no | .34 |
| 6 | H.R. 5118 (Unemployment Insurance for Federal Employees): Forand motion to suspend rules and pass bill. | yes | .47 |
| 7 | H.R. 3880: Adoption of second conference report. | yes | .71 |
| 8 | H.R. 3193 (Veterans' Disability Pension Increase): Passage over veto. | yes | .91 |
| 9 | H.R. 7800 (Social Security Act Amendments): Doughty motion to suspend rules and pass with amendment deleting FSA authority to determine disability. | yes | .91 |
| 10 | (No positive responses) | | |

*Ideological Classifications:* Strong liberal, 0–1; moderate liberal, 2–3; uncommitted, 4–6; moderate conservative, 7–8; strong conservative, 9–10.

POWER AND RESOURCE DEVELOPMENT

*Senate*

| | | | |
|---|---|---|---|
| 0 | H.R. 7268 (Army Civil Functions Appropriations for 1953): Ferguson amendment to cut funds for rivers and harbors by $8 million. | no | .15 |
| 1 | H.R. 4386 (Army Civil Functions Appropriations for 1952): Douglas amendment to cut funds for rivers and harbors by 10 percent. | no | .18 |
| 2 | H.R. 7072 (Independent Offices Appropriations for 1953): Ferguson amendment to cut TVA funds by $45 million. | no | .20 |

| Scale Type Defined | Roll Call | Positive Response | P+ |
|---|---|---|---|
| 3 | S.J. Res. 20 (Tidelands Leases): Connally, Holland amendment confirming and establishing title of states to Tidelands. | no | .24 |
| 4 | H.R. 3790 (Interior Department Appropriations for 1952): Hayden amendment to add $12 million for eight reclamation projects. | yes | .33 |
| 5 | S. 75 (Central Arizona Project): Knowland, Nixon amendment prohibiting construction of irrigation works unless net revenues equal irrigation distribution costs plus 25 percent of other costs. | no | .41 |
| 6 | H.R. 3973 (Agriculture Department Appropriations for 1952): Douglas amendment to cut funds for soil and water conservation by $20 million. | no | .42 |
| 7 | H.R. 4386: Ferguson motion to recommit with instructions to cut funds for rivers and harbors by $50 million. | no | .42 |
| 8 | H.R. 3790: Ferguson amendment to cut Bureau of Land Management funds by $238,304. | no | .47 |
| 9 | ———: Ferguson amendment to cut Bureau of Reclamation funds by $10 million. | no | .48 |
| 10 | H.R. 7268: Douglas amendment to cut funds for rivers and harbors by $100 million. | no | .48 |
| 11 | H.R. 3790: Douglas amendment to cut Bureau of Reclamation funds by $16 million. | no | .71 |
| 12 | H.R. 7176 (Interior Department Appropriations for 1953): Benton amendment to cut Bureau of Reclamation funds by $31 million. | no | .72 |
| 13 | (No positive responses) | | |

*Ideological Classifications:* Strong liberal, 0–2; moderate liberal, 3–5; uncommitted, 6–8; moderate conservative, 9–11; strong conservative, 12–13.

*House*

| | | | |
|---|---|---|---|
| 0 | H.R. 3790 (Interior Department Appropriations for 1952): Short amendment prohibiting expenditures for development of western Missouri project. | no | .06 |
| | H.R. 4484 (Submerged Lands Act): Passage. | no | .10 |

| Scale Type Defined | Roll Call | Positive Response | P+ |
|---|---|---|---|
| 1 | S.J. Res. 20 (Tidelands Leases): Adoption of conference report giving title to states. | no | .10 |
| 2 | H.R. 3790: Ford amendment cutting $5.5 million from Bonneville Power Administration construction funds. | no | .10 |
| 3 | ——: Taber amendment cutting $10 million from funds for Bureau of Reclamation construction and rehabilitation. | no | .12 |
| 4 | ——: Keating amendment prohibiting expenditures for construction of power transmission facilities in areas covered by power wheeling contracts serving federal establishments and preferred customers. | no | .16 |
| 5 | H.R. 7176 (Interior Department Appropriations for 1953): Rogers amendment to reduce by $816,800 Bureau of Mines conservation and mineral resource development funds. | no | .18 |
| 6 | H.R. 3973 (Agriculture Department Appropriations for 1952): Conference report. Aspinall motion to concur in Senate provision of $1.9 million for control of spruce-bark beetles, amended to $900,000. | yes | .62 |
| 7 | (No positive responses) | | |

*Ideological Classifications:* strong liberal, 0–1; moderate liberal, 2–3; uncommitted, 4–5; moderate conservative, 6; strong conservative, 7.

| Member | Foreign Policy | Fiscal and Economic Policy | Welfare Policy | Power and Resource Development |
|---|---|---|---|---|
| | | SENATE | | |
| Aiken, Vt. | 5 MI | 2 SL | o SL | 2 SL |
| Bennett, Utah | 12 MN | 13 SC | 8 SC | 9 MC |
| Bricker, Ohio | 17 SN | 11 MC | 8 SC | 13 SC |
| Bridges, N.H. | 12 MN | 8 U | 7 MC | 13 SC |
| Butler, H., Neb. | 17 SN | 12 SC | 8 SC | 8 U |
| Butler, J. M., Md. | 10 U | 9 MC | 8 SC | 10 MC |
| Capehart, Ind. | 17 SN | 9 MC | 8 SC | 6 U |
| Carlson, Kans. | 8 U | 11 MC | 6 MC | 5 ML |
| Case, S.Dak. | 14 MN | 11 MC | not scaled | 8 U |
| Cordon, Ore. | not scaled | 11 MC | 5 U | 6 U |
| Dirksen, Ill. | 16 SN | 13 SC | 8 SC | 12 SC |
| Duff, Pa. | 2 SI | 4 ML | 4 U | not scaled |
| Dworshak, Idaho | 16 SN | 9 MC | 7 MC | 4 ML |
| Ferguson, Mich. | 13 MN | 7 U | 8 SC | 13 SC |
| Flanders, Vt. | 4 MI | 8 U | 4 U | 12 SC |
| Hendrickson, N.J. | not scaled | 3 ML | 8 SC | 13 SC |
| Hickenlooper, Iowa | 13 MN | 11 MC | 7 MC | 10 MC |
| Ives, N.Y. | 1 SI | 1 SL | 1 SL | 13 SC |
| Jenner, Ind. | 17 SN | 12 SC | 8 SC | not scaled |
| Knowland, Calif. | 7 U | 12 SC | 5 U | 7 U |
| Langer, N.Dak. | 17 SN | not scaled | 1 SL | 3 ML |
| Malone, Nev. | 17 SN | 12 SC | not scaled | o SL |
| Martin, Pa. | 15 SN | not scaled | 8 SC | not scaled |
| McCarthy, Wis. | 13 MN | 10 MC | 6 MC | not scaled |
| Millikin, Colo. | 9 U | 10 MC | 8 SC | 4 ML |
| Morse, Ore. | o SI | o SL | 1 SL | 2 SL |
| Mundt, S.Dak. | 9 U | 11 MC | 7 MC | 4 ML |
| Saltonstall, Mass. | 2 SI | 4 ML | 2 ML | 13 SC |
| Schoeppel, Kans. | 17 SN | 9 MC | 6 MC | 5 ML |
| Smith, H. A., N.J. | 1 SI | 3 ML | 3 ML | 12 SC |
| Smith, M., Maine | 12 MN | 3 ML | 5 U | 13 SC |
| Taft, Ohio | 11 MN | 8 U | 3 ML | 11 MC |
| Thye, Minn. | 6 MI | 6 U | 4 U | 9 MC |
| Tobey, N.H. | o SI | 6 U | 1 SL | not scaled |
| Watkins, Utah | 11 MN | 5 ML | 8 SC | 3 ML |
| Welker, Idaho | 16 SN | 13 SC | 7 MC | 4 ML |
| Wiley, Wis. | 3 MI | 11 MC | 8 SC | not scaled |
| Williams, Del. | 15 SN | 13 SC | 8 SC | 13 SC |
| Young, N.Dak. | 16 SN | 12 SC | 7 MC | 1 SL |

* Abbreviations used: SI and MI—strong and moderate internationalist; SN
and MN—strong and moderate nationalist; SL and ML—strong and moderate
liberal; SC and MC—strong and moderate conservative; U—uncommitted.

| Member | Foreign Policy | Fiscal and Economic Policy | Welfare Policy | Power and Resource Development |
|---|---|---|---|---|
| | | HOUSE | | |
| Adair, Ind.—4 | 13 MN | 11 MC | 6 U | 6 MC |
| Allen, J., Calif.—7 | 8 U | 12 MC | 6 U | 6 MC |
| Allen, L., Ill.—16 | 15 SN | 16 SC | 8 MC | 6 MC |
| Andersen, Minn.—7 | 15 SN | 12 MC | 7 MC | not scaled |
| Andresen, Minn.—1 | 14 SN | 12 MC | 9 SC | 7 SC |
| Angell, Ore.—3 | 6 MI | 1 SL | 0 SL | 2 ML |
| Arends, Ill.—17 | 14 SN | 15 SC | 7 MC | 6 MC |
| Auchincloss, N.J.—3 | 4 MI | 7 U | 3 ML | 7 SC |
| Ayres, Ohio—14 | 8 U | 4 ML | 3 ML | 6 MC |
| Baker, Tenn.—2 | 15 SN | 10 U | 4 U | 5 U |
| Bates, Mass.—6 | 8 U | 9 U | 7 MC | 7 SC |
| Beamer, Ind.—5 | 12 MN | 14 SC | 8 MC | 6 MC |
| Belcher, Okla.—1 | 13 MN | 16 SC | 8 MC | 6 MC |
| Bender, Ohio—23 | 6 MI | 2 SL | 1 SL | 7 SC |
| Bennett, Mich.—12 | 14 SN | 3 ML | 3 ML | 4 U |
| Berry, S.Dak.—2 | 15 SN | 16 SC | 7 MC | 3 ML |
| Betts, Ohio—8 | 16 SN | 16 SC | 7 MC | 6 MC |
| Bishop, Ill.—25 | 16 SN | 16 SC | 8 MC | 5 U |
| Bolton, F., Ohio—22 | 6 MI | 3 ML | 1 SL | 6 MC |
| Bow, Ohio—16 | 15 SN | 16 SC | 8 MC | 6 MC |
| Bramblett, Calif.—13 | 13 MN | 16 SC | 7 MC | 6 MC |
| Bray, Ind.—7 | 12 MN | not scaled | 3 ML | 5 U |
| Brown, Ohio—7 | not scaled | 16 SC | 7 MC | 6 MC |
| Brownson, Ind.—11 | 8 U | 8 U | 7 MC | 7 SC |
| Budge, Idaho—2 | 14 SN | 15 SC | 7 MC | 5 U |
| Burdick, N.Dak.—A.L. | 13 MN | not scaled | 3 ML | 1 SL |
| Busbey, Ill.—3 | 14 SN | 16 SC | not scaled | 7 SC |
| Bush, Pa.—17 | 15 SN | 13 MC | 7 MC | 7 SC |
| Byrnes, Wis.—8 | not scaled | 12 MC | 9 SC | 7 SC |
| Canfield, N.J.—8 | 1 SI | 1 SL | 0 SL | not scaled |
| Case, N.J.—6 | 0 SI | 0 SL | 1 SL | not scaled |
| Chenoweth, Colo.—3 | 12 MN | 16 SC | 7 MC | 5 U |
| Chiperfield, Ill.—19 | 8 U | 16 SC | 8 MC | 6 MC |
| Church, Ill.—13 | 12 MN | 16 SC | 8 MC | 7 SC |
| Clevenger, Ohio—5 | 16 SN | 16 SC | 10 SC | 7 SC |
| Cole, W.S., N.Y.—37 | 7 MI | 12 MC | 9 SC | not scaled |
| Corbett, Pa.—29 | 6 MI | not scaled | 3 ML | not scaled |
| Cotton, N.H.—2 | 6 MI | 8 U | 8 MC | 7 SC |
| Coudert, N.Y.—17 | 6 MI | 3 ML | 2 ML | 7 SC |
| Crumpacker, Ind.—3 | 8 U | 8 U | 7 MC | 6 MC |

| Member | Foreign Policy | Fiscal and Economic Policy | Welfare Policy | Power and Resource Development |
|---|---|---|---|---|
| Cunningham, Iowa—5 | 8 U | 16 SC | 8 MC | 6 MC |
| Curtis, C., Neb.—1 | 15 SN | 16 SC | 7 MC | 7 SC |
| Curtis, T., Mo.—2 | 12 MN | 5 ML | 3 ML | 7 SC |
| Dague, Pa.—9 | 7 MI | 10 U | 7 MC | 7 SC |
| Davis, Wis.—2 | 14 SN | 14 SC | 9 SC | 7 SC |
| Devereux. Md.—2 | 8 U | 11 MC | 4 U | 7 SC |
| D'Ewart, Mont.—2 | 14 SN | 13 MC | 7 MC | 5 U |
| Dolliver, Iowa—6 | 12 MN | 16 SC | 7 MC | 6 MC |
| Dondero, Mich.—18 | 16 SN | 11 MC | 8 MC | 6 MC |
| Ellsworth, Ore.—4 | 8 U | 16 SC | not scaled | not scaled |
| Fenton, Pa.—12 | 10 U | 8 U | 6 U | 7 SC |
| Ford, Mich.—5 | 4 MI | 2 SL | 9 SC | 7 SC |
| Fulton, Pa.—27 | 0 SI | 3 ML | 1 SL | 7 SC |
| Gamble, N.Y.—26 | 8 U | 9 U | 5 U | 7 SC |
| Gavin, Pa.—23 | 14 SN | 13 MC | 6 U | 7 SC |
| George, Kans.—3 | 14 SN | 15 SC | 7 MC | 5 U |
| Golden, Ky.—8 | not scaled | 16 SC | 7 MC | 5 U |
| Goodwin, Mass.—8 | 10 U | 12 MC | 7 MC | 7 SC |
| Graham, Pa.—25 | 14 SN | 13 MC | 7 MC | 7 SC |
| Gross, Iowa—3 | 15 SN | 16 SC | 8 MC | not scaled |
| Gwinn, N.Y.—27 | not scaled | 16 SC | 8 MC | 7 SC |
| Hagen, Minn.—9 | 12 MN | 16 SC | 4 U | 2 ML |
| Hale, Maine—1 | 4 MI | 6 ML | 9 SC | 6 MC |
| Halleck, Ind.—2 | 8 U | 14 SC | 6 U | 6 MC |
| Hand, N.J.—2 | 12 MN | 6 ML | 1 SL | 6 MC |
| Harden, Ind.—6 | 12 MN | 14 SC | 6 U | 6 MC |
| Harrison, W., Wyo.—A.L. | 13 MN | 16 SC | 7 MC | 5 U |
| Harvey, Ind.—10 | 16 SN | 16 SC | 7 MC | 6 MC |
| Heselton, Mass.—1 | 2 SI | 1 SL | 0 SL | 7 SC |
| Hess, Ohio—2 | 11 MN | 9 U | 3 ML | 7 SC |
| Hill, Colo.—2 | 12 MN | 13 MC | 7 MC | 5 U |
| Hillings, Calif.—25 | 9 U | 16 SC | 7 MC | 6 MC |
| Hinshaw, Calif.—20 | 8 U | 15 SC | not scaled | 7 SC |
| Hoeven, Iowa—8 | 15 SN | 16 SC | 8 MC | 6 MC |
| Hoffman, C., Mich.—4 | 16 SN | 16 SC | 9 SC | 7 SC |
| Hoffman, R., Ill.—10 | 14 SN | 16 SC | 8 MC | 6 MC |
| Holmes, Wash.—4 | 5 MI | 10 U | 0 SL | 2 ML |
| Hope, Kans.—5 | 4 MI | 12 MC | 7 MC | 7 SC |
| Horan, Wash.—5 | 12 MN | 10 U | 6 U | 2 ML |
| Hunter, Calif.—12 | 7 MI | 12 MC | 6 U | 6 MC |

| Member | Foreign Policy | Fiscal and Economic Policy | Welfare Policy | Power and Resource Development |
|---|---|---|---|---|
| Jackson, Calif.—16 | 10 U | 13 MC | 9 SC | 6 MC |
| James, Pa.—7 | 8 U | 8 U | 7 MC | 7 SC |
| Javits, N.Y.—21 | 0 SI | 0 SL | 0 SL | 0 SL |
| Jenkins, Ohio—10 | 12 MN | 16 SC | 6 U | 5 U |
| Jensen, Iowa—7 | 15 SN | 16 SC | 7 MC | 6 MC |
| Johnson, Calif.—11 | 11 MN | 5 ML | 6 U | 2 ML |
| Jonas, E., Ill.—12 | 14 SN | 13 MC | 8 MC | 6 MC |
| Judd, Minn.—5 | 4 MI | 6 ML | 1 SL | 6 MC |
| Kean, N.J.—12 | 2 SI | 1 SL | 0 SL | 7 SC |
| Kearney, N.Y.—32 | 7 MI | 5 ML | 8 MC | 7 SC |
| Kearns, Pa.—24 | not scaled | 16 SC | not scaled | 5 U |
| Keating, N.Y.—38 | 5 MI | 3 ML | 6 U | 7 SC |
| Kersten, Wis.—5 | 5 MI | 2 SL | 6 U | 6 MC |
| Kilburn, N.Y.—33 | 8 U | 14 SC | 8 MC | 7 SC |
| Latham, N.Y.—4 | 8 U | 5 ML | 7 MC | 7 SC |
| LeCompte, Iowa—4 | 8 U | 15 SC | 8 MC | 7 SC |
| Lovre, S.Dak.—1 | 12 MN | 16 SC | 8 MC | 6 MC |
| Mack, Wash.—3 | 8 U | 6 ML | 6 U | 2 ML |
| Martin, J., Mass.—14 | 8 U | 10 U | 6 U | not scaled |
| Martin, T., Iowa—1 | 14 SN | 16 SC | 8 MC | 5 U |
| Mason, Ill.—15 | 14 SN | 16 SC | not scaled | 7 SC |
| McConnell, Pa.—13 | 8 U | 7 U | 6 U | 7 SC |
| McCulloch, Ohio—4 | 12 MN | 13 MC | 7 MC | 7 SC |
| McDonough, Calif.—15 | 10 U | 12 MC | 8 MC | 7 SC |
| McGregor, Ohio—17 | 12 MN | 16 SC | 7 MC | 7 SC |
| McVey, Ill.—4 | 14 SN | 15 SC | 8 MC | 6 MC |
| Meader, Mich.—2 | 8 U | 9 U | 7 MC | 7 SC |
| Merrow, N.H.—1 | 6 MI | 8 U | 2 ML | 6 MC |
| Miller, A., Neb.—4 | 15 SN | 16 SC | 7 MC | 7 SC |
| Miller, E., Md.—1 | 8 U | 16 SC | 7 MC | 7 SC |
| Miller, W., N.Y.—40 | 8 U | 5 ML | 6 U | 6 MC |
| Morano, Conn.—4 | 3 SI | 1 SL | 2 ML | 6 MC |
| Mumma, Pa.—16 | 15 SN | 12 MC | 2 ML | 7 SC |
| Nelson, Maine—2 | 12 MN | not scaled | 7 MC | 6 MC |
| Nicholson, Mass.—9 | 16 SN | 16 SC | 8 MC | 7 SC |
| Norblad, Ore.—1 | 6 MI | not scaled | 6 U | 4 U |
| O'Hara, Minn.—2 | 14 SN | 16 SC | 8 MC | 6 MC |
| O'Konski, Wis.—10 | 15 SN | 11 MC | 0 SL | 0 SL |
| Ostertag, N.Y.—39 | 8 U | 7 U | 7 MC | 6 MC |
| Patterson, Conn.—5 | 7 MI | 1 SL | 4 U | 6 MC |
| Phillips, Calif.—29 | 14 SN | 16 SC | 10 SC | 6 MC |
| Prouty, Vt.—A.L. | 4 MI | not scaled | 5 U | 6 MC |

| Member | Foreign Policy | Fiscal and Economic Policy | Welfare Policy | Power and Resource Development |
|---|---|---|---|---|
| Radwan, N.Y.—41 | 7 MI | 5 ML | 6 U | 6 MC |
| Reece, Tenn.—1 | 14 SN | 16 SC | 8 MC | 6 MC |
| Reed, C., Ill.—14 | 15 SN | 16 SC | 8 MC | 7 SC |
| Reed, D., N.Y.—43 | 14 SN | 16 SC | 10 SC | 6 MC |
| Rees, Kans.—4 | 13 MN | 13 MC | 6 U | 6 MC |
| Riehlman, N.Y.—35 | 7 MI | 3 ML | 3 ML | 6 MC |
| Rogers, Mass.—5 | 9 U | 1 SL | 5 U | 7 SC |
| Sadlak, Conn.—A.L. | 9 U | 6 ML | not scaled | 7 SC |
| St. George, N.Y.—28 | 13 MN | 13 MC | 7 MC | 7 SC |
| Saylor, Pa.—22 | 10 U | 9 U | 0 SL | 5 U |
| Scott, Pa.—6 | 2 SI | 0 SL | 0 SL | 7 SC |
| Scrivner, Kans.—2 | 16 SN | 16 SC | 7 MC | 7 SC |
| Scudder, Calif.—1 | 13 MN | 14 SC | 7 MC | 6 MC |
| Seely-Brown, Conn.—2 | 3 SI | 1 SL | 2 ML | 7 SC |
| Shafer, Mich.—3 | 15 SN | 16 SC | 8 MC | 6 MC |
| Sheehan, Ill.—11 | 15 SN | 16 SC | 10 SC | 6 MC |
| Short, Mo.—7 | 16 SN | 16 SC | 7 MC | 6 MC |
| Simpson, R., Pa.—18 | 15 SN | 16 SC | 6 U | 7 SC |
| Simpson, S., Ill.—20 | 14 SN | 16 SC | 8 MC | 6 MC |
| Smith, L., Wis.—1 | 14 SN | 16 SC | 8 MC | 6 MC |
| Smith, W., Kans.—6 | 16 SN | 16 SC | 10 SC | 7 SC |
| Springer, Ill.—22 | 8 U | 16 SC | 8 MC | 6 MC |
| Taber, N.Y.—36 | 16 SN | 16 SC | 10 SC | 7 SC |
| Talle, Iowa—2 | 9 U | 12 MC | 8 MC | 7 SC |
| Taylor, N.Y.—31 | 7 MI | 5 ML | 1 SL | 6 MC |
| Thompson, Mich.—9 | 12 MN | 16 SC | 7 MC | 7 SC |
| Tollefson, Wash.—6 | 5 MI | 5 ML | 0 SL | 2 ML |
| Van Pelt, Wis.—6 | 14 SN | 14 SC | 9 SC | 7 SC |
| Van Zandt, Pa.—20 | 8 U | 8 U | 5 U | 7 SC |
| Velde, Ill.—18 | 14 SN | 16 SC | 8 MC | 6 MC |
| Vorys, Ohio—12 | 8 U | 13 MC | 7 MC | 7 SC |
| Vursell, Ill.—23 | 14 SN | 16 SC | 8 MC | 5 U |
| Weichel, Ohio—13 | 8 U | 10 U | 6 U | 6 MC |
| Wharton, N.Y.—29 | 15 SN | 16 SC | 8 MC | 6 MC |
| Widnall, N.J.—7 | 4 MI | 6 ML | 1 SL | 6 MC |
| Wigglesworth, Mass.—13 | 4 MI | 1 SL | 4 U | 7 SC |
| Williams, N.Y.—34 | not scaled | 11 MC | 3 ML | 6 MC |
| Wilson, E., Ind.—9 | 13 MN | 16 SC | 5 U | 7 SC |
| Withrow, Wis.—3 | 13 MN | 1 SL | 0 SL | 0 SL |
| Wolcott, Mich.—7 | 16 SN | 12 MC | 8 MC | 6 MC |
| Wolverton, N.J.—1 | 7 MI | 1 SL | 0 SL | 6 MC |

| Senator | | Scale Score and Ideological Classification | Ideological Classification, Foreign Policy* |
|---|---|---|---|
| | | INDIVIDUAL SCORES | |
| Aiken, Vt. | 0 | Strong pro-executive | MI |
| Bennett, Utah | 6 | Strong anti-executive | MN |
| Bricker, Ohio | 6 | Strong anti-executive | SN |
| Bridges, N.H. | 5 | Moderate anti-executive | MN |
| Butler, H., Neb. | 6 | Strong anti-executive | SN |
| Butler, J. M., Md. | 6 | Strong anti-executive | U |
| Capehart, Ind. | 6 | Strong anti-executive | SN |
| Carlson, Kans. | 6 | Strong anti-executive | U |
| Case, S.Dak. | 6 | Strong anti-executive | MN |
| Cordon, Ore. | 5 | Moderate anti-executive | not scaled |
| Dirksen, Ill. | 6 | Strong anti-executive | SN |
| Duff, Pa. | 1 | Moderate pro-executive | SI |
| Dworshak, Idaho | 6 | Strong anti-executive | SN |
| Ferguson, Mich. | 5 | Moderate anti-executive | MN |
| Flanders, Vt. | 1 | Moderate pro-executive | MI |
| Hendrickson, N.J. | 5 | Moderate anti-executive | not scaled |
| Hickenlooper, Iowa | 6 | Strong anti-executive | MN |
| Ives, N.Y. | 0 | Strong pro-executive | SI |
| Jenner, Ind. | 6 | Strong anti-executive | SN |
| Knowland, Calif. | 3 | Uncommitted | U |
| Langer, N.Dak. | 6 | Strong anti-executive | SN |
| Malone, Nev. | 6 | Strong anti-executive | SN |
| Martin, Pa. | 6 | Strong anti-executive | SN |
| McCarthy, Wis. | 5 | Moderate anti-executive | MN |
| Millikin, Colo. | 4 | Uncommitted | U |
| Morse, Ore. | 2 | Moderate pro-executive | SI |
| Mundt, S.Dak. | 6 | Strong anti-executive | U |
| Saltonstall, Mass. | 1 | Moderate pro-executive | SI |
| Schoeppel, Kans. | 6 | Strong anti-executive | SN |
| Smith, H. A., N.J. | 1 | Moderate pro-executive | SI |
| Smith, M., Maine | 5 | Moderate anti-executive | MN |
| Taft, Ohio | 6 | Strong anti-executive | MN |
| Thye, Minn. | 3 | Uncommitted | MI |
| Tobey, N.H. | 0 | Strong pro-executive | SI |
| Watkins, Utah | 6 | Strong anti-executive | MN |
| Welker, Idaho | 6 | Strong anti-executive | SN |
| Wiley, Wis. | 3 | Uncommitted | MI |
| Williams, Del. | 5 | Moderate anti-executive | SN |
| Young, N.Dak. | 6 | Strong anti-executive | SN |

* Abbreviations used: SI and MI—strong and moderate internationalist, U—uncommitted, MN and SN—moderate and strong nationalist.

255

| Scale Type Defined † | Roll Call | Positive (Pro-Executive) Response | P+‡ |
|---|---|---|---|
| | ROLL CALLS USED AS BASIS FOR SCALE, EIGHTY-SECOND CONGRESS | | |
| 0 | S. Res. 99 (Troops to Europe): Lehman amendment approving policy and stating the sense of the Senate that there should be the "fullest collaboration" between Congress and the President on such matters. | yes | .08 |
| 1 | ———: Reconsideration of Ives amendment approving the policy but providing for review of future policy by Senate Foreign Relations and House Foreign Affairs Committees. | no | .18 |
| 2 | H.R. 4550 (Mutual Defense Assistance Control Act of 1951): Kem amendment to make mandatory the termination of economic and military aid for any country shipping strategic materials to Soviet bloc. | no | .24 |
| 3 | S. Res. 99: Bricker motion to recommit with instructions that committees report it as a joint resolution in statutory form. | no | .32 |
| 4 | U.S.-Japanese Security Pact: Jenner, M. Smith reservation that no administrative agreement regarding disposition of U.S. armed forces shall be binding unless ratified as a treaty by the Senate, or approved by an act of Congress. | no | .35 |
| 5 | S. Res. 99: Kem amendment stating the sense of the Senate that before additional ground troops are sent to Europe, the Joint Chiefs of Staff must certify to Congress that sufficient air strength will be available. | no | .47 |

† Scale score assigned to legislators responding positively on given roll call and all those following (allowing for permissible scale "errors"). Scale type 6 defined by no positive responses.

‡ Proportion of total Republican legislators with recorded responses taking the positive position on given roll call.

| Roll Call | Total Vote | Republican Vote |
|---|---|---|
| **SENATE** | | |
| H.R. 6391 (Mutual Security Appropriations for 1954): Long amendment to limit obligation of funds to $6.2 billion (Eisenhower opposed) | 35–53 | 18–27 |
| ————: McCarthy motion to suspend rules to offer amendment reducing aid to any recipient nation by the amount of any goods shipped to Communist China prior to Chinese agreement to Korean peace settlement (Eisenhower opposed) | 34–50 | 19–24 |
| ————: Ellender amendment reducing European military aid by $500 million. (Eisenhower opposed) | 32–52 | 19–24 |
| ————: Ellender amendment reducing European economic aid by $71.8 million. (Eisenhower opposed) | 37–45 | 21–21 |
| ————: Jenner motion to limit expenditures in fiscal 1954 to $5.5 billion. (Eisenhower opposed) | 33–49 | 17–25 |
| ————: Gore amendment eliminating $50 million for mutual special weapons planning. (Eisenhower opposed) | 23–55 | 2–38 |
| ————: Passage. (Eisenhower supported) | 69–10 | 32–9 |
| S. 2128 (Mutual Security Authorization for 1954): Dirksen amendment making available up to $25 million in surplus agricultural commodities for use of Asia Pacific countries. (Eisenhower supported) | 28–42 | 23–10 |
| ————: Humphrey amendment making available up to $50 million in surplus agricultural commodities to any friendly nation to meet famine or crisis. (Eisenhower supported) | 12–54 | 3–28 |
| ————: McClellan amendment making available part of military assistance funds for use in a currency conversion program under which foreign currency would be accepted in exchange for surplus farm commodities. (Eisenhower supported) | 49–35 | 14–30 |
| ————: Case motion to table Long motion to recommit with instructions to reduce authorization by $2 billion. (Eisenhower supported) | 48–34 | 30–13 |

| Roll Call | Total Vote | Republican Vote |
|---|---|---|
| ———: Long motion to recommit with instructions to reduce total authorization by $1 billion. (Eisenhower opposed) | 34–48 | 21–22 |
| ———: Long motion to recommit with instructions to reduce total to House-approved figure of $4,998,732,500. (Eisenhower opposed) | 38–42 | 22–18 |
| H.R. 6481 (Refugee Act of 1953): Passage. (Eisenhower supported) | 69–30 | 39–8 |
| Knowland motion to recess on July 17, 1953, to give committee time to study refugee immigration bill. (Eisenhower supported) | 40–31 | 34–4 |
| S. 2911 (Wool Supports): Malone amendment to substitute tariff protection for direct payments. (Eisenhower opposed) | 7–76 | 7–38 |
| H.R. 9678 (Mutual Security Authorization for 1955): Malone amendment to strike out text of bill and put in language authorizing $13 billion for construction of military aircraft for U.S. armed forces. (Eisenhower opposed) | 7–81 | 7–40 |
| ———: Long amendment reducing total authorization by $1 billion. (Eisenhower opposed) | 38–48 | 20–25 |
| ———: Long amendment reducing total authorization by $500 million (Eisenhower opposed) | 45–41 | 19–26 |
| ———: Passage. (Eisenhower supported) | 67–19 | 30–15 |
| H.R. 9474 (Reciprocal Trade Act Extension): Gore amendment to extend presidential authority three years instead of one, and permit further reductions of duties. (Eisenhower supported) | 32–45 | 0–39 |
| ———: Passage. (Eisenhower supported) | 71–3 | 37–2 |
| Exec. B. (International Sugar Agreement): Ratification. (Eisenhower supported) | 60–16 | 39–5 |

HOUSE

| Roll Call | Total Vote | Republican Vote |
|---|---|---|
| H.R. 6391 (Mutual Security Appropriation for 1954): Conference Report. Passman motion to recommit with instructions to cut European military aid by $211 million. (Eisenhower opposed) | 192–200 | 97–101 |

| Roll Call | Total Vote | Republican Vote |
|---|---|---|
| ———: Adoption of conference report. (Eisenhower supported) | 237–156 | 115–84 |
| H.R. 6200 (First Supplemental Appropriations for 1954): Rooney motion to recommit with instructions to increase Voice of America funds from $60 to $80 million, and delete personnel reduction provision. (Eisenhower supported) | 154–244 | 24–177 |
| H.R. 5495 (1953 Reciprocal Trade Act Extension): Smith motion to recommit with instructions to delete section increasing Tariff Commission membership from six to seven. (Eisenhower opposed) | 185–215 | 6–200 |
| ———: Passage. (Eisenhower supported) | 363–34 | 179–25 |
| H.R. 5894 (Second Simpson Trade Bill): Curtis motion to recommit to Ways and Means Committee. (Eisenhower supported) | 242–161 | 104–105 |
| H.R. 5710 (Mutual Security Authorization for 1954): Passage. (Eisenhower supported) | 280–108 | 119–81 |
| ———: Adoption of conference report. (Eisenhower supported) | 222–109 | 95–80 |
| H.R. 6481 (Refugee Act of 1953): Wilson motion to recommit. (Eisenhower opposed) | 186–222 | 73–133 |
| ———: Passage. (Eisenhower supported) | 221–185 | 132–74 |
| H.R. 6016 (Emergency Famine Relief Authority): Sutton motion to recommit. (Eisenhower opposed) | 82–322 | 10–194 |
| H.R. 5659 (Wheat for Pakistan): Passage. (Eisenhower supported) | 310–75 | 164–29 |
| H.R. 9474 (Reciprocal Trade Act Extension of 1954): Rule providing for consideration. (Eisenhower opposed) | 273–63 | 145–27 |
| ———: Passage. (Eisenhower supported) | 281–53 | 126–39 |
| H.R. 9678 (Mutual Security Authorization for 1955): Passage. (Eisenhower supported) | 260–126 | 118–79 |

| Roll Call | Total Vote | Republican Vote |
|---|---|---|
| SENATE | | |
| S. 1081 (Economic Controls): Byrd amendment that emergency controls not be imposed unless Congress declares war or state of national emergency. (Eisenhower opposed) | 45–41 | 34–13 |
| ———: Bricker amendment deleting stand-by authority. (Eisenhower opposed) | 26–61 | 24–24 |
| ———: Adoption of conference report. (Eisenhower supported) | 42–47 | 42–4 |
| S. 2047 (Sale of Government-owned Rubber Plants): Passage. (Eisenhower supported) | 65–16 | 40–3 |
| H.J. Res. 238 (Discharge Indebtedness of Commodity Credit Corporation): Adoption of conference report. (Eisenhower supported) | 49–10 | 23–1 |
| H.R. 8224 (Excise Tax Reductions): Capehart amendment to retain 5 percent excises on household appliances. (Eisenhower opposed) | 64–23 | 29–15 |
| ———: Douglas amendment lowering manufacturer's excise on vehicles. (Eisenhower opposed) | 25–63 | 6–39 |
| ———: Douglas amendment lowering excise on radios, televisions, phonographs, and musical instruments. (Eisenhower opposed) | 23–64 | 5–39 |
| ———: McClellan amendment to set aside revenues from highway fuel tax for road-building (Eisenhower supported) | 27–61 | 7–37 |
| ———: Byrd, Williams amendment to extend all excises except admissions taxes. (Eisenhower supported) | 34–54 | 18–27 |
| H.R. 8300 (Internal Revenue Code Revision): George amendment to increase personal exemption to $700 and delete dividend exclusions and tax credit. (Eisenhower opposed) | 46–49 | 3–45 |
| ———: Johnson amendment to delete tax credit on dividends. (Eisenhower opposed) | 71–13 | 34–10 |

| Roll Call | Total Vote | Republican Vote |
|---|---|---|
| ————: Long amendment granting each taxpayer a $20 credit each year and deleting dividend exclusion. (Eisenhower opposed) | 33–50 | 3–41 |
| ————: Morse amendment deleting provision permitting accelerated depreciation. (Eisenhower opposed) | 20–60 | 2–40 |
| ————: Douglas motion to recommit with instructions to add provisions for individual income-tax relief. (Eisenhower opposed) | 15–62 | 1–41 |
| ————: Monroney amendment to delete all provisions except one-year extension of corporate tax. (Eisenhower opposed) | 15–58 | 2–40 |
| ————: Passage. (Eisenhower supported) | 63–9 | 41–1 |
| ————: Adoption of conference report. (Eisenhower supported) | 61–26 | 42–4 |

HOUSE

| Roll Call | Total Vote | Republican Vote |
|---|---|---|
| H.R. 5728 (Sale of Rubber Plants): Patman motion to recommit. (Eisenhower opposed) | 58–316 | 2–190 |
| H.R. 5898 (Excess Profits Tax Extension): Passage. (Eisenhower opposed) | 325–77 | 169–38 |
| H.R. 6672 (Debt Limit Increase): Mills motion to recommit with instructions to make increase temporary. (Eisenhower opposed) | 173–225 | 0–203 |
| ————: Passage. (Eisenhower supported) | 239–158 | 169–33 |
| H.R. 5141 (Small Business Administration): Spence motion to recommit with instructions not to terminate Reconstruction Finance Corporation. (Eisenhower opposed) | 161–227 | 2–197 |
| H.R. 9756 (Commodity Credit Corporation): Passage of joint resolution discharging indebtedness. (Eisenhower supported) | 323–27 | 178–12 |
| ————: Increase borrowing authority of CCC. (Eisenhower supported) | 317–57 | 170–27 |
| H.R. 8300 (Internal Revenue Code Revision): Cooper motion to recommit with instructions to increase personal exemption and delete dividend credit. (Eisenhower opposed ) | 204–210 | 10–201 |

| Roll Call | Total Vote | Republican Vote |
|---|---|---|
| ——: Passage. (Eisenhower supported) | 339–80 | 208–5 |
| ——: Conference report. Cooper motion to recommit with instructions to delete 4 percent dividend tax credit. (Eisenhower opposed) | 169–227 | 3–204 |
| ——: Adoption of conference report. (Eisenhower supported) | 315–77 | 201–3 |
| H.R. 8224 (Excise Tax Reductions): Lyle motion to recommit with instructions to exempt from tax admission tickets costing less than 50 cents. (Eisenhower opposed) | 200–213 | 0–210 |

| Roll Call | *Total Vote* | *Republican Vote* |
|---|---|---|
| **SENATE** | | |
| H.R. 7839 (Housing Redevelopment): Knowland amendment providing authority to construct 140,000 public housing units over a four-year period. (Eisenhower supported) | 66–16 | 38–3 |
| ———: Adoption of conference report. (Eisenhower supported) | 59–21 | 38–4 |
| H.R. 5173 (Employment Security): Kennedy amendment increasing amount and duration of benefits. (Eisenhower opposed) | 30–56 | 4–42 |
| ———: Adoption of conference report. (Eisenhower supported) | 78–3 | 44–0 |
| **HOUSE** | | |
| H.R. 4663 (First Independent Offices Appropriation for 1954): Yates motion to recommit with instructions to provide for 35,000 public housing starts in fiscal 1954. (Eisenhower supported) | 157–245 | 34–176 |
| ———: Conference report. Phillips motion that House concur in Senate amendment authorizing 20,000 public housing starts in fiscal 1954. (Eisenhower supported) | 239–161 | 173–36 |
| H.R. 7839 (Housing Redevelopment): Bolling motion to recommit with instructions to authorize 140,000 public housing starts over a four-year period. (Eisenhower supported) | 176–211 | 48–150 |
| ———: Passage. (Eisenhower supported) | 353–36 | 189–9 |
| ———: Rule disagreeing with Senate bill and sending to conference. (Eisenhower supported) | 361–19 | 192–1 |
| ———: Conference report. Spence motion to recommit with instructions to provide authority for 140,000 public housing starts over a four-year period. (Eisenhower supported) | 156–234 | 50–155 |
| ———: Adoption of conference report. (Eisenhower supported) | 358–30 | 196–7 |

| Roll Call | Total Vote | Republican Vote |
|---|---|---|
| H.R. 8356 (Health Reinsurance): Rule providing for consideration. (Eisenhower supported) | 274–88 | 175–18 |
| ———: Williams motion to recommit. (Eisenhower opposed) | 238–134 | 75–120 |
| H.R. 9366 (Social Security Amendments): Passage. (Eisenhower supported) | 356–8 | 181–2 |
| H.R. 9709 (Unemployment Compensation): Forand motion to recommit with instructions to increase benefits. (Eisenhower opposed) | 110–241 | 17–173 |
| ———: Passage. (Eisenhower supported) | 309–36 | 178–7 |

| Roll Call | Total Vote | Republican Vote |
|---|---|---|
| **SENATE** | | |
| S. 3052 (Omnibus Farm Bill): McCarthy amendment to support five basic commodities at 90 to 100 percent of parity. (Eisenhower opposed) | 12–81 | 5–43 |
| ———: Schoeppel amendment to support five basic commodities at 82.5 to 90 percent of parity. (Eisenhower supported) | 49–44 | 37–11 |
| ———: Thye amendment to support dairy products at between 80 and 90 percent. (Eisenhower opposed) | 44–48 | 11–37 |
| ———: Aiken amendment to continue to support dairy products at 75 to 90 percent. (Eisenhower supported) | 49–43 | 37–11 |
| ———: Young amendment to establish mandatory support for non-basic grains and soy beans at between 75 and 90 percent. (Eisenhower opposed) | 33–54 | 8–38 |
| ———: Aiken amendment deleting provisions for non-basic grains. (Eisenhower supported) | 52–29 | 38–5 |
| ———: Anderson amendment to encourage holders of range grazing permits to construct improvements. (Eisenhower supported) | 45–41 | 40–7 |
| ———: Thye amendment to insert House language on disposal of dairy surpluses. (Eisenhower opposed) | 30–56 | 13–34 |
| ———: Humphrey amendment prohibiting Secretary of Agriculture from limiting the number of terms which members of county conservation committees can serve. (Eisenhower opposed) | 45–44 | 5–43 |
| ———: Johnston motion to table reconsideration of Humphrey amendment. (Eisenhower opposed) | 46–43 | 5–43 |
| H.R. 9680 (Omnibus Farm Bill): Passage. (Eisenhower supported) | 62–28 | 44–4 |
| ———: Adoption of conference report. (Eisenhower supported) | 44–28 | 31–6 |
| S. 2911 (Wool Supports): Ellender amendment to continue rigid 90 percent price supports on six basic commodities through 1955. (Eisenhower opposed) | 40–48 | 8–37 |

| Roll Call | Total Vote | Republican Vote |
|---|---|---|
| **SENATE** | | |
| ————: Humphrey amendment providing for support of dairy products at 90 percent of parity. (Eisenhower opposed) | 32–60 | 8–40 |
| ————: Thye amendment setting dairy supports at 85 percent and limiting reductions to 5 percent per year. (Eisenhower opposed) | 38–53 | 10–37 |
| ————: Passage. (Eisenhower supported) | 69–17 | 40–4 |
| **HOUSE** | | |
| H.R. 9680 (Omnibus Farm Bill): Harrison amendment to support five basic commodities at between 82.5 and 90 percent of parity. (Eisenhower supported) | 228–170 | 182–23 |

| Roll Call | Total Vote | Republican Vote |
|---|---|---|
| **SENATE** | | |
| S.J. Res. 13 (Submerged Lands): Anderson motion to lay bill aside temporarily. (Eisenhower opposed) | 21–61 | 4–42 |
| ———: Taft motion to table Anderson substitute. (Eisenhower supported) | 56–33 | 38–8 |
| ———: Douglas amendment limiting all states to ownership within three miles, and designating federal revenues from offshore oil to education. (Eisenhower opposed) | 26–58 | 6–39 |
| ———: Monroney amendment limiting all states to three-mile title, providing for federal leasing of the outer continental shelf, and devoting federal royalties to reducduction of national debt. (Eisenhower opposed) | 22–59 | 3–41 |
| ———: Douglas amendment requiring that state limits be measured from coast of main continent, and limiting to three miles the seaward boundaries of islands lying off coastal states. (Eisenhower opposed) | 26–50 | 9–34 |
| ———: Lehman amendment providing for federal title to submerged lands, and devoting revenues to aid for education, etc. (Eisenhower opposed) | 30–60 | 6–38 |
| ———: Kefauver amendment to set up a federal study commission on submerged lands question. (Eisenhower opposed) | 32–59 | 7–38 |
| ———: Neely amendment providing for federal title to submerged lands, and designating revenues in specified ways. (Eisenhower opposed) | 27–64 | 3–42 |
| ———: Langer amendment providing that 87.5 percent of all offshore royalties accruing to states be used to reduce national debt. (Eisenhower opposed) | 34–56 | 9–36 |
| ———: Committee amendment with substitute wording (virtually the original bill). (Eisenhower supported) | 56–35 | 35–10 |
| S. 1901 (Continental Shelf): Hendrickson, Case amendment to apply revenues from federal leases in outer shelf to national defense expenses during national emergency, and thereafter to education. (Eisenhower opposed) | 37–42 | 37–3 |

| Roll Call | Total Vote | Republican Vote |
|---|---|---|
| SENATE *(cont.)* | | |
| ————: Adoption of conference report. (Eisenhower supported) | 45–43 | 37–7 |
| S. 3690 (Atomic Energy): Anderson amendment limiting Atomic Energy Commission power contracts to power supplied directly to AEC. (Eisenhower opposed) | 36–55 | 3–44 |
| ————: Knowland motion to table reconsideration of vote authorizing AEC contract for power to be supplied to the TVA. (Eisenhower supported) | 56–35 | 44–3 |
| ————: Stennis amendment to strike from bill all provisions except those related to international pooling. (Eisenhower opposed) | 31–51 | 2–40 |
| H.R. 9757 (Atomic Energy): Passage. (Eisenhower supported) | 57–28 | 44–3 |
| ————: First conference report. (Eisenhower supported) | 41–48 | 39–6 |
| ————: Second conference report. (Eisenhower supported) | 59–17 | 39–1 |
| HOUSE | | |
| H.R. 4198 (Submerged Lands): Celler motion to recommit. (Eisenhower opposed) | 106–283 | 15–191 |
| ————: Passage. (Eisenhower supported) | 285–108 | 188–18 |
| ————: Adoption of rule concurring in Senate amendments. (Eisenhower supported) | 287–116 | 184–17 |
| H.R. 5134 (Continental Shelf): Passage. (Eisenhower supported) | 309–91 | 193–12 |
| H.R. 9757 (Atomic Energy): Cole amendment granting normal patent rights. (Eisenhower opposed) | 203–161 | 190–6 |
| ————: Holifield motion to recommit. (Eisenhower opposed) | 165–222 | 7–196 |
| ————: Passage. (Eisenhower supported) | 231–154 | 195–7 |

| Roll Call | Total Vote | Republican Vote |
|---|---|---|
| **SENATE** | | |
| S.J. Res. 1 (Bricker Amendment): Bricker substitute that a treaty can become internal law only after legislation, unless Senate stipulates otherwise. (Eisenhower opposed) | 42–50 | 29–17 |
| ———: George substitute providing that only non-treaty executive agreements would require implementing legislation. (Eisenhower opposed) | 61–30 | 30–17 |
| ———: Passage of resolution, with wording of George substitute. (Eisenhower opposed; two-thirds majority required) | 60–31 | 32–15 |
| Nomination of Charles E. Bohlen: Vote on confirmation. (Eisenhower supported) | 74–13 | 35–11 |
| S. 2650 (Revision of Taft-Hartley Act): Hill motion to recommit. (Eisenhower opposed) | 50–42 | 3–42 |
| S. 2150 (St. Lawrence Seaway): Flanders motion to recommit. (Eisenhower opposed) | 32–51 | 14–28 |
| ———: Passage of bill. (Eisenhower supported) | 51–33 | 26–15 |
| **HOUSE** | | |
| S. 2150 (St. Lawrence Seaway): Fallon motion to recommit. (Eisenhower opposed) | 157–242 | 62–144 |
| ———: Passage of bill. (Eisenhower supported) | 241–158 | 144–64 |

*Appendix J* LEADING EISENHOWER SUPPORTERS AND OPPONENTS AMONG DEMOCRATS IN THE EIGHTY-THIRD CONGRESS, BY ISSUE AREA

| SENATE | | | |
|---|---|---|---|
| *Supporters* | | *Opponents* | |
| *Foreign Policy* | | | |
| Humphrey, Minn. | .96 | *Byrd, Va. | .14 |
| *Fulbright, Ark. | .94 | *Russell, Ga. | .19 |
| Lehman, N.Y. | .93 | Frear, Del. | .22 |
| *Kefauver, Tenn. | .92 | *McClellan, Ark. | .24 |
| Murray, Mont. | .91 | *Johnston, S.C. | .26 |
| *Hennings, Mo. | .91 | Hunt, Wyo. | .27 |
| Jackson, Wash. | .91 | | |
| *Fiscal-Economic* | | | |
| *Holland, Fla. | .78 | McCarran, Nev. | .06 |
| E. Johnson, Colo. | .76 | Magnuson, Wash. | .18 |
| *Daniel, Tex. | .72 | Lehman, N.Y. | .20 |
| *Symington, Mo. | .71 | Mansfield, Mont. | .22 |
| *Robertson, Va. | .69 | Jackson, Wash. | .22 |
| *L. Johnson, Tex. | .67 | *Kerr, Okla. | .25 |
| *Long, La. | .67 | | |
| *Welfare* | | | |
| *L. Johnson, Tex. | 1.00 | Kennedy, Mass. | .00 |
| *Daniel, Tex. | 1.00 | Douglas, Ill. | .25 |
| *Ervin, N.C. | 1.00 | Green, R.I. | .25 |
| Frear, Del. | 1.00 | Humphrey, Minn. | .25 |
| *Holland, Fla. | 1.00 | Jackson, Wash. | .25 |
| E. Johnson, Colo. | 1.00 | *Kilgore, W. Va. | .25 |
| *Lennon, N.C. | 1.00 | Lehman, N.Y. | .25 |
| *Robertson, Va. | 1.00 | Magnuson, Wash. | .25 |
| *Smathers, Fla. | 1.00 | Mansfield, Mont. | .25 |
| *Stennis, Miss. | 1.00 | Murray, Mont. | .25 |
| *Power and Resources* | | | |
| *Byrd, Va. | 1.00 | Douglas, Ill. | .06 |
| *Hoey, N.C. | 1.00 | *Gore, Tenn. | .06 |
| *W. Smith, N.C. | 1.00 | *Hennings, Mo. | .06 |
| *Ellender, La. | .94 | *Hill, Ala. | .06 |
| *Holland, Fla. | .94 | Jackson, Wash. | .06 |
| *Robertson, Va. | .94 | *Kefauver, Tenn. | .06 |
| | | Lehman, N.Y. | .06 |
| | | Magnuson, Wash. | .06 |
| | | Mansfield, Mont. | .06 |
| | | *Monroney, Okla. | .06 |
| | | *Symington, Mo. | .06 |

* Indicates Southern or border-state congressman.

| HOUSE | | | |
|---|---|---|---|
| *Supporters* | | *Opponents* | |

### Foreign Policy

| Supporters | | Opponents | |
|---|---|---|---|
| O'Neill, Mass. | 1.00 | *Willis, La. | .00 |
| Doyle, Calif. | .93 | *Dowdy, Tex. | .13 |
| C. King, Calif. | .93 | *Gentry, Tex. | .13 |
| Moss, Calif. | .93 | *Dorn, S.C. | .14 |
| Yorty, Calif. | .93 | *T. A. Thompson, La. | .15 |
| 16 tied with | .92 | *Sutton, Tenn. | .18 |

### Fiscal-Economic

| Supporters | | Opponents | |
|---|---|---|---|
| *Boykin, Ala. | 1.00 | Buckley, N.Y. | .00 |
| *Rivers, S.C. | .89 | Powell, N.Y. | .00 |
| *Durham, N.C. | .82 | Eberharter, Pa. | .08 |
| *Chatham, N.C. | .80 | Green, Pa. | .08 |
| *D. Rogers, Fla. | .75 | E. Kelly, N.Y. | .09 |
| *J. F. Wilson, Tex. | .75 | Keogh, N.Y. | .09 |
| | | Klein, N.Y. | .09 |
| | | Machrowicz, Mich. | .09 |
| | | Multer, N.Y. | .09 |

### Welfare

| Supporters | | Opponents | |
|---|---|---|---|
| H. Miller, Kans. | .92 | *Robeson, Va. | .20 |
| L. Johnson, Wis. | .90 | *H. W. Smith, Va. | .25 |
| H. Williams, N.J. | .90 | *Teague, Tex. | .27 |
| Yorty, Calif. | .86 | *Willis, La. | .29 |
| *Brooks, La. | .83 | *W. Rogers, Tex. | .33 |
| *P. Brown, Ga. | .83 | *Tuck, Va. | .33 |
| Engle, Calif. | .83 | *J. B. Williams, Miss. | .33 |
| Howell, N.J. | .83 | *Winstead, Miss. | .33 |
| Moss, Calif. | .83 | | |
| *Vinson, Ga. | .83 | | |

### Power and Resources

| Supporters | | Opponents | |
|---|---|---|---|
| 19 tied with (includes 18*) | 1.00 | Buckley, N.Y. | .00 |
| | | Dawson, Ill. | .00 |
| | | Dingell, Mich. | .00 |
| | | Hart, N.J. | .00 |
| | | Heller, N.Y. | .00 |
| | | Powell, N.Y. | .00 |

| Member | Foreign Policy | Fiscal and Economic Policy | Welfare Policy | Power and Resource Development |
|---|---|---|---|---|
| | | SENATE | | |
| Aiken, Vt. | .83 | .78 | .75 | .56 |
| Barrett, Wyo. | .52 | .78 | 1.00 | 1.00 |
| Beall, Md. | .74 | .83 | 1.00 | .94 |
| Bennett, Utah | .70 | .78 | 1.00 | .94 |
| Bowring, Neb. | .88* | .88* | 1.00 | 1.00* |
| Bricker, Ohio | .11 | .71 | 1.00 | .94 |
| Bridges, N.H. | .79 | .82 | 1.00 | 1.00 |
| Bush, Conn. | .85 | .94 | 1.00 | .94 |
| Butler, H., Neb. | .29* | .75* | 1.00* | .92 |
| Butler, J., Md. | .57 | .71 | 1.00 | .94 |
| Capehart, Ind. | .20 | .68 | 1.00 | .92 |
| Carlson, Kans. | .83 | .78 | 1.00 | .94 |
| Case, S.Dak. | .65 | .83 | 1.00 | .65 |
| Cooper, Ky. | .87 | .94 | 1.00 | .39 |
| Cordon, Ore. | .80 | .83 | 1.00 | .94 |
| Crippa, Wyo. | .50* | .88* | 1.00 | 1.00* |
| Dirksen, Ill. | .73 | .78 | 1.00 | .94 |
| Duff, Pa. | .94 | .72 | 1.00 | .94 |
| Dworshak, Idaho | .30 | .72 | 1.00 | .89 |
| Ferguson, Mich. | .78 | .67 | 1.00 | .78 |
| Flanders, Vt. | .85 | .88 | .75 | .94 |
| Goldwater, Ariz. | .32 | .76 | 1.00 | .94 |
| Griswold, Neb. | .82* | .67 | .00* | .64 |
| Hendrickson, N.J. | .78 | .72 | 1.00 | .94 |
| Hickenlooper, Iowa | .65 | .78 | 1.00 | .94 |
| Ives, N.Y. | .94 | .75 | .50 | .88 |
| Jenner, Ind. | .25 | .68 | 1.00 | .94 |
| Knowland, Calif. | .83 | .71 | 1.00 | .94 |
| Kuchel, Calif. | .85 | .67 | 1.00 | .94 |
| Langer, N.Dak. | .32 | .39 | .33 | .00 |
| Malone, Nev. | .10 | .65 | 1.00 | .69 |
| Martin, E., Pa. | .55 | .78 | 1.00 | .94 |
| McCarthy, Wis. | .22 | .67 | 1.00 | .94 |
| Millikin, Colo. | .87 | .65 | 1.00 | .94 |
| Morse, Ore. | .68 | .11 | .25 | .06 |
| Mundt, S.Dak. | .57 | .71 | 1.00 | .82 |
| Payne, Maine | .91 | .83 | 1.00 | .94 |
| Potter, Mich. | .71 | .65 | 1.00 | 1.00 |
| Purtell, Conn. | .78 | .72 | 1.00 | 1.00 |

* Indicates incomplete record (responses on fewer than half the roll calls) in the policy area.

| Member | Foreign Policy | Fiscal and Economic Policy | Welfare Policy | Power and Resource Development |
|---|---|---|---|---|
| Reynolds, Neb. | .40* | 1.00* | 1.00 | .67* |
| Saltonstall, Mass. | .83 | .75 | .75 | 1.00 |
| Schoeppel, Kans. | .42 | .72 | 1.00 | .94 |
| Smith, H. A., N.J. | .83 | .89 | 1.00 | .94 |
| Smith, M. C., Maine | .65 | .72 | 1.00 | .89 |
| Taft, Ohio | .67* | .25* | .00* | 1.00 |
| Thye, Minn. | .83 | .71 | 1.00 | .94 |
| Tobey, N.H. | .00* | .75* | .00* | .00 |
| Upton, N.H. | .88* | .85 | 1.00 | 1.00* |
| Watkins, Utah | .53 | .65 | 1.00 | .94 |
| Welker, Idaho | .18 | .78 | 1.00 | .94 |
| Wiley, Wis. | .91 | .75 | 1.00 | .47 |
| Williams, Del. | .30 | .56 | .75 | .94 |
| Young, N.Dak. | .35 | .53 | .67 | .31 |
| HOUSE | | | | |
| Adair, Ind.—4 | .36 | .92 | .75 | .86 |
| Allen, J., Calif.—7 | .93 | 1.00 | .74 | .86 |
| Allen, L., Ill.—16 | .87 | 1.00 | .73 | .86 |
| Andersen, Minn.—7 | .27 | .75 | .67 | .29 |
| Andresen, Minn.—1 | .29 | .92 | .67 | .86 |
| Angell, Ore.—3 | .64 | .89 | .78 | 1.00* |
| Arends, Ill.—17 | .87 | 1.00 | .75 | .86 |
| Auchincloss, N.J.—3 | .87 | 1.00 | 1.00 | .86 |
| Ayres, Ohio—14 | .92 | 1.00 | .92 | .86 |
| Baker, Tenn.—2 | .60 | 1.00 | .92 | .86 |
| Bates, Mass.—6 | .87 | .92 | .75 | .86 |
| Beamer, Ind.—5 | .47 | 1.00 | .67 | .86 |
| Becker, N.Y.—3 | .77 | .91 | .73 | .86 |
| Belcher, Okla.—1 | .36 | 1.00 | .73 | .86 |
| Bender, Ohio—23 | .79 | 1.00 | .90 | .86 |
| Bennett, Mich.—12 | .27 | .78 | .67 | .57 |
| Bentley, Mich.—8 | .53 | .91 | .70 | .86 |
| Berry, S.Dak.—2 | .33 | 1.00 | .64 | .67 |
| Betts, Ohio—8 | .43 | 1.00 | .58 | .86 |
| Bishop, Ill.—25 | .13 | .82 | .58 | .86 |
| Bolton, F., Ohio—22 | .86 | 1.00 | .92 | .86 |
| Bolton, O., Ohio—11 | .87 | 1.00 | .75 | .86 |
| Bonin, Pa.—11 | .79 | 1.00 | .63 | .86 |
| Bosch, N.Y.—5 | .79 | .83 | .75 | .86 |
| Bow, Ohio—16 | .27 | 1.00 | .55 | .86 |
| Bramblett, Calif.—13 | .73 | 1.00 | .70 | .86 |

| Member | Foreign Policy | Fiscal and Economic Policy | Welfare Policy | Power and Resource Development |
|---|---|---|---|---|
| Bray, Ind.—7 | .46 | .83 | .75 | .86 |
| Brown, C., Ohio—7 | .33 | .92 | .58 | .86 |
| Brownson, Ind.—11 | .73 | 1.00 | .83 | .86 |
| Broyhill, Va.—10 | .73 | 1.00 | .75 | .86 |
| Budge, Idaho—2 | .20 | 1.00 | .67 | .83 |
| Burdick, N.Dak.—A.L. | .50 | .55 | .73 | .14 |
| Busbey, Ill.—3 | .15 | .82 | .33 | .86 |
| Bush, Pa.—17 | .40 | 1.00 | .70 | .86 |
| Byrnes, Wis.—8 | .53 | .92 | .75 | .86 |
| Canfield, N.J.—8 | .87 | .92 | .75 | .29 |
| Carrigg, Pa.—10 | .79 | 1.00 | .83 | .86 |
| Case, N.J.—6 | .86 | 1.00 | 1.00* | .00 |
| Cederberg, Mich.—10 | .40 | 1.00 | .67 | .86 |
| Chenoweth, Colo.—3 | .53 | 1.00 | .75 | .86 |
| Chiperfield, Ill.—19 | .64 | .92 | .75 | .86 |
| Church, Ill.—13 | .40 | .83 | .67 | .86 |
| Clardy, Mich.—6 | .20 | .80 | .50 | .86 |
| Clevenger, Ohio—5 | .21 | .92 | .64 | .86 |
| Cole, W. C., Mo.—6 | .13 | .92 | .75 | .86 |
| Cole, W. S., N.Y.—37 | .71 | 1.00 | .75 | .86 |
| Coon, Ore.—2 | .27 | 1.00 | .70 | .86 |
| Corbett, Pa.—29 | .87 | 1.00 | .75 | .40 |
| Cotton, N.H.—2 | .85 | .89 | .57 | 1.00 |
| Coudert, N.Y.—17 | .64 | .73 | 1.00 | .86 |
| Cretella, Conn.—3 | .93 | .91 | .92 | .86 |
| Crumpacker, Ind.—3 | .53 | .92 | .75 | .86 |
| Cunningham, Iowa—5 | .80 | 1.00 | .67 | .86 |
| Curtis, C., Neb.—1 | .50 | 1.00 | .50 | .86 |
| Curtis, L., Mass.—10 | .87 | 1.00 | .92 | .86 |
| Curtis, T., Mo.—2 | .73 | .92 | .75 | .86 |
| Dague, Pa.—9 | .71 | 1.00 | .83 | .86 |
| Davis, Wis.—2 | .33 | .92 | .75 | .86 |
| Dawson, Utah—2 | .87 | .83 | .75 | .43 |
| Derounian, N.Y.—2 | .80 | .92 | .75 | .86 |
| Devereux, Md.—2 | .87 | 1.00 | .67 | .86 |
| D'Ewart, Mont.—2 | .47 | 1.00 | .75 | .80 |
| Dolliver, Iowa—6 | .40* | 1.00 | .33 | .86 |
| Dondero, Mich.—18 | .40 | 1.00 | .55 | .86 |
| Dorn, N.Y.—12 | .87 | .83 | .83 | .86 |
| Ellsworth, Ore.—4 | .50 | 1.00 | .73 | .86 |
| Fenton, Pa.—12 | .73 | 1.00 | .67 | .86 |
| Fino, N.Y.—25 | .80 | .67 | .82 | .60 |

| Member | Foreign Policy | Fiscal and Economic Policy | Welfare Policy | Power and Resource Development |
|---|---|---|---|---|
| Ford, Mich.—5 | .87 | 1.00 | .75 | .86 |
| Frelinghuysen, N.J.—5 | .93 | 1.00 | .83 | .86 |
| Fulton, Pa.—27 | .80 | .82 | .83 | .80 |
| Gamble, N.Y.—26 | .92 | .90 | .75 | .86 |
| Gavin, Pa.—23 | .33 | .92 | .67 | .86 |
| George, Kans.—3 | .73 | 1.00 | .67 | .57 |
| Golden, Ky.—8 | .42 | 1.00 | .64 | .86 |
| Goodwin, Mass.—8 | .87 | 1.00 | .83 | .86 |
| Graham, Pa.—25 | .67 | 1.00 | .75 | .86 |
| Gross, Iowa—3 | .13 | .83 | .58 | .00 |
| Gubser, Calif.—10 | 1.00 | .92 | .73 | .86 |
| Gwinn, N.Y.—27 | .58 | .91 | .67 | .83 |
| Hagen, Minn.—9 | .27 | 1.00 | .67 | .71 |
| Hale, Maine—1 | .80 | 1.00 | .73 | .86 |
| Halleck, Ind.—2 | .87 | 1.00 | .92 | .86 |
| Hand, N.J.—2 | .17 | .92 | .92 | .86 |
| Harden, Ind.—6 | .73 | 1.00 | .92 | .86 |
| Harrison, R., Neb.—3 | .46 | 1.00 | .67 | .86 |
| Harrison, W. H., Wyo.—A.L. | .27 | 1.00 | .50 | .83 |
| Harvey, Ind.—10 | .53 | 1.00 | .60 | .86 |
| Heselton, Mass.—1 | .87 | .92 | .92 | .29 |
| Hess, Ohio—2 | .67 | .92 | .75 | .86 |
| Hiestand, Calif.—21 | .60 | .92 | .75 | .86 |
| Hill, Colo.—2 | .64 | 1.00 | .82 | .86 |
| Hillelson, Mo.—4 | .47 | 1.00 | .75 | .86 |
| Hillings, Calif.—25 | .87 | 1.00 | .57 | .86 |
| Hinshaw, Calif.—20 | .92 | .92 | .67 | .86 |
| Hoeven, Iowa—8 | .33 | 1.00 | .67 | .86 |
| Hoffman, C., Mich.—4 | .14 | .75 | .42 | .83 |
| Hoffman, R., Ill.—10 | .47 | .91 | .75 | .86 |
| Holmes, Wash.—4 | .93 | 1.00 | .92 | .86 |
| Holt, Calif.—22 | .93 | 1.00 | .75 | .86 |
| Hope, Kans.—5 | .93 | 1.00 | .75 | .86 |
| Horan, Wash.—5 | .75 | 1.00 | .75 | .86 |
| Hosmer, Calif.—18 | .80 | 1.00 | .75 | .86 |
| Hruska, Neb.—2 | .50 | 1.00 | .67 | .86 |
| Hunter, Calif.—12 | .43 | 1.00 | .75 | .86 |
| Hyde, Md.—6 | .86 | 1.00 | .75 | .86 |
| Jackson, Calif.—16 | 1.00 | 1.00 | .64 | .86 |
| James, Pa.—7 | .69 | 1.00 | .70 | .86 |
| Javits, N.Y.—21 | .87 | .58 | .67 | .14 |
| Jenkins, Ohio—10 | .38 | 92 | .67 | .86 |

| Member | Foreign Policy | Fiscal and Economic Policy | Welfare Policy | Power and Resource Development |
|---|---|---|---|---|
| Jensen, Iowa—7 | .50 | .90 | .67 | .86 |
| Johnson, Calif.—11 | .93 | 1.00 | .70 | .86 |
| Jonas, C., N.C.—10 | .73 | 1.00 | .58 | .86 |
| Jonas, E., Ill.—12 | .50 | .92 | .67 | .86 |
| Judd, Minn.—5 | .93 | 1.00 | .82 | .86 |
| Kean, N.J.—12 | .87 | .83 | .92 | .86 |
| Kearney, N.Y.—32 | 1.00 | .82 | .83 | .86 |
| Kearns, Pa.—24 | .64 | 1.00 | .75 | .86 |
| Keating, N.Y.—38 | .87 | .83 | .75 | .43 |
| Kersten, Wis.—5 | .92 | 1.00 | 1.00 | .83 |
| Kilburn, N.Y.—33 | .71 | 1.00 | .58 | .86 |
| King, Pa.—8 | .33 | .91 | .67 | .86 |
| Knox, Mich.—11 | .31 | 1.00 | .80 | .86 |
| Krueger, N.Dak.—A.L. | .50 | .92 | .70 | .83 |
| Laird, Wis.—7 | .31 | .92 | .75 | .86 |
| Latham, N.Y.—4 | .79 | .83 | .75 | .86 |
| LeCompte, Iowa—4 | .87 | 1.00 | .58 | .86 |
| Lipscomb, Calif.—23 | .67* | 1.00 | .78 | .67* |
| Lovre, S.Dak.—1 | .47 | 1.00 | .67 | .67 |
| Mack, Wash.—3 | .47 | 1.00 | .67 | .86 |
| Mailliard, Calif.—4 | .92 | 1.00 | 1.00 | 1.00 |
| Martin, T., Iowa—1 | .36 | 1.00 | .67 | .86 |
| Mason, Ill.—15 | .13 | .64 | .17 | .80 |
| McConnell, Pa.—13 | .83 | 1.00 | .73 | .86 |
| McCulloch, Ohio—4 | .36 | 1.00 | .58 | .86 |
| McDonough, Calif.—15 | .71 | 1.00 | .67 | .86 |
| McGregor, Ohio—17 | .33 | .83 | .67 | .86 |
| McIntire, Maine—3 | .31 | .91 | .73 | .33 |
| McVey, Ill.—4 | .30 | 1.00 | .64 | .71 |
| Meader, Mich.—2 | .82 | 1.00 | .67 | .50 |
| Merrill, Ind.—8 | .87 | 1.00 | .75 | .86 |
| Merrow, N.H.—1 | .92 | 1.00 | .80 | .86 |
| Miller, A. L., Neb.—4 | .50 | .92 | .67 | .86 |
| Miller, E. T., Md.—1 | .53 | 1.00 | .67 | .86 |
| Miller, W., N.Y.—40 | .79 | .91 | .73 | .86 |
| Morano, Conn.—4 | .86 | .92 | .91 | 1.00 |
| Mumma, Pa.—16 | .64 | 1.00 | .75 | .86 |
| Neal, W.Va.—4 | .27 | 1.00 | .58 | .86 |
| Nelson, Maine—2 | .29 | .91 | .70 | .83 |
| Nicholson, Mass.—9 | .47 | .92 | .67 | .86 |
| Norblad, Ore.—1 | .71 | 1.00 | .63 | .83 |
| Oakman, Mich.—17 | .93 | 1.00 | .75 | .86 |

| Member | Foreign Policy | Fiscal and Economic Policy | Welfare Policy Fiscal | Power and Resource Development |
|---|---|---|---|---|
| O'Hara, Minn.—2 | .00* | .89 | .64 | .86 |
| O'Konski, Wis.—10 | .15 | .44 | .60 | .00 |
| Osmers, N.J.—9 | .93 | .92 | .73 | .86 |
| Ostertag, N.Y.—39 | .80 | 1.00 | .75 | .86 |
| Patterson, Conn.—5 | .86 | 1.00 | .91 | .86 |
| Pelly, Wash.—1 | .79 | 1.00 | .75 | .86 |
| Phillips, Calif.—29 | .18 | .91 | .64 | .86 |
| Pillion, N.Y.—42 | .69 | .83 | .75 | .86 |
| Poff, Va.—6 | .60 | .92 | .67 | .86 |
| Prouty, Vt.—A.L. | 1.00 | 1.00 | .67 | .43 |
| Radwan, N.Y.—41 | .87 | .92 | .92 | .29 |
| Ray, N.Y.—15 | .87 | .92 | .75 | .86 |
| Reece, Tenn.—1 | .58 | 1.00 | .75 | .80 |
| Reed, C., Ill.—14 | .11 | 1.00 | .75 | .86 |
| Reed, D., N.Y.—43 | .33 | .91 | .50 | .86 |
| Rees, Kans.—4 | .40 | 1.00 | .75 | .86 |
| Rhodes, Ariz.—1 | .85 | 1.00 | .58 | 1.00 |
| Riehlman, N.Y.—35 | .86 | 1.00 | .67 | .86 |
| Robsion, Ky.—3 | .87 | 1.00 | .82 | .43 |
| Rogers, Mass.—5 | .93 | .92 | .92 | .86 |
| Sadlak, Conn.—A.L. | .87 | 1.00 | .91 | .86 |
| St. George, N.Y.—28 | .87 | 1.00 | .83 | .86 |
| Saylor, Pa.—22 | .67 | .92 | .92 | 1.00 |
| Schenck, Ohio—3 | .50 | 1.00 | .73 | .86 |
| Scherer, Ohio—1 | .58 | .83 | .64 | .86 |
| Scott, Pa.—6 | 1.00 | .91 | .89 | .86 |
| Scrivner, Kans.—2 | .27 | 1.00 | .67 | .86 |
| Scudder, Calif.—1 | .80 | 1.00 | .67 | .86 |
| Seely-Brown, Conn.—2 | .87 | 1.00 | .91 | .86 |
| Shafer, Mich.—3 | .14 | 1.00 | .40 | .83 |
| Sheehan, Ill.—11 | .54 | .75 | .73 | .86 |
| Short, Mo.—7 | .14 | 1.00 | .57 | .86 |
| Simpson, R., Pa.—18 | .79 | 1.00 | .70 | .86 |
| Simpson, S., Ill.—20 | .33 | .91 | .67 | .86 |
| Small, Md.—5 | .71 | .92 | .75 | .86 |
| Smith, L., Wis.—1 | .20 | .83 | .50 | .86 |
| Smith, W., Kans.—6 | .13 | .82 | .33 | .86 |
| Springer, Ill.—22 | .87 | .92 | .92 | 1.00 |
| Stauffer, Pa.—19 | .83 | 1.00 | .67 | .86 |
| Stringfellow, Utah—1 | .63 | 1.00 | .75 | .86 |
| Taber, N.Y.—36 | .80 | 1.00 | .50 | .86 |
| Talle, Iowa—2 | .47 | 1.00 | .67 | .86 |

| Member | Foreign Policy | Fiscal and Economic Policy | Welfare Policy | Power and Resource Development |
|---|---|---|---|---|
| Taylor, N.Y.—31 | .73 | .82 | .78 | .86 |
| Thompson, Mich.—9 | .31 | .92 | .67 | .86 |
| Tollefson, Wash.—6 | .93 | 1.00 | .83 | .86 |
| Utt, Calif.—28 | .40 | .92 | .50 | .86 |
| Van Pelt, Wis.—6 | .21 | 1.00 | .67 | .86 |
| Van Zandt, Pa.—20 | .53 | .92 | .75 | .86 |
| Velde, Ill.—18 | .33 | .83 | .70 | .86 |
| Vorys, Ohio—12 | .87 | 1.00 | .67 | .86 |
| Vursell, Ill.—23 | .58 | 1.00 | .67 | .86 |
| Wainwright, N.Y.—1 | 1.00 | .92 | .91 | .86 |
| Wampler, Va.—9 | .67 | 1.00 | .75 | .86 |
| Warburton, Del.—A.L. | .87 | 1.00 | .75 | .86 |
| Weichel, Ohio—13 | .62 | 1.00 | .40* | .83 |
| Westland, Wash.—2 | .86 | 1.00 | .73 | .86 |
| Wharton, N.Y.—29 | .53 | .83 | .73 | .86 |
| Widnall, N.J.—7 | .87 | 1.00 | .92 | .86 |
| Wigglesworth, Mass.—13 | .82 | 1.00 | 1.00 | .86 |
| Williams, N.Y.—34 | .67 | 1.00 | .73 | .86 |
| Wilson, E., Ind.—9 | .50 | .91 | .82 | .86 |
| Wilson, R., Calif.—30 | .80 | .92 | .83 | .86 |
| Withrow, Wis.—3 | .29 | 1.00 | .75 | .00 |
| Wolcott, Mich.—7 | .58 | .92 | .73 | .80 |
| Wolverton, N.J.—1 | .87 | 1.00 | .92 | .86 |
| Young, Nev.—A.L. | .80 | 1.00 | .67 | .86 |
| Younger, Calif.—9 | .80 | .92 | .83 | .86 |

## Manuscript Sources

Sherman Adams Papers. Baker Library, Dartmouth College, Hanover, N.H.

John W. Bricker Papers. In possession of Senator Bricker, Columbus, Ohio.

————. Ohio Historical Society, Columbus.

Dwight D. Eisenhower Papers. Dwight D. Eisenhower Library, Abilene, Kans.

Ralph E. Flanders Papers. George Arents Research Library, Syracuse Univ., Syracuse, N.Y.

Charles A. Halleck Papers. Lilly Library, Indiana Univ., Bloomington.

Irving M. Ives Papers. Collection of Regional History and University Archives, Olin Library, Cornell Univ., Ithaca, N.Y.

I. Jack Martin Papers. In possession of Mrs. I. Jack Martin, Kensington, Md.

Daniel A. Reed Papers. Collection of Regional History and University Archives, Olin Library, Cornell Univ., Ithaca, N.Y.

H. Alexander Smith Papers. Princeton Univ. Library, Princeton, N.J.

John Taber Papers. Collection of Regional History and University Archives, Olin Library, Cornell Univ., Ithaca, N.Y.

Robert A. Taft Papers. Division of Manuscripts, Library of Congress, Washington, D.C.

John M. Vorys Papers. Ohio Historical Society, Columbus.
Alexander Wiley Papers. Wisconsin State Historical Society, Madison.

*Newspapers*

Unless otherwise noted, references are to the issues in Sept.–Nov. 1952.
Baltimore *Sun.*
Bangor (Maine) *Daily News,* June–Sept. 1952.
Bay City (Mich.) *Times.*
Boston *Daily Globe.*
Bristol (Tenn.-Va.) *Herald-Courier.*
Charlotte *Observer.*
Cincinnati *Enquirer.*
Detroit *Free Press.*
*East Oregonian* (Pendleton).
Evansville (Ind.) *Courier.*
Fargo (N.Dak.) *Forum.*
Hartford *Courant.*
Hazelton (Pa.) *Standard-Sentinel.*
Huntington (W.Va.) *Herald-Dispatch.*
Kansas City *Star.*
Laramie (Wyo.) *Republican and Boomerang.*
Los Angeles *Times.*
Louisville *Courier-Journal.*
Meriden (Conn.) *Record.*
*New York Times,* 1952–54.
Ogden (Utah) *Standard-Examiner.*
Omaha *Morning World Herald.*
Phoenix *Gazette.*
Reno (Nev.) *Evening Gazette.*
Roanoke (Va.) *Times.*
Saginaw (Mich.) *News.*
St. Joseph (Mo.) *News-Press.*
Salt Lake *Tribune.*
San Diego *Union.*
San Francisco *Chronicle.*
San Jose (Calif.) *Mercury.*
San Mateo (Calif.) *Times.*

Santa Ana (Calif.) *Register.*
Sault Ste. Marie (Mich.) *Evening News.*
Seattle *Daily Times.*
*The State Journal* (Lansing, Mich.)
Warren (Ohio) *Tribune-Chronicle.*
Washington *Post,* 1952–54.
Wausau (Wis.) *Daily Record Herald.*
Wilmington (Del.) *Journal-Every Evening.*


## Public Documents

U.S. Congress. *Congressional Record.* Vols. xcix and c.
U.S. President. *Public Papers of the Presidents of the United States: Dwight D. Eisenhower.* Washington: Government Printing Office, 1960. Vols. 1953 and 1954.


## Books

Adams, Sherman. *Firsthand Report: The Story of the Eisenhower Administration.* New York: Harper, 1961.
Altmyer, Arthur J. *The Formative Years of Social Security.* Madison: Univ. of Wisconsin Press, 1966.
Anderson, Lee F., Meredith W. Watts, Jr., and Allen R. Wilcox. *Legislative Roll Call Analysis.* Evanston: Northwestern Univ. Press, 1966.
Barnard, Ellsworth. *Wendell Willkie: Fighter for Freedom.* Marquette: Northern Michigan Univ. Press, 1966.
Bartley, Ernest R. *The Tidelands Oil Controversy: A Legal and Historical Analysis.* Austin: Univ. of Texas Press, 1953.
Bauer, Raymond A., Ithiel deSola Pool, and Lewis Dexter. *American Business and Public Policy: The Politics of Foreign Trade.* New York: Atherton, 1963.
Benson, Ezra Taft. *Cross Fire: The Eight Years With Eisenhower.* Garden City, N.Y.: Doubleday, 1962.
Bohlen, Charles E. *Witness to History, 1929–1969.* With the editorial assistance of Robert H. Phelps. New York: Norton, 1973.
Bone, Hugh A. *Party Committees and National Politics.* Seattle: Univ. of Washington Press, 1958.

Burns, James M. *The Deadlock of Democracy: Four-Party Politics in America.* Englewood Cliffs, N.J.: Prentice-Hall, 1963.

Campbell, Angus, Gerald Gurin, and Warren E. Miller. *The Voter Decides.* Evanston: Row, Peterson, 1954.

Caridi, Ronald J. *The Korean War and American Politics: The Republican Party as a Case Study.* Philadelphia: Univ. of Pennsylvania Press, 1968.

Carroll, Holbert N. *The House of Representatives and Foreign Affairs.* Pittsburgh: Univ. of Pittsburgh Press, 1958.

Childs, Marquis. *Eisenhower: Captive Hero; A Critical Study of the General and the President.* New York: Harcourt, 1958.

*Congressional Quarterly Almanac.* Vols. VII–X. Washington: Congressional Quarterly Service, 1951–54.

Crabb, Cecil V., Jr. *Bipartisan Foreign Policy: Myth or Reality?* Evanston: Row, Peterson, 1957.

Dale, Edwin L., Jr. *Conservatives in Power: A Study in Frustration.* Garden City, N.Y.: Doubleday, 1960.

David, Paul T., Malcolm Moos, and Ralph M. Goldman, eds., *Presidential Nominating Politics in 1952.* 5 vols. Baltimore: Johns Hopkins Univ. Press, 1954.

DeGrazia, Alfred. *The Western Public: 1952 and Beyond.* Stanford: Stanford Univ. Press, 1954.

Donovan, Robert J. *Eisenhower: The Inside Story.* New York: Harper, 1956.

Eisenhower, Dwight D. *The White House Years: Mandate for Change, 1953–1956.* Garden City, N.Y.: Doubleday, 1963.

————. *The White House Years: Waging Peace, 1956–1961.* Garden City, N.Y.: Doubleday, 1965.

Farnsworth, David N. *The Senate Committee on Foreign Relations.* Vol. XLIX of Illinois Studies in the Social Sciences. Urbana: Univ. of Illinois Press, 1961.

Fenno, Richard F., Jr. *The Power of the Purse: Appropriations Politics in Congress.* Boston: Little, Brown, 1966.

Froman, Lewis A., Jr. *Congressmen and Their Constituencies.* Chicago: Rand McNally, 1963.

Goldman, Eric F. *The Crucial Decade—And After: America, 1945–1960.* New York: Vintage Books, 1960.

Goodwin, George, Jr. *The Little Legislatures: Committees of Congress.* [Amherst]: Univ. of Massachusetts Press, 1970.

Graebner, Norman A. *The New Isolationism: A Study in Politics and Foreign Policy Since 1950.* New York: Ronald, 1956.

Green, Harold P., and Alan Rosenthal. *Government of the Atom: The Integration of Powers.* New York: Atherton, 1963.

Harris, Louis. *Is There a Republican Majority? Political Trends, 1952–1956.* New York: Harper, 1954.

Henry, Laurin L. *Presidential Transitions.* Washington: Brookings Institution, 1960.

Holtzman, Abraham. *Legislative Liaison: Executive Leadership in Congress.* Chicago: Rand McNally, 1970.

Horn, Stephen. *The Cabinet and Congress.* New York: Columbia Univ. Press, 1960.

———. *Unused Power: The Work of the Senate Committee on Appropriations.* Washington: Brookings Institution, 1970.

Hughes, Emmet J. *The Ordeal of Power: A Political Memoir of the Eisenhower Years.* New York: Atheneum, 1963.

Humphrey, George M. *The Basic Papers of George M. Humphrey, Secretary of the Treasury, 1953–1957,* ed. by Nathaniel R. Howard. Cleveland: Western Reserve Historical Society, 1965.

Janowitz, Morris, and Dwaine Marvick. *Competitive Pressure and Democratic Consent: An Interpretation of the 1952 Presidential Election.* No. 32 in Michigan Governmental Studies. Ann Arbor: Univ. of Michigan Institute of Public Administration, 1956.

Jewell, Malcolm E. *Senatorial Politics and Foreign Policy.* Lexington: Univ. of Kentucky Press, 1962.

Johnson, Donald B. *The Republican Party and Wendell Willkie.* Vol. XLVI of Illinois Studies in the Social Sciences. Urbana: Univ. of Illinois Press, 1960.

Joyner, Conrad. *The Republican Dilemma: Conservatism or Progressivism.* Tucson: Univ. of Arizona Press, 1963.

Kessel, John H. *The Goldwater Coalition: Republican Strategies in 1964.* Indianapolis: Bobbs-Merrill, 1968.

Key, V. O., Jr. *The Responsible Electorate: Rationality in Presidential Voting, 1936–1960.* With the assistance of Milton C. Cummings, Jr. Cambridge: Harvard Univ., Belknap Press, 1966.

Larson, Arthur. *A Republican Looks at His Party.* New York: Harper, 1956.

———. *Eisenhower: The President Nobody Knew.* New York: Scribners, 1968.

Lubell, Samuel. *The Future of American Politics*, 3rd ed., rev. New York: Harper, Colophon Books, 1965.

Lyons, Barrow. *Tomorrow's Birthright: A Political and Economic Interpretation of Our Natural Resources*. New York: Funk & Wagnalls, 1955.

Mabee, Carleton. *The Seaway Story*. New York: Macmillan, 1961.

MacRae, Duncan, Jr. *Dimensions of Congressional Voting: A Statistical Study of the House of Representatives in the Eighty-first Congress*. Berkeley: Univ. of California Press, 1958.

————. *Issues and Parties in Legislative Voting: Methods of Statistical Analysis*. New York: Harper, 1970.

Martin, Joseph W. *My First Fifty Years in Politics*. As told to Robert J. Donovan. New York: McGraw-Hill, 1960.

Matthews, Donald R. *U.S. Senators & Their World*. New York: Vintage Books, 1960.

Mayer, George H. *The Republican Party, 1854–1966*, 2nd ed. New York: Oxford Univ. Press, 1967.

Mayhew, David R. *Party Loyalty Among Congressmen: The Difference Between Democrats and Republicans, 1947–1962*. Cambridge: Harvard Univ. Press, 1966.

Miller, William L. *Piety Along the Potomac: Notes on Politics and Morals in the Fifties*. Boston: Houghton, 1964.

Moos, Malcolm. *Politics, Presidents and Coattails*. Baltimore: Johns Hopkins Univ. Press, 1952.

————. *The Republicans: A History of Their Party*. New York: Random, 1956.

Neustadt, Richard E. *Presidential Power: The Politics of Leadership*, rev. ed. New York: Wiley, 1968.

Parmet, Herbert S. *Eisenhower and the American Crusades*. New York: Macmillan, 1972.

Patterson, James T. *Mr. Republican: A Biography of Robert A. Taft*. Boston: Houghton, 1972.

Porter, Kirk H., and Donald B. Johnson, comps. *National Party Platforms, 1840–1964*. Urbana: Univ. of Illinois Press, 1966.

Pusey, Merlo J. *Eisenhower the President*. New York: Macmillan, 1956.

Rieselbach, Leroy N. *The Roots of Isolationism: Congressional Voting and Presidential Leadership in Foreign Policy*. Indianapolis: Bobbs-Merrill, 1966.

Ripley, Randall B. *Majority Party Leadership in Congress.* Boston: Little, Brown, 1969.

———. *Party Leaders in the House of Representatives.* Washington: Brookings Institution, 1967.

———. *Power in the Senate.* New York: St. Martin's Press, 1969.

Rogin, Michael P. *The Intellectuals and McCarthy: The Radical Specter.* Cambridge, Mass.: M.I.T. Press, 1967.

Roper, Elmo. *You and Your Leaders: Their Actions and Your Reactions, 1936–1956.* New York: Morrow, 1957.

Rosenau, James N. *The Nomination of "Chip" Bohlen.* Case 1 in the Eagleton Institute Cases in Practical Politics. [New York]: McGraw-Hill, 1960.

Rostow, Walt W. *The United States in the World Arena: An Essay in Recent History.* New York: Harper, 1960.

Rovere, Richard H. *Affairs of State: The Eisenhower Years.* New York: Farrar, 1956.

Scheele, Henry Z. *Charlie Halleck: A Political Biography.* New York: Exposition Press, 1966.

Schlesinger, Arthur M., Jr., and Fred L. Israel, eds. *History of American Presidential Elections.* 4 vols. New York: Chelsea House, 1971.

Stein, Herbert. *The Fiscal Revolution in America.* Chicago: Univ. of Chicago Press, 1969.

Strauss, Lewis. *Men and Decisions.* Garden City, N.Y.: Doubleday, 1962.

Theoharis, Athan G. *The Yalta Myths: An Issue in U.S. Politics, 1945–1955.* Columbia: Univ. of Missouri Press, 1970.

Truman, David B. *The Congressional Party: A Case Study.* New York: Wiley, 1959.

Vatter, Harold G. *The U.S. Economy in the 1950s: An Economic History.* New York: Norton, 1963.

Viorst, Milton. *Fall From Grace: The Republican Party and the Puritan Ethic.* New York: New American Library, 1968.

Westerfield, H. Bradford. *Foreign Policy and Party Politics: Pearl Harbor to Korea.* New Haven: Yale Univ. Press, 1955.

White, William S. *The Taft Story.* New York: Harper, 1954.

Wildavsky, Aaron. *Dixon-Yates: A Study in Power Politics.* New Haven: Yale Univ. Press, 1962.

Wilkinson, Joe R. *Politics and Trade Policy.* Washington: Public Affairs Press, 1960.

Willoughby, William R. *The St. Lawrence Seaway: A Study in Politics and Diplomacy.* Madison: Univ. of Wisconsin Press, 1961.

Young, James P. *The Politics of Affluence: Ideology in the United States Since World War II.* Scranton, Pa.: Chandler Publishing, 1968.


*Articles and Periodicals*

Belknap, George M. "A Method for Analyzing Legislative Behavior," *Midwest Journal of Political Science* 2, No. 4 (Nov. 1958), 377–402.

Blackwood, George D. "Let's Look at the Record," *The Reporter* 7, No. 2 (July 22, 1952), 14–16.

Burns, James M. "Congressional Contests and the Presidential Election," *Annals of the American Academy of Political and Social Science* 283 (Sept. 1952), 115–21.

Carleton, William G. "Triumph of the Moderates," *Harper's Magazine* 210, No. 1259 (Apr. 1955), 31–37.

Cater, Douglass. " 'Mr. Conservative'—Eugene Millikin of Colorado," *The Reporter* 8, No. 6 (Mar. 17, 1953), 26–31.

Clausen, Aage R. "Measurement Identity in the Longitudinal Analysis of Legislative Voting," *American Political Science Review* 41, No. 4 (Dec. 1967), 1020–35.

———— and Richard B. Cheney. "A Comparative Analysis of Senate-House Voting on Economic and Welfare Policy, 1953–1964," *American Political Science Review* 44, No. 1 (Mar. 1970), 138–52.

Commager, Henry Steele. "The Republican Dilemma," *The Reporter* 7, No. 8 (Oct. 14, 1952), 6–9.

DeVoto, Bernard. "The Easy Chair—Preliminary Forecast," *Harper's Magazine* 206, No. 1232 (Jan. 1953), 52–55.

Farris, Charles D. "A Method of Determining Ideological Groupings in the Congress," *Journal of Politics* 20, No. 2 (May 1958), 308–38.

Harsch, Joseph C. "Which Road? The Chicago Choice," *The Reporter* 7, No. 2 (July 22, 1952), 5–8.

Havens, Murray C. "Metropolitan Areas and Congress: Foreign Policy and National Security," *Journal of Politics* 26, No. 4 (Nov. 1964), 758–74.

Hyman, Sidney. "Eisenhower's Presidency—the Known and the Foreseeable," *The Reporter* 14, No. 6 (Mar. 22, 1956), 13–17.

Kelso, Paul. "The 1952 Elections in Arizona," *The Western Political Quarterly* 6, No. 1 (Mar. 1953), 100–102.

Kempton, Murray. "The Underestimation of Dwight Eisenhower," *Esquire* 68, No. 3 (Sept. 1967), 108–109+.

Masters, Nicholas A. "Committee Assignments in the House of Representatives," *American Political Science Review* 55, No. 2 (June 1961), 345–57.

Miller, Joe. "The Battle for Hell's Canyon," *The Reporter* 10, No. 10 (May 11, 1954), 23–26.

———. "Oregon: Can the Issues be Ignored?", *The Reporter* 11, No. 8 (Nov. 4, 1954), 33–35.

Miller, Warren, and Donald E. Stokes. "Constituency Influence in Congress," in Angus Campbell et al. (eds.), *Elections and the Political Order*. New York: Wiley, 1966.

Murphy, Charles J. V. "The Eisenhower Shift," 4 parts, *Fortune* 53, No. 1 (Jan. 1956), 83–87+; No. 2 (Feb. 1956), 110–13+; No. 3 (Mar. 1956), 110–12+; No. 4 (Apr. 1956), 112–16+.

Neustadt, Richard. "Presidency and Legislation: Planning the President's Program," *American Political Science Review* 49, No. 4 (Dec. 1955), 980–1021.

*Newsweek*. Vols. 41–44 (1953–54).

Nieburg, H. L. "The Eisenhower AEC and Congress: A Study in Executive-Legislative Relations," *Midwest Journal of Political Science* 6, No. 2 (May 1962), 115–48.

Pennock, J. Roland. "Party and Constituency in Postwar Agricultural Price-Support Legislation," *Journal of Politics* 18, No. 2 (May 1956), 167–210.

Pomper, Gerald. " 'If Elected, I Promise': American Party Platforms," *Midwest Journal of Political Science* 11, No. 3 (Aug. 1967), 318–52.

Prothro, James W. "Verbal Shifts in the American Presidency: A Content Analysis," *American Political Science Review* 50, No. 3 (Sept. 1956), 726–39.

Ranney, Austin. "The Platforms, the Parties, and the Voter," *Yale Review* 40, No. 1 (Sept. 1952), 10–20.

Schoenbrun, David F. "The Ordeal of General Ike," *Harper's Magazine* 205, No. 1229 (Oct. 1952), 25–34.

Schubert, Glendon A. "Politics and the Constitution: The Bricker Amendment During 1953," *Journal of Politics* 16, No. 2 (May 1954), 257–98.

Smuckler, Ralph H. "The Region of Isolationism," *American Political Science Review* 47, No. 2 (June 1953), 386–401.

Truman, David B. "The Domestic Politics of Foreign Aid," *Proceedings of the Academy of Political Science* 27, No. 2 (Jan. 1962), 62–72.

*U.S. News & World Report.* Vols. 33–37 (1952–54).

Watson, Richard A. "The Tariff Revolution: A Study of Shifting Party Attitudes," *Journal of Politics* 18, No. 4 (Nov. 1956), 678–701.

White, William S. "The Fight for the Senate," *Harper's Magazine* 209, No. 1251 (Aug. 1954), 23–29.

———. "Has Eisenhower Changed the G.O.P.?" *New York Times Magazine* (Mar. 18, 1956), 11+.

## Unpublished Sources

Annunziata, Frank A. "The Attack on the Welfare State: Patterns of Anti-Statism from the New Deal to the New Left." Diss., Ohio State Univ., 1968.

Koo, Youngnok. "Dissenters from American Involvement in World Affairs: A Political Analysis of the Movement for the Bricker Amendment." Diss., Univ. of Michigan, 1966.

Mahood, Harry R. "The St. Lawrence Seaway Bill of 1954: A Case Study in Decision-Making in American Foreign Policy." Diss., Univ. of Illinois, 1960.

## Oral Sources

Bohlen, Charles E. Transcript of a tape-recorded interview conducted by Philip A. Crowl, John Foster Dulles Oral History Project, Princeton Univ. Library, Princeton, N.J.

Bricker, John W. Interview conducted by author, Feb. 2, 1971, Columbus, Ohio.

Eisenhower, Dwight D. Transcript of interview by Philip A. Crowl, Dulles Project, Princeton Univ. Library.

Halleck, Charles A. Transcript of interview [by Philip A. Crowl], Dulles Project, Princeton Univ. Library.

———. Transcript of interview by John Luter, Dwight D. Eisenhower Oral History Project, Dwight D. Eisenhower Library, Abilene, Kans.

Javits, Jacob. Transcript of interview by Peter A. Corning, Eisenhower Project, Eisenhower Library.

Jones, Roger W. Transcript of interview by Paul L. Hopper, Eisenhower Project, Eisenhower Library.

Lawrence, William H. Transcript of interview by John Luter, Eisenhower Project, Eisenhower Library.

Morton, Thruston B. Transcript of interview by Philip A. Crowl, Dulles Project, Princeton Univ. Library.

Saltonstall, Leverett. Transcript of interview by Ed Edwin, Eisenhower Project, Eisenhower Library.

Vorys, John M. Transcript of interview by Richard D. Challener, Dulles Project, Princeton Univ. Library.

*Twentieth-Century America Series*
DEWEY W. GRANTHAM, GENERAL EDITOR

Each volume in this series will focus on some aspect of the politics of social change in recent American history, utilizing new approaches to clarify the response of Americans to the dislocating forces of our own day—economic, technological, racial, demographic, and administrative.

.

This book has been set on the Linotype in eleven-point Baskerville with two-point line spacing. Foundry Baskerville and Bulmer were used as display. The book was designed by Jim Billingsley, and composed and printed letterpress by Heritage Printers, Inc., Charlotte, North Carolina. The paper on which the book is printed bears the watermark of the S. D. Warren Company and is designed for an effective life of at least three hundred years.

THE UNIVERSITY OF TENNESSEE PRESS
KNOXVILLE